The Organization of Political Interest Groups

Interest groups form an important part of the development of political and social systems. This book goes beyond current literature in examining the survival and 'careers' of such groups beyond their formation.

The author introduces the concept of organizational form and develops a framework to describe and evaluate organizations, and uncover how they adapt to survive. Using example case studies from the UK, US and Australia, the book presents extensive historical analyses of specific groups, to better understand the organization and position of such groups within their political system. It analyses how groups differentiate themselves from each other, how they develop differently and what impact this has on policy implementation and democratic legitimacy.

The Organization of Political Interest Groups will be of interest to students and scholars of political science, comparative politics, public representation, and public policy.

Darren R. Halpin is Associate Professor at The Australian National University, Australia.

Routledge research in comparative politics

1 **Democracy and Post-communism**
Political change in the
post-communist world
Graeme Gill

2 **Sub-state Nationalism**
A comparative analysis of
institutional design
*Edited by Helena Catt and
Michael Murphy*

3 **Reward for High Public Office**
Asian and Pacific Rim States
*Edited by Christopher Hood and
B. Guy Peters*

4 **Social Democracy and Labour
Market Policy**
Developments in Britain and
Germany
Knut Roder

5 **Democratic Revolutions**
Asia and Eastern Europe
Mark R. Thompson

6 **Democratization**
A comparative analysis of 170
countries
Tatu Vanhanen

7 **Determinants of the Death
Penalty**
A comparative study of the world
Carsten Anckar

8 **How Political Parties Respond
to Voters**
Interest aggregation revisited
*Edited by Kay Lawson and
Thomas Poguntke*

9 **Women, Quotas and Politics**
Edited by Drude Dahlerup

10 **Citizenship and Ethnic Conflict**
Challenging the nation-state
Haldun Gülalp

11 **The Politics of Women's
Interests**
New comparative and
international perspectives
*Edited by Louise Chappell and
Lisa Hill*

12 **Political Disaffection in
Contemporary Democracies**
Social capital, institutions and
politics
*Edited by Mariano Torcal and
José Ramón Montero*

13 **Representing Women in
Parliament**
A comparative study
*Edited by Marian Sawer,
Manon Tremblay and
Linda Trimble*

14 **Democracy and Political Culture in Eastern Europe**
Edited by Hans-Dieter Klingemann, Dieter Fuchs and Jan Zielonka

15 **Social Capital and Associations in European Democracies**
A comparative analysis
Edited by William A. Maloney and Sigrid Roßteutscher

16 **Citizenship and Involvement in European Democracies**
A comparative analysis
Edited by Jan van Deth, José Ramón Montero and Anders Westholm

17 **The Politics of Foundations**
A comparative analysis
Edited by Helmut K. Anheier and Siobhan Daly

18 **Party Policy in Modern Democracies**
Kenneth Benoit and Michael Laver

19 **Semi-Presidentialism Outside Europe**
A comparative study
Edited by Robert Elgie and Sophia Moestrup

20 **Comparative Politics**
The principal-agent perspective
Jan-Erik Lane

21 **The Political Power of Business**
Structure and information in public policymaking
Patrick Bernhagen

22 **Women's Movements**
Flourishing or in abeyance?
Edited by Marian Sawer and Sandra Grey

23 **Consociational Theory**
McGarry and O'Leary and the Northern Ireland conflict
Edited by Rupert Taylor

24 **The International Politics of Democratization**
Comparative perspectives
Edited by Nuno Severiano Teixeira

25 **Post-communist Regime Change**
A comparative study
Jørgen Møller

26 **Social Democracy in Power**
The capacity to reform
Wolfgang Merkel, Alexander Petring, Christian Henkes and Christoph Egle

27 **The Rise of Regionalism**
Causes of regional mobilization in Western Europe
Rune Dahl Fitjar

28 **Party Politics in the Western Balkans**
Edited by Věra Stojarová and Peter Emerson

29 **Democratization and Market Reform in Developing and Transitional Countries**
Think tanks as catalysts
James G. McGann

30 **Political Leadership, Parties and Citizens**
The personalisation of leadership
Edited by Jean Blondel and Jean-Louis Thiebault

31 **Civil Society and Activism in Europe**
Contextualizing engagement and political orientation
Edited by William A. Maloney and Jan W. van Deth

32 **Gender Equality, Citizenship and Human Rights**
Controversies and challenges in China and the Nordic countries
Edited by Pauline Stoltz, Marina Svensson, Zhongxin Sun and Qi Wang

33 **Democratization and the European Union**
Comparing Central and Eastern European post-Communist countries
Edited by Leonardo Morlino and Wojciech Sadurski

34 **The Origin of Electoral Systems in the Postwar Era**
A worldwide approach
Krister Lundell

35 **The Globalization of Motherhood**
Deconstruction and reconstructions of biology and care
Edited by Wendy Chavkin and JaneMaree Maher

36 **Parties, Elections, and Policy Reforms in Western Europe**
Voting for social pacts
Kerstin Hamann and John Kelly

37 **Democracy and Famine**
Olivier Rubin

38 **Women in Executive Power**
A global overview
Edited by Gretchen Bauer and Manon Tremblay

39 **Women and Representation in Local Government**
International case studies
Edited by Barbara Pini and Paula McDonald

40 **The Politics of Charity**
Kerry O'Halloran

41 **Climate Policy Changes in Germany and Japan**
A path to paradigmatic policy change
Rie Watanabe

42 **African Parliamentary Reform**
Edited by Rick Stapenhurst, Rasheed Draman and Andrew Imlach with Alexander Hamilton and Cindy Kroon

43 **The Politics of International Law and Compliance**
Serbia, Croatia and The Hague tribunal
Edited by Nikolas Rajkovic

44 **The Funding of Political Parties**
Where now?
Edited by Keith Ewing, Joo-Cheong Tham and Jacob Rowbottow

45 **Parliamentary Oversight Tools**
A comparative analysis
Riccardo Pelizzo and Frederick Stapenhurst

46 **Inclusion and Exclusion in the Liberal Competition State**
The cult of the individual
Richard Münch

47 **New Challenger Parties in Western Europe**
A comparative analysis
Airo Hino

48 **Metropolitan Governance and Policy**
Jen Nelles

49 Rewards for High Public Office in Europe and North America
Edited by B. Guy Peters and Marleen Brans

50 International Security, Conflict and Gender
'HIV/AIDS is another war'
Hakan Seckinelgin

51 Young People and Politics
Comparing Anglo-American democracies
Aaron J. Martin

52 Immigration and Public Opinion in Liberal Democracies
Gary P. Freeman, Randall Hansen, and David L. Leal

53 Russia's Regions and Comparative Subnational Politics
Comparing Anglo-American democracies
Edited by William M. Reisinger

54 Protecting Immigrant Rights in Mexico
Understanding the state-civil society nexus
Laura Valeria González-Murphy

55 Public Sector Performance and Reform in Developing Countries
Pockets of effectiveness
Edited by Michael Roll

56 The Organization of Political Interest Groups
Designing advocacy
Darren R. Halpin

The Organization of Political Interest Groups
Designing advocacy

Darren R. Halpin

LONDON AND NEW YORK

First published 2014
by Routledge
2 Park Square, Milton Park, Abingdon, Oxfordshire OX14 4RN

and by Routledge
711 Third Avenue, New York, NY 10017

First issued in paperback 2015

Routledge is an imprint of the Taylor & Francis Group, an informa business

© 2014 Darren R. Halpin

The right of Darren R. Halpin to be identified as author of this work has been asserted by him in accordance with the Copyright, Designs and Patent Act 1988.

All rights reserved. No part of this book may be reprinted or reproduced or utilized in any form or by any electronic, mechanical, or other means, now known or hereafter invented, including photocopying and recording, or in any information storage or retrieval system, without permission in writing from the publishers.

Trademark notice: Product or corporate names may be trademarks or registered trademarks, and are used only for identification and explanation without intent to infringe.

British Library Cataloguing in Publication Data
A catalogue record for this book is available from the British Library

Library of Congress Cataloging in Publication Data
A catalog record for this book has been requested

ISBN 13: 978-1-138-94527-2 (pbk)
ISBN 13: 978-0-415-59680-0 (hbk)

Typeset in Times
by Wearset Ltd, Boldon, Tyne and Wear

For Jenny, Matilda and Skye

Contents

List of figures		xii
List of tables		xiii
Acknowledgements		xiv
1	Studying interest groups as 'organizations': a lacuna?	1
2	Where is 'organization' in the group literature?	18
3	Interest groups and organizational form	37
4	Revisiting population-level analysis: a feature-based approach	56
5	Interest group 'careers' (I): formation	79
6	Interest group 'careers' (II): group adaptation and change over time	99
7	Niche theories: differentiation *through* 'form'?	122
8	Assembling group identities in nascent fields: revisiting a population-level perspective	144
9	Evolving group identities: the role of 'categories' and audience	161
10	Interest group policy capacities	176
11	Conclusions: technological change and the (ongoing) importance of organization	196
	References	206
	Index	219

Figures

6.1	Interest group evolutionary sequences	105
9.1	Measures of category strength (various years)	170
9.2	Trends in category spanning, selected years	172
9.3	Complexity of group identity: average identity niche-width, over time	173

Tables

2.1	Existing group scholarship approach to organization	19
3.1	Summary of approaches to conceptualizing organizational form	41
4.1	Summary of generic group forms and their characteristics	63
4.2	Summary of group cases	72–3
4.3	Hypothesized variation on institutional field variables	74
5.1	How was the group formed?	81
6.1	Has your organization undertaken any of the following strategies in the past five years?	100
6.2	Type of organizational change among surviving groups (1970–2005)	101
6.3	Group organizational form and change	108
6.4	Scope of change	110
6.5	Ideal type style of radical change	111
6.6	Composition of executive council of RNIB 1966–2001, selected years	118
7.1	Deployment of niche concept in group literature, summary	127
7.2	Ideal-type identity niche positioning	139
8.1	Generic forms and their core features	151
8.2	Frequency of features amongst population	154
8.3	Correlations among group features, WCL members	155
8.4	Borrowing of features across generic forms	156–7
8.5	Measures of form fuzziness and contrast	159
9.1	Category measures of fuzziness and label contrast, DBA entries selected years	169
9.2	Frequency of realized category combination, all years	174
10.1	The policy capacity concept and its link to organizational form in the existing literature	189
10.2	Policy strategy and group capacity development	193

Acknowledgements

As book project are wont to do, this volume took considerably longer to complete than first promised. In my defence this was not aided by having been employed at three universities in three different countries during the writing phase. Thus, I would like to thank the incredible patience and perseverance of the editorial staff at Routledge. Specifically Heidi Bagtazo who commissioned the book (but has since left Routledge) and Alex Quayle who never let on that he thought this book would never arrive!

Some of the work reported in this book was supported by the Leverhulme Trust (UK) funded Research Fellowship 'Interest Group Organizations: A case-study analysis' (2008–9) and the ESRC grant 'The mobilisation of organised interests in policy making: Access activity and bias in the group system' (2006–9). It was also massively assisted by a Visiting Fellowship to Stanford in 2011, where I was privileged to work at the Scandinavian Centre for Organizational Research (SCANCOR). I would like to thank the myriad scholars and students for engaging with my work so actively and to those who commented on a paper I presented (now appearing as Chapter 4 in this volume). I would single out Mitchel Stevens, Mike Hannan and Kurt Sandholtz (a then Ph.D. student) who all shared time willingly. The visit was funded by the Department of Political Science at Aarhus University, where I was then employed, and I am grateful for their support.

The intellectual task set here is something I have to take sole responsibility for. However, knowingly or otherwise, several scholars have been highly influential in making this book happen. David Lowery has been a key figure in encouraging my work in this direction and I look forward to future collaborations. As always Grant Jordan cajoled me to keep moving on to the next thing: whether this is what he had in mind is another matter. Some of the work included in this volume has been a result of research collaborations: here I would single out work with Tony Nownes and Carsten Daugbjerg. I have and continue to work with both, and it is always a joy (and lots of fun).

In recent years I have been lucky enough to make the acquaintance and spend some time talking about my work with a range of colleagues. People like McGee Young, Michael Heaney, and Matt Grossman have been generous with their time. Others in Europe such as Caelesta Poppelars, Bert Fraussen, Joost Berhkout and Jan Beyers have discussed these ideas robustly and assisted my thinking.

I presented work that found its way into this book at conferences including, the Southern Political Science Association (2009 and 2011), Midwest Political Science Association (2011) and the European Consortium for Political Research (2011). I thank discussants and chairs of these panels for providing helpful feedback and insights.

I always read acknowledgements from colleagues thanking their students and wondered how that might be – but, as it happens, several classes at both Aarhus and ANU have been my guinea pigs in this case. I thank them for their candour and willingness to ask difficult questions. I have in particular profited from discussions with Helene Fisker, one of my students at Aarhus who has gone on to doctoral studies.

Last, but not least, thanks to Jenny and the two dog-children for letting me hide away on weekends to get this thing finished.

1 Studying interest groups as 'organizations'

A lacuna?

Introduction

In his classic treatment of interest groups, James Q. Wilson claimed that 'Whatever else organizations seek, they seek to survive' (1995, 10). His point was a simple one: before groups could actually get on with their job of engaging in policy they needed to establish themselves and secure resources sufficient to be an ongoing organizational concern. Yet, Wilson – and his contemporaries – largely left this important observation at that. Missing was an explicit problematization of the 'choice' of style, format or design of group organizations. Survival 'yes'; but in what *form*?

The premise of this book is that this basic observation ought to provoke a range of rather crucial questions for the way we understand and interpret groups and the group system more generally. Specifically, if taken seriously, it challenges us to look at those aspects of group life we are well used to studying – namely, formation, maintenance and population dynamics and influence – in new, important and revealing ways. It calls for taking the terrain of organizational design seriously.

As will become evident, the classic group literature is not particularly attentive to issues of organizational design. Scholars would no doubt accept them as salient, but they are under-examined. They are – and remain – themes for the footnotes of studies of 'other' things like influence, formation, maintenance, and population-level analysis. This book sets out to identify this lacuna in the literature and, in so doing, seeks to reinvigorate an organizational perspective on group life. It puzzles over both the origins and processes driving the adoption of specific forms by single groups and the diversity of forms among group populations.

It is commonplace to rue the lack of progress in group studies, particularly compared to the apparent sophistication and progress of electoral and party studies (see Baumgartner and Leech 1998; Richardson 1999). This assessment likely underplays the extent to which recent group research has been able to start to accumulate conclusions. Moreover, it understates the extent to which group studies have been channeled into a few discrete – albeit largely independent – streams of scholarly inquiry. There are established cannons of research with

2 *Studying interest groups as 'organizations'*

respect to formation and maintenance, population dynamics and influence. Yet, against this considerable progress, one particular feature of group study has, however, been left to one side: namely, the question of group organization. Put simply, group entrepreneurs *cannot* avoid asking the question 'how should we organize?', nor can they avoid dealing with its consequences for things like influence and survival prospects. This book develops an organizational perspective on group life, and then offers illustrations as to how it might give new insights to each compartment of the interest group canon.

The aim pursued in this book is timely. In discussing research on civic participation and US democracy, Theda Skocpol makes the point that in recent decades scholars – armed with survey data on individual citizen behaviour – pursued questions about why individual citizens did (or did not) participate in voluntary associations; yet they were far less focused on 'the kinds of organizations leaders were creating [or] ... what sorts of groups were available for citizens to join' (2003, 16). This is unsatisfactory when, as Skocpol maintains, there is much diversity (not to mention substantial historical flux) in the way groups themselves are assembled. Much the same omission has existed in interest group scholarship. Perhaps influenced by the strong legacy of Mancur Olson's work on collective action (problems), the literature has pursued a largely context-free discussion of incentive structures and the rationality of individual joining decisions, with far less attention placed on the organizational substance of the groups that individuals actually joined.

A recent review by a set of senior scholars in the field argues that the shadow cast by Olson may be lifting. It is suggested that one of the hallmarks of the recent literature has been that it has left behind the Olsonian focus on the decisions of individuals – and on group joining – and thus 'the unit of analysis becomes the group rather than the individual' (Hojnacki *et al.* 2012, 10; see also Lowery and Gray 2004a, 166). And, as a consequence, studies take contextual social, economic and political variables as explanations of group organizational behaviour (such as formation, strategy or influence) (Hojnacki *et al.* 2012, 10). This is undoubtedly true, and to be welcomed. However, the tone struck by this book is that the practice of treating groups as the unit of analysis has some way to evolve. Not only is current work mostly stuck with a (convenient) unitary assumption – namely that groups are functionally equivalent but, in turn, the group field operates with few heuristics with which to guide describe, analyse or develop expectations as to how groups 'decide' to organize themselves.

Take the recent waves of population ecology work. It rightly places emphasis on identifying those factors that shape the aggregate size of the group universe, but there is little concern with the ways in which those groups constituting populations are themselves constituted as organizations (a point accepted by key authors, see Gray and Lowery 2000). In short, the existing group literature – by and large – 'black boxes' the question of group organizational form, and in so doing, deprives scholars of an insight into what are important questions of organizational crafting and design. While few if challenged would actually suggest it is empirically the case, one must assume (for the purposes of analysis) that

Studying interest groups as 'organizations' 3

groups are more or less homogenous and substitutable. While progress has been made, and there is cause for optimism, there is more that can be done to move the treatment of organization as the unit of analysis on further.

The marginalization of questions of organization is not a disease that singularly or disproportionally afflicts group scholarship. As Terry Moe (1991) eloquently argues, this state of affairs reflects the broad political science disciplines tendency to avoid studying parties, legislatures *and* groups *as organizations*.[1] As Moe explains, the choice to pursue a theory of groups, and not seek to embed this in a broader concern with organization, means that political science is borrowing – and not contributing – to the broader organizational social science literature (and vice versa). This book explicitly sets out to turn this around, by showing how organizational social science can support and rejuvenate group scholarship (and vice versa). In so doing, acknowledgement is made of a frequent complaint that there is a lack of accumulation in the interest group literature owing to a lack of common, broad or overarching theoretical questions framing the empirical work of group scholars (Hojnacki *et al.* 2012). At least so far as group organizing goes, this book aims to address these concerns.

In so doing, the intent here is not to replace or argue down existing stances. The tone I wish to strike here is of building progress and adding extra layers to existing approaches. Recent reviews of the group literature explain, with some cause, that this sub-literature is on an upswing (see Lowery and Gray 2004a). A new cohort of scholars – in the US, Europe and further afield – are engaged in large-scale data collection activities that share core questions. Whether this work can be satisfactorily subsumed by tags like 'neo-pluralist' or not, there is plenty of cause for optimism. This book seeks to plug into this emerging scholarly milieu and to make it richer. The story here is not what is wrong with scholarship, but how often-discussed and referred-to dimensions of group life might be taken up and addressed more centrally and explicitly by group scholars. In short, it is about *adding* to the conceptual toolkit from which a new generation of researchers will generate novel research questions, formulate hypotheses and hunches, and thence develop empirical accounts.

Old questions, new perspectives

The primary aim of this book is to prompt scholars to look at long-standing questions in new ways. One way to approach this task is to think about the key aspects of groups that have garnered research attention, and to recast these from the perspective of organizational form. As will be discussed in Chapter 2, the group literature might helpfully be split up into concerns with, formation, maintenance, population-level dynamics, and policy influence (which maps quite nicely onto Lowery and Gray's [2004a] influence production process). How might each of these be addressed from a fresh organizational perspective?

Let's take formation for a start. Orthodox examinations of formation are typically concerned with 'whether' or 'if' a particular group – or set of groups – is born. Put another way, the dependent variable here is the event of group

4 *Studying interest groups as 'organizations'*

creation. However, we know precious little about the types of groups that are created: what are their organizational properties?

Early work on interest groups contended, rather straightforwardly, that social change and political disturbances would lead to group formation (Bentley 1908; Truman 1971). The next generation of scholars established that external disturbance and shared interests are rarely enough to stimulate collective action and group formation. As such, the dominant framework inherited by contemporary scholars is focused on explaining *how* collective-action problems associated with group formation are overcome. The key works of Olson (1965) and Salisbury (1969) emphasized the central task of group survival or 'maintenance' as entrepreneurs managing (selective) incentives to secure member support. Inherent in this argument is the idea that groups producing only political 'goods' are vulnerable – members may not all agree on political goals, political goals may be unachievable or lose relevance over time, and politics may not be enough to attract sufficient numbers of supporters. In the face of such vulnerabilities, so the argument goes, the stability and survival of the group is secured by managing incentives, and typically by supplying non-political inducements by way of *selective* material incentives. Once created, groups are often presumed to drift into predictable oligarchy, professionalization and bureaucratization as they age (see discussion in Wilson 1995). The formation and maintenance account concerns itself with organization only to the extent that a group makes a transition from a *latent* to *formal* organization. Explanatory focus is on overcoming collective action problems so that an organization might be established. Yet there is almost no concern with the qualitative nature of the organization that is established. Put simply, we should ask not 'Was a group organization born?', but 'What style of group was born?'

The suggestion that groups have not been satisfactorily studied as adaptive organizations in their own right tends to attract the retort that this is a question of 'group maintenance'. And, it is true, the 'maintenance' literature is perhaps the only approach which explicitly sets out to study group 'organizations' and their qualitative development (Wilson 1995; Moe 1980). But where group scholars *have* been explicitly concerned with group organizations, they have utilized a model that assumes organizational practices are shaped (primarily) by the overriding need to satisfy the motivational orientations of members. Like formation, the maintenance literature is dominated by the study of incentive exchange. The maintenance literature contends that group organizations will reflect the incentive structures leaders believe are needed to maintain support, and thus survive. Consequently, there is a certain degree of inevitability that entrepreneurs will tend to 'build' group organizations that are founded on non-political incentives (those that are less vulnerable to rapid destabilization outside of the entrepreneur's control). Leaders are sketched in as key agents in group maintenance, yet their actions are to more or less 'automatically' respond to shifting motivations using stylized rational routines. The maintenance account suggests that survival will likely demand conformance to a form of group organization that matches the demand for non-political commitment among citizens, with the provision of

Studying interest groups as 'organizations' 5

selective incentives by entrepreneurs. The approach pursued in this volume eschews a reliance on teleological processes like bureaucratization and professionalization as drivers of change over group careers, whereby all groups might manifest high or low levels of each. Instead the focus is on understanding the models of organization utilized by specific groups (and sets of groups) and how these change over time.

It is not as though there is insufficient evidence that groups can transform themselves organizationally. For instance, there are studies that show small business groups in the UK transforming from activist-led outsider groups to sensible and reasoned insiders (Jordan and Halpin 2004a). Studies of poverty groups in the US found non-uniform responses to the very same challenging operating environment (Imig 1992). Others note considerable 'group transformation' in the way environmental groups operate in the UK and US (Jordan and Maloney 1997a, 17; Bosso 2005). Indeed, the wallpaper for Salisbury's (1969) classic discussion of incentive management in the US is a narrative about the way farm groups attempted – and sometimes failed – to adapt to shifting circumstances. Thus it seems worthwhile asking not how groups adjust incentive strategies, but how groups adjust or modify the organizational models they commence their 'careers' with to survive.

A related, yet somewhat distinctive, approach to the question of maintenance is provided by niche theories. This literature proposes that competition among groups over various resource dimensions might stimulate individual groups to seek out 'clear water' to operate in (see Wilson 1995; Browne 1990). Typically this meant that groups would specialize on policy issues, thus increasingly crowded group systems would lead to increased policy specialization. This approach directs analytical attention beyond straightforward questions of membership resources, and towards the way groups craft policy strategies. Yet abstract resource competition keeps us remote from the tussle over organization design within specific groups (or sets of related groups). Moreover, the mechanism underpinning this type of strategic positioning behaviour among groups is a vague notion that leaders respond to environmental resource constraints. The approach pursued in this book looks at organizational design as one potential basis of niche-building – thus distinguishing it from the usual explanation of niche-building as competition around a finite resource or policy space.

The centre of gravity in the literature's discussion of group survival has, in the past two decades, shifted to the population level. This can be attributed to the influence of the population ecology approach (see for instance Gray and Lowery 2000; Nownes 2004). This literature has been highly productive. Among other things, it has underlined the fundamental point that survival *is* precarious, not all groups born survive. This is in contrast to the formation and maintenance literature's focus on explaining *individual* group existence. Moreover, the population ecology (PE) approach emphasizes the types of general environmental factors – operating at the population level – that shape group survival prospects. Yet, the approach is not immediately helpful in illuminating or probing choices and changes in the way specific groups are organized. This is partly theoretical:

6 Studying interest groups as 'organizations'

ecological theories, as applied in the PE literature, tended to emphasize selection processes and assume some basic homogeneity in organizational formats. The other key stumbling block is methodological: the data source used involves a count of organizational births and deaths (or entry and exit from lobby populations). Indeed, key proponents freely explain that the approach is not geared up to focus on variations in individual group-level organizational configurations (see discussion in Gray and Lowery 2000, 59, 250). Existing population work focuses upon the question of *if* groups survive but say little about in what organizational form they survive. Moreover, there is little attention to the prospects for adaptation by groups *between* the events of birth and death. Whether entry and exit into and out of populations is based on an assessment of organizational persistence and disbandment (see Nownes and Lipinski 2005), or the emergence and atrophying of a lobbying function (see Gray and Lowery 2000), the basic concern is with the population as a unit of analysis. Again, the analysis is concerned with explaining aggregate population levels, and not the form in which those individual organizations survive (or whether they had to reorganize to survive).

If questions of group organization are superficially addressed in the literature concerning formation, maintenance, and population dynamics, then matters are no better in the literature concerning the policy-directed activity of groups. The recent resurgence of work focusing on the public-policy influence activities of groups makes precious little connection between the qualitative form a group exists in and its policy impact. Instead, work has been intent on explaining the types of strategies that groups utilize to seek influence, and the types of factors that 'explain' policy influence or success (whether operationalized as access or as preference attainment). It is in this explanatory exercise where organizational issues are perhaps most underdeveloped. Much basic work assumes that groups are equally capable, and compares relative policy success. However, an assumption of analytical equivalence is likely to be very misleading. Groups confront the task of influence from vastly different resource positions. Understandably, better accounts suggest that not all groups are equally *well resourced* and will likely have very different sets of 'access goods'. If one accepts that access and influence are likely to flow to the most 'politically useful' groups, then the diverse sets of goods held by groups will be a key factor in explaining access (and influence). But where do access goods come from? Access goods are not a simple case of natural endowment; rather, they have to be generated purposefully by groups. Thus they are closely linked to the organizational design of groups. Put simply, the ability of groups to generate and supply access goods is in part down to how they are organized (see Bouwen 2004; Culpepper 2001). Yet this element of influence is largely absent in the current wave of influence-based group studies.

The cost of ignoring organizational questions is even more apparent if one accepts that groups fulfill a wide range of policy-relevant roles aside from straight-up lobbying for members' interests on well-defined issues. It has been argued that groups are perhaps better understood as 'service bureaus' to policy makers (Leech 2011). The Scandinavian corporatist literature suggests that policy formulation committees – the core of administrative corporatism – can only work where groups are 'capable' partners, by which they refer to various organizational design features and their derivate functions (Öberg *et al.* 2011). If one seeks to explain the success of groups within this expanded conception of group policy work, then organizational design becomes an even more directly relevant variable. Put simply, when scholarship tries to explain the policy capacities that groups possess to fulfill important policy roles – rather than more narrowly on influence over policy outcomes – then the question of group organizational design becomes a more obvious topic (and its omission more troublesome).

To summarize, for different reasons, existing approaches to questions of formation, maintenance, population dynamics/survival and influence do not explicitly concern themselves with uncovering the organizational design of a group. Most studies are content to note straightforward group existence. Of course, 'mere' existence is a very important phenomenon to explain. Yet, a concern with entry (or entry and exit) into a population of groups does not tell us what, if any, organizational changes have been undertaken to achieve survival (or to prolong life and postpone death). Nor does it tell us anything about the organizational capabilities of those groups (or the group populations) that do survive. This all points to somewhat of a lacuna in group scholarship. Some time ago Mundo (1992, 18) noted

> despite abundant documentation of the number and types of interest groups as well as of their political activities and strategies, little is known about their organizational character. Interest groups tend to be lumped together functionally, as though they all perform essentially the same tasks in the political system.

This holds as much for today. This book seeks to address existing facets of the group canon in new ways. This is achieved by building a vocabulary and associated conceptual scaffolding for making sense of group *organizational* life.

An organizational (re)turn in group studies?

Timeliness is a critical ingredient in academic scholarship. While there may be a lacuna around the place of organization in the literature, there are also contemporary signs of a growing momentum towards taking organization seriously. In that sense, this book aims at gathering together disparate elements already sitting within the literature, and in drawing connections between literatures, as much as claiming it delivers on a new paradigm. Several contributions, from admittedly diverse directions, provide cues for the task pursued in this book.

At one end of the spectrum, we have the population ecology approach, which has emphasized the pursuit of group survival as a key driver of behaviour. While the aggregate emphasis means the approach has not explicitly unpacked group form – except to differentiate between the 'forms' of firms and associations – there

8 *Studying interest groups as 'organizations'*

have been calls from *within* population ecology to deal with the way broad environmental forces (selection pressures) are 'interpreted' and acted upon by individual group entrepreneurs, and a firm suggestion to utilize comparative case studies and group histories to do so (see Gray and Lowery 2000). Work exploring survival chances of groups and 'mortality anxiety' has included organizational variables (Halpin and Thomas 2012b). This has been extended to a more explicit concern with what *type* of group we get in our populations. We are starting to move beyond headcounts or roll-calls of survival (as valuable as they might be) (see Halpin and Jordan 2009). This is consistent with a broader rethink in the literature calling for an 'organizational' perspective to be adopted on group life (see for instance Lowery 2007; Beyers 2008; Lang *et al*. 2008); albeit, this call comes with little by way of either empirical illustrations nor middle-range theories that may guide analysis. In sum, there is accumulating evidence that noting groups exist is not enough, we need to know something about their composition and design.

This instinct is far more evident beyond what we might call the core orthodox group literature. Those concerned with broad questions of the democratic health of modern societies also counsel a closer look at the nature of 'organization building'. The long-standing practice of counting group populations – in part to assess pattern of 'bias' (Schlozman *et al*. 2012) – have become more concerned with qualitative variations in *how* these groups are organized. Highly influential accounts point to a series of generational shifts in the ways interest groups organize. There is a concern that groups – and the group system in aggregate – are becoming less capable as democratic actors in their own right. Some have argued that the set of groups formed in the early 1900s (based on local branch structures and face-to-face membership engagement) have been transformed into organizations run by professional staff, empty of membership involvement and with a single-issue policy agenda, leading to a 'diminished democracy' (Skocpol 2003) in which integrative policy capacities, important to strategic policy making, are lost. Further, the advent of direct mail and other recruitment processes have, it is argued, undermined the logic of a 'membership' model and supported a 'professionalized' model. Skocpol suggests that the answer to this broad shift in the group universe is not driven by the fact that individual citizens no longer wish to be involved in federations, but more that the types of organizational designs selected by new generations of organizers has shifted (2003, 176). While there has been a focus on the advocacy explosion, Skocpol suggests we pay attention also to the 'kinds of groups' where growth has taken place (2003, 140). Whether you buy into the particulars of Skocpol's substantive argument – and there is some considerable debate as to the empirical accuracy of her account of organizational change at the population level (see McCarthy 2005; Minkoff *et al*. 2008; Walker *et al*. 2011) – she makes the valid point that we have become somewhat obsessed with the bottom line as to 'how many' groups and unduly disinterested in 'what types' of groups we are counting.

While this debate continues, additional complications arise from the potential role of recent and rapid changes in communication technologies such as the

Internet and social media. A new generation of scholars are suggesting that the Internet and associated social media have created a third – perhaps 'better adapted' – generation of groups that foster 'virtual' participation of activists and use technology to keep the transaction costs of organizing at a minimum (Karpf 2012). Unlike professionalized models, such groups allegedly pursue a broad generalized policy agenda. Groups like MoveOn (USA) and GetUp! (Australia) are cited as exemplars of a group model that provides cheap and efficient ways to re-engage citizens with the policy process. More generally, some claim that these new technologies will overcome many collective action problems (especially for diffuse interests) thus enabling a broader, larger, and more diverse organized interest system to develop (Bimber 2003; Bimber *et al.* 2012). These claims are heavily contested, with some suggesting this technology will likely reproduce the same passive participation and professional advocacy associated with second-generation 'professionalized' models.

A key take-home from this literature is the anticipation of real diversity in the models applied by group architects. The discussion of blending among different models of group organization, and of hybrid models that borrow elements from here and there, conveys a dynamism and creativity about group organization that is sadly missing from the orthodox group literature. Yet, when one talks to groups it is hard not to see its direct relevance. It is precisely these models of association-building that this book suggests ought to be the explicit concern of group scholars.

While very much the exception, some very recent work among an emerging generation of group scholars has *explicitly* sought to incorporate and engage with organizational approaches to groups. This provides broad encouragement for the endeavours reported in the pages that follow. A recent collection exploring international advocacy organizations frames its work against classical approaches to groups that have tended to 'black box' the question of organization which ends up 'assuming that groups will have undifferentiated responses to the same external stimuli' (Prakash and Gugarty 2010, 300). It is argued that a fresh engagement with organizational theories can throw new light on the different ways that groups decide to organize themselves, even when confronted with similar contexts (Prakash and Gugarty 2010, 303). This is a key insight taken up here.

In a similar vein, several scholars have explicitly problematized the presumed uniformity of group organizational designs. Some work looks at organizational form through the lens of identity, linking it to choices over what issues to engage in and when (Engel 2007; Heaney 2004, 2007; Young 2010; Halpin and Nownes 2011). Others talk about the way groups – much like firms – consciously develop 'brands' to help differentiate themselves in crowded markets (Barakso 2011a). These contributions serve as important inspiration for what follows in this book.

Moreover, recent work has started to focus in on why and how we get the *type* of interest group organizations we find in front of us. Some have chosen to unpack the way groups develop over time as organizations, paying attention to why groups formed in the organizational configurations they did, and how this may shape subsequent evolution in a path-dependant manner (see Engel 2007; Young 2010; Halpin and Daugbjerg 2013). While for others, a focus has been on

10 *Studying interest groups as 'organizations'*

the variation in design of internal decision making processes (Barakso 2011b; Halpin 2006, 2010). What they have in common is a desire to explore the mechanisms that are responsible for explaining the organizational diversity in the group universe. These emerging threads are followed up in the chapters to come.

Still others have started to question whether competition underpins group population dynamics (Holyoake 2012) and point to the importance of the way entrepreneurs interpret environments (as either competitive or collaborative) (Halpin and Jordan 2009). Work exploring the role of firm-based metaphors and theories arrives at the way 'markets' exist for advocacy of 'products' that might be 'sold' to 'willing buyers', prompting new questions about how groups differentiate themselves from one another (Prakash and Gugarty 2010, 297). Others argue that we have become so concerned with assessing bias in the group system by focusing on relative headcounts of the number of *organizations* speaking for those with disadvantage that we have not acknowledged that these same groups are likely to address the concerns of their most advantaged subgroups over those of the more marginalized or disadvantaged subgroups (Strolovich 2007). Such an observation points to the possibility of an organizational layer to representational bias in the group system. All this provides further weight to the notion that organizational work on groups is in somewhat of an upswing: we are witnessing an organizational (re)turn in group scholarship.

At the same time as group scholars might be turning away from individuals and to organization as the unit of analysis (Hojnacki *et al.* 2012), it is, however, important to acknowledge that this is not all one-way traffic. A very dynamic, nevertheless young, literature is emerging in the area of political communication, which is focused on assessing the impact of Web-based technologies on, among other things, collective action. Within this literature there *is* pushback against the style of work pursued in this book that must be recognized. The key charge levelled at group scholars is that they remain focused on organizations as the unit of analysis, when technology increasingly renders this obsolete and redundant. They ask why the focus on groups as organizational entities when the literature increasingly discusses collective efforts that seem to rely little on any formal organization? The ubiquity of weblogs, chat rooms and email campaigns that *seem* to be a growing (if not dominant) mode of organizing suggest to some the irrelevance of standing political organizations. Thus, one might suggest a focus on 'organizing', as opposed to simply 'organizations' (see Bimber *et al.* 2009, 2012). Some also suggest that organizations no longer dictate the parameters of political action in this technological age. They argue that technology has enabled individuals enhanced agency to negotiate their own boundaries of belonging and participation with organizations, as opposed to conceptualizing such boundaries as settled or determined by the group organization itself (Bimber *et al.* 2012, 21). Others engaged in analysing the role of Web technologies for protest and collective action argue that group categorization or the application of organizational typologies makes little sense because the hallmark of extant groups in such a technological environment is an ability to project multiple identities or forms (Bennett and Segerberg 2012; Bimber *et al.* 2012).

Studying interest groups as 'organizations' 11

It is no doubt true that in some contexts technology has shifted the locus of control with respect to the nature of membership or 'affiliation' away from groups and towards the active choices of individuals. And, as such, individuals might 'experience' the same organization in different ways (Bimber *et al.* 2012). Yet formal organizations remain the predominant agents of political representation and public policy activity. And moreover, organizations need to be there for individuals to 'experience' them. Further, while hybridity is evident, the borrowing of features from across generic organizational forms is as we will see routine, and not a by-product per se of technological innovations alone (Chapters 8 and 9). Thus, in my estimation, a more sensible view, and one closer to the approach pursued here, is to see the impact of new communications technologies 'not through "organizing without organizations," but through organizing *with different* organizations' (Karpf 2012, 3 italics in original).

The approach

How to proceed? It has recently been observed that while it had been recommended for some decades that group scholars take up and adopt an economic understanding of group life, this had not been overwhelmingly the case (Lowery and Gray 2004a). Consistent with Moe's point made at the outset, this book suggests borrowing theories and concepts from the interdisciplinary field of organizational social science to help firm-up our existing hunches. In realizing the aspiration to develop a truly organizational approach to group survival and evolution, this book will introduce and develop several interrelated concepts. The purpose of this section is to briefly introduce three concepts that I suggest will provide a useful way to explore interest groups as organizations.

The key and focal concept is group 'organizational form'. In its most general sense, it is used as an umbrella term to say that we are interested in problematizing the way specific groups organize themselves: opening up the black box. It is in this manner that group scholars have idiosyncratically deployed this term in the past. But, beyond that, it is unpacked further as a series of specific usages anchored in the organizational social science literature. These are elaborated fully in Chapter 3. A distinction is made between 'generic' organizational forms – that exist as constructs, models or institutions – that serve as guides for the design of 'realized' organizational forms.

The concept can be operationalized to describe the specific form of a given group at points in time, and to describe generic forms that exist as constructs or recipes that frame and shape the way specific forms emerge. For instance, group *organizational form* can be operationalized as the organizational configuration – the set of features (strategies and tactics) and identity – a group manifests at any point in time (see Chapter 6). The basic proposition is that groups, at birth and thereafter, have to confront some basic choices around 'how should we organize?'. This involves broad questions such as 'What is our broad mission and purpose?', plus more practical concerns such as 'How should we engage in policy?' and 'From where and by what means should we garner financial

12   *Studying interest groups as 'organizations'*

resources?'. The answers to such questions – and changes to these answers – are often times heavily interdependent and, as such, are best explored together.

The form concept is also relevant at the population level. Groups most often have to answer 'Who are we?' or 'What is our mission?' in the context of the way other groups that might be similar or otherwise occupy a abutting or overlapping space answer the same question. Thus, we might seek to examine the diversity of group forms, understood broadly as their features or architecture. Or, we may also seek to examine how groups fashion more or less unique group 'identities' that distinguish themselves in the crowd, but also secure valuable resources. The approach is committed to a population perspective, whereby actions of a single group are studied against those of their 'peers'.

A 'group career', the second concept, refers to the organizational history of a single case group. It can be conceptualized as the string or sequence of specific organizational forms through which a group travels. They establish a 'form' at birth, at the start of their career, which is subsequently adapted and changed. Each new form is a step in the group's career. In general terms, it is possible to identify generic types of sequences or careers that groups tend to travel. We ought to pay attention not only to whether groups are born, and if they survive, but the organizational *configurations* in which they survive and adaptations made to such configurations in the search for survival. In so doing, the presumption is that there is more than one way to survive in the same set of circumstances: more than one 'recipe' for a viable organizational group form. I pursue an account that maps what I call group 'careers'.

Finally, the concept of 'group capacity' is developed. The focus on group organizational form may be interesting in and of itself, but how does it relate to questions of public policy? One answer to the above question is that the way a group engages in policy life (and its prospects for its success) is heavily, if not decisively, shaped by its *capacities* at any given time. *Group capacity* here is defined as the generalized abilities and skills that a group possesses to contribute to – and affect – the process of policy formulation and/or implementation at a given point in time (see Halpin *et al.* 2011). But how are capacities arrived at? It is suggested that the capacities a group possesses (or can generate) are *coupled* to the specific organizational form it embodies at a given point in time.

Several sets of questions arise from deploying these concepts and will be pursued variously in this volume:

- How might we describe groups as organizations at any one time? What language and organizing frameworks can we deploy to map group configurations?
- What types of adaptive processes go on to underpin group survival? What types of procedures, processes and systems are commonly changed?
- What dimensions allow groups to differentiate themselves from other similar groups?
- At a population or system level, do all groups survive the same? What variations and commonality is there in organizational change?

Studying interest groups as 'organizations' 13

- And what implications do such changes have for overall group capacities (e.g. policy implementation, democratic legitimacy)?

Plan for the book

The focus of this book is on addressing what is a historic gap in the group literature, namely the ways in which groups organize themselves. As will become evident, this is not so much due to a lack of attention, but that other agendas have dominated. As such, this book is as much about retrieving hidden gems in the literature as it is about offering a shiny new approach. Having said that, it is also the case that an emerging number of scholars are working in this area, and one might even go so far as to say there is some kind of momentum from which this book might positively profit.

Some books present tightly spun arguments, with a small number of narrow yet clear hypotheses which are then tested with 'new' empirical data. This is not one of those books. The purpose here is to develop a broad organizational perspective – emphasizing links with existing work as far as is possible – and then to illustrate its application to well-established areas of group research endeavour. As such this is self-consciously designed as an initial word on the matter. That being said, as far as is possible each chapter develops ideas in ways that are amenable to this kind of 'testing' style of research. Indeed, one of the basic motivations for this book is to provide momentum to an emerging thread of organizationally sensitive work in the group field.

The book first sets out to develop a broad organizational approach/perspective on interest groups guided by the concept of organizational form. With this perspective in hand, the balance of the book is designed to illustrate its utility by showing how it provides new ways of addressing core areas in the canon of group scholarship. There are no established sets of areas in group scholarship. So in this respect I am broadly guided by Lowery and Gray's (2004a) 'influence production process' heuristic from which I identify the core areas as formation, maintenance, population and influence. Each chapter explores how one of these areas might look when viewed through the broad lens of organizational form. The emphasis is on deploying varied usages and conceptualizations of organizational form, rather than privileging one over another. The next chapter is a review of the group literature. There are many excellent reviews available (see for example, Baumgartner and Leech 1998; Lowery and Brasher 2004), yet there is a lack of focus on the place of organizations within the existing canon. Thus, the purpose of Chapter 2 is to set out the various themes examined by the literature and to examine the way in which (explicitly or implicitly) the question of organization is treated.

If nothing else, this volume seeks to establish the value of group scholars speaking the language of organizational form. Chapter 3 presents an extended development of the organizational form concept. It is argued that this concept can be traced back to the work of Truman, and that as such it is a thread to be rediscovered rather than a case of importing something entirely foreign to the

14 *Studying interest groups as 'organizations'*

field. Having said that, the chapter sets out to establish and clarify the varied usages of the term in organizational social sciences, as a platform from which group scholars might then choose from and apply. Two broad approaches are evident – feature- and identity-based – under which different variations are discussed. The emphasis here is on mapping different usages, rather than legislating approaches. Indeed, the chapters that come draw selectively from many of these approaches, signalling that the intention is to promote and provoke usage of all these different approaches. It is horses for courses.

What comes next are a series of substantive chapters, each one exploring how a lens of organizational form might reshape the way we address classic questions and aspects of group life: formation, maintenance, population dynamics and influence. Chapters run in this sequence – from formation to influence – with the exception of Chapter 4.

Chapter 4 is the first substantive empirical chapter. And, out of order, it plunges us straight into the issue of population-level dynamics. Before starting with questions of formation, it is crucial to bed down the concept of organizational form – to let readers imagine what it might look like when in use. Thus, Chapter 4 starts by setting out a feature-based approach to form by describing four ideal-type generic forms. This approach takes direct inspiration from the party literature which has models like 'mass' and 'cartel' parties to make sense of and discuss party organization. To illustrate their application, the chapter tests the proposition that groups survive in *different forms* when facing the *same* objective environmental challenges and conditions. This proposition is important for several reasons. First, if it is found that groups survive using different recipes, then it suggests that adaptive mechanisms – in addition to selective mechanisms – are driving population-level survival strategies. Second, and following on from the first, it would suggest that there is no 'default' or 'natural' form for groups to survive in. Third, by varying the type of populations we examine, and examining levels of variation in form, we can try and narrow in on the ways that environmental factors matter for explaining group form.

Chapters 5 and 6 approach the classic themes of group formation and maintenance. Both chapters conceptualize groups as organizations with 'careers'. Here the focus is on understanding the organizational lives of individual group cases. Group careers consist of strings of changes in organizational form and together constitute adaptive sequences. This is not an unusual approach to political organizations generally. Long-standing observers of political parties talk of a need to focus on party careers (Rose and Mackie 1988). In so doing, they suggest that attention be paid to the way parties persist by changing form: for instance, the way a mass party transforms itself into a cartel party. The party approach to careers is also evident in the social movement literature. Scholars ask, for example, whether it is possible to document the 'natural history' of a social movement (Curtis and Zurcher 1974).

Chapter 5 revisits perhaps the most frequently examined theme in the group literature, namely formation. Here, it is (re)conceptualized as a process of identity formation, where entrepreneurs work with generic models or designs in

Studying interest groups as 'organizations' 15

order to find a desired design. First steps are tentative, conflict over designs is likely and early successes are decisive in crystallizing identity. Chapter 6 views maintenance as about adaptation of initial forms through a career, which is conceptualized as a type of path-dependent sequence. In addition, it fleshes out types of change and ideal-type change processes by developing an identity-based heuristic for describing organizational form.

Chapter 7 revisits a classic maintenance-based approach, namely niche theory. This theory suggests groups differentiate themselves from other like-groups to survive. The chapter outlines several ways in which the lens of organizational form has important lessons for this current understanding of niche theories. First, adopting an identity-based approach to form, it is argued that the space being partitioned can be reconceptualized not as 'resource' space but as 'identity' space. Second, it suggests that niche-building is achieved through (variations in) organizational design, and not through competition among groups manifesting the same design. Finally, the chapter develops a dynamic account for how the modal group in an n-dimensional identity-space might be expected to strategize over niche-building.

Chapters 8 and 9 return to the population level of analysis, taking two different approaches to utilizing organizational form in this genre of research. For ease of interpretation, and convenience, these chapters examine the same population as in Chapter 4; but the treatment is rather different. Chapter 8 addresses the question of how groups settle on an organizational design where there are no obvious generic forms to follow. Drawing on identity-based institutional and ecological approaches to conceptualizing form, the chapter develops a theory of how this borrowing and recombinational design process is undertaken. Taking the case of environmental groups in the UK, it examines the way organizational forms are created from cues from related fields such as science, campaigning and conservation groups. Drawing on categorical theories to understanding organizational form and identity, Chapter 9 explores how audiences and intermediaries have a role in shaping the value and meaning of the raw materials that groups use to fashion identities. This pushes the work in Chapter 8 further, by examining the way the generic forms or categories from which groups build identities themselves evolve. Both these chapters draw on notions of hybridity and bricolage to reflect the idea that group entrepreneurs, when building their specific and unique identities, often combine generic group forms.

The final substantive chapter addresses how we might approach the question of influence differently from an organizational perspective. It links the discussion of organizational form – and changes therein – to policy behaviour by virtue of a discussion of group policy capacity. Group capacity is defined as the generalized abilities and skills that a group possesses to contribute to – and affect – the process of policy formulation and/or implementation at a given point in time. It is argued that the obsession with influence – understood as preference attainment – underplays the variety of policy work groups engage in. When one takes a broader view of the policy work groups engage in, and the capacities required to engage in it, then considerations raised from the perspective of organizational

16 *Studying interest groups as 'organizations'*

form become central. Like many other concepts discussed in this book, capacity *has* a latent currency in the literature: the argument here is simply that it ought to be explicitly utilized and developed.

A (short) word on data

The task of this book is to develop and deploy the broad concept of organizational form – and associated heuristic devices and frameworks – in order to revisit the standard group themes of group formation, maintenance, population dynamics and influence from a new perspective. Thus, the primary purpose of the empirical discussion presented in the remainder of the book is purely illustrative: to show how this approach might work, and to promote further work by others. Thus, I utilize a wide range of empirical data sources for this task.

Group case histories

In this volume I utilize case histories to illustrate the broad approach. This does swim against somewhat of a tide towards population-level data sets. For instance, some in the organizational and population ecology literatures see population-level studies as superseding individual case-study work (see Minkoff 1999). More generally, it has often been remarked that the group literature has been held back by stand alone case-studies (see Baumgartner and Leech 1998). However, there is also a call for such work to better inform the discussion around survival. In the conclusion to their seminal population ecology study Gray and Lowery say that

> The most important opportunities for further analysis, however, may entail examining some less obvious implications of our population level findings for the survival and influence strategies and life histories of *individual* interest organizations…. Several such questions arise from our findings and merit further research, questions that will require both further elaboration of the population ecology theory of interest organizations and research design and data different from those employed here.
>
> (2000, 250)

The work reported here accepts that descriptive cases alone are not going to accumulate research findings, but that well-crafted cases can support theoretical development.

For the most part I have selected cases from among English-speaking democracies, primarily the UK, with some from the US and Australia. This was down to familiarity with the contexts, availability of data and funding sources. The UK and Australian cases are derived from data collected myself, with US cases deriving mostly from the existing literature. Primary data consists of interviews with key leadership figures. There are obvious problems in relying on interview data for historical facts – above all that in old groups no one is around to actually say what happened, and memories fade. Thus, I also use multiple secondary sources – typically annual reports, AGM proceedings, group newsletters or magazines, published histories and media coverage – to triangulate with interview recollections and to flesh out timelines and events. Again, the extent of archival resources (and my time to utilize them) are key variables in the comprehensiveness of my cases. This is inevitable, and all I can say is that I have developed cases that are broadly accepted by those who know about the context. However, I do not discount that other researchers may arrive at different views, whether by finding new records or by interpreting and collating the same material in a different manner.

Population data

One of the key propositions in this book is that groups survive differently. To address this style of claim, I need population-level data. Thus, in three chapters I present data collected on several sets of related UK environmental interest groups. Unless indicated otherwise in the chapters, the data was compiled from a range of secondary sources, including websites, annual reports and submission to the UK Charities Commission. In some instances, additional details were gathered from direct discussions with group officials (mostly via email).

Survey data

In some selected instances the results of a survey of Scottish groups is presented to substantiate and illustrate claims. In May 2008, questionnaires were sent to a sample of 1,459 non-governmental organizations identified as having responded to at least one Scottish Executive consultation exercise during the post-devolution period of June 1999 to May 2007. By the end of August 2008, 469 completed questionnaires had been returned, giving a response rate of 32 per cent (respectable for a postal survey). Questions were asked about their structure and pattern of policy engagement, but also about adapative change and mortality anxiety. While these results cannot be expected to generalize to all groups in all political systems, they are the best currently available and serve as an exemplar of how work of this nature might be replicated elsewhere.

Note

1 By way of corroboration, one can cite the rueful plea from a senior party scholar 'Why don't more people study party organizations?' (Janda 1983, 319). It may well be, as Janda noted, that studies of party organizations *only* fill a briefcase. But from a group perspective the party literature on organizations looks positively burgeoning.

2 Where is 'organization' in the group literature?

Introduction

This book is based on the premise that concerns with organization have played second fiddle in group scholarship. As evident in Chapter 1, this is not because group researchers are blinded to the salience of organization. Rather it is the case that the classic literature has focused much more on individuals and collective action than on the nature of group organizations that individuals participate in. First principle deductions about how groups are organized have often been a convenient substitute for embracing differentiated organizational models, designs and capacities. The argument developed is that such considerations should be brought out of the footnotes – where they *do* reside – and made an explicit *part* of our scholarly endeavours. Against this backdrop, the purpose of the present chapter is to briefly review and (importantly) order the group literature. This provides evidence for the above assertions in addition to providing important context for the approaches developed in succeeding chapters.

Ordering the group literature

The group literature seems to cover two general dimensions of group life particularly well. On the one hand, it conceives of the group lifespan in terms of questions around formation, maintenance and mortality (death). These three events or phases in the group life cycle are most often used to count group populations. On the other hand, the literature conceives of groups in relation to policy influence.

Table 2.1 outlines an initial ordering of the literature in the fashion described. Care is taken to identify the key questions pursued by each component, and offer some examples of well-utilized articles and books that could be said to be representative of each perspective. In the section that follows these approaches are reviewed, with attention paid to weaknesses and identifying promising leads that might be taken up.

Table 2.1 Existing group scholarship approach to organization

Perspective	Key question(s)	Key theories/publications
Formation	• How are groups formed?	• Automatic formation? (Truman 1971) • Role of entrepreneur? (Salisbury 1969) • Role of patrons? (Walker 1991) • Incentive mix? (Olson 1965)
Maintenance	• How do groups obtain membership/ support? • How are group organizations maintained?	• Dominated by collective action question (incentive mixes) (e.g. Clark and Wilson 1961; Olson 1965; Moe 1980) • Shift from political to 'other' incentives key to stable group (e.g. Wilson 1995; Moe 1980) • Viable niche? (Browne 1990; Gray and Lowery 2000; Heaney 2007)
Population dynamics	• How are group populations regulated? • What explains density?	• Population ecology approach (e.g. Gray and Lowery 2000; Nownes 2004)
Policy influence	• How do groups exercise policy influence?	Most public policy literature • Strategy choice? (Grant 1978; Binderkrantz 2006) • Influence? (Dür 2008; Mahoney 2007)

20   *'Organization' in the group literature?*

Group formation

The group literature is well developed with respect to issues of group formation. The early group theorists concerned themselves primarily with formation. Social change and disturbances led to the formation of organized interest groups (Truman 1971). The group theorists had the 'naive' proposition of more or less automatic formation. Once formed, the presumption was that a group would continue surviving until such time that the group's social or economic base disbursed or shifted. This implied the almost infinite growth of the group system.

However, rational choice approaches challenged these theories of formation. Olson (1965) argued that identifying interests did not automatically lead to formation: the failure of formation may reflect the lack of selective incentives, rather than the absence of collective interest. This implies that formation is a by-product of successful incentive structures, but where do such structures come from? Who devises and tinkers with such structures? The answer is the group entrepreneur. It was Salisbury (1969) who described how formation was predicated on the capacities of 'entrepreneurs' to construct incentive systems that attract the support of members. Others have emphasized the role of patronage and benefactors in forming groups, which effectively sidesteps rather than resolves the collective action problem (Walker 1991; Nownes and Neeley 1996).

No matter how one conceives of formation, the core concern is with establishing how it is that individuals come together and establish an organization. By contrast scant attention is paid to the characteristics of the *type* of organization that is established, and why one versus another style of group was chosen. The word organization is uttered, but it is the process of moving from a latent to a realized organization (irrespective of type) that remains *the* central question in this literature. The incentive-focus of much group theory does foster an expectation that groups most often form in a 'protest' or 'expressive' style: a form that is inherently unstable, and thus needs to be promptly transformed by a selective incentive-focused mix of inducements (see the discussion in the maintenance section below). The presumption is that formation is driven by activists, but long-term organization relies on engaging a different set of individuals (see Cigler 1986).

A broader conceptual issue concerns how to identify when a group is formed. Is it an event or a process? While the literature insists on a distinction between formation and maintenance, in practice these have been conflated. Nownes and Neeley claim that 'there is little theoretical or empirical work suggesting when formation ends and maintenance begins' (1996, 120). They suggest group formation be defined as 'the *process* by which a group comes into existence' (ibid., italics added). However, they then rest on the founding date (an event) as a proxy for formation. In a response to their paper, Imig and Berry (1996, 149) agree that there is much conceptual confusion between formation and maintenance. They suggest a move away from an event focus and back towards a process approach. In so doing they speak of a group's 'formative period', which is longer than 'the brief period when a group is formally founded' (ibid.). But

'Organization' in the group literature? 21

how this is operationalized remains unclear. This entire debate provides a strong rationale for the approach pursued in this book, which is to pursue group analysis focusing upon group careers.

In the formation (and maintenance, see below) literatures interest groups are typically assumed to wish to maximize resources via increases in membership numbers.[1] Consequently, they undertake recruitment campaigns and manage organizational incentives such that members continue contributing resources and non-members take up membership. As such, the interest group's interactions are guided by what they believe motivates people to join and stay a member.

The emergent consensus in the literature is that members respond to a mix of motives in joining. It is generally conceded that interest groups offer four types of incentives: material, solidary, expressive and purposive (Clark and Wilson 1961; Salisbury 1969; Moe 1980; Knoke 1990; Prestby *et al.* 1990). Consequently, interest group activity aimed at securing support often includes exclusive individual incentives (such as provision of services and discounts on certain items), the sponsorship of meetings that foster and support social interaction, and the provision of activities (such as participation in branch meetings and internal decision-making functions, protesting, letter-writing, voting or election to leadership roles) which promote a feeling amongst members that they have directly or indirectly influenced the policy agenda. The relationship between members and leaders is also potentially underwritten by the exchange of representation for support.[2] That is, the support of members is directly linked to their agreement with the groups policy manifesto.

The advocated 'developmental' (Young and Forsyth 1993), 'group identity' (Dunleavy 1988, 1991) and 'experiential' (Rothenberg 1988) approaches imply that interest-group leaders must constantly attend to members' changing needs. The 'supply side' approach highlights the pivotal role of leaders in structuring joining opportunities (see Jordan and Maloney 1998). The general point made is that the manner by which a constituency joins and the depth of their engagement as a member is largely constrained by the offerings made by leaders.

The ease and means with which member support is developed depends, in part, on the environment within which these members operate. The constituency's geographic dispersion, level of education, social isolation, economic prosperity and potential size are amongst many of the characteristics that determine the degree of difficulty in generating support because they may hamper the ease with which members of a constituency identify with one another and from this can begin organizing. The number of groups competing for the support of the same constituency is also a major factor (Gray and Lowery 2000).

Of course, there is an intuitive appeal to suggesting that mobilization is a matter of tweaking incentive mixes. It offers a technocratic façade on what is often a highly political process. It is not as if individual citizens simply make passive choices over what 'membership product' to consume, as if choosing toothpaste. Of course, group leaders may wish for group membership to be approached in such a superficial manner – for instance in mass membership mail-order groups – but this is a specific instance of a broader phenomena that

22 *'Organization' in the group literature?*

has to be explained. Why would a group try to foster this type of decision environment for would-be members? How easy is it to fashion such a decision environment? These types of questions are not encouraged by an incentive 'exchange' approach. I return to this in the maintenance section below.

Group maintenance

Formation may have preoccupied the group literature for some decades, but what happens after this formative phase has come to pass? As it happens, the literature is far less adept at assessing or explaining group life *post*-formation. The most direct attempt to engage with organization in a more integrated fashion is the discussion about maintenance and survival.

Lowery and Brasher (2004, 49) observe, 'Once formed, organizations must survive if they are to influence public policy. But organizational survival has not always seemed an important issue.' It is certainly true that group survival post-formation is an understudied phenomenon. Yet the issue of survival *has* been introduced under the rather benign-sounding term of group 'maintenance'. The topic of maintenance has been unfashionable for some time, and the literature is poorly structured. And, as will become evident, key contributors seem to offer contrasting – some may even say incompatible – approaches. However, Lowery and Brasher (2004) suggest it has two core threads: (i) exchange theory and (ii) niche theory.

Maintenance as 'exchange'

The exchange account – also referred to as 'incentive theory' – suggests maintenance is about leaders fostering an exchange of incentives and representation from the group to potential (plus existing) members, who in return provide the group a mix of material and political support (key works include Olson 1965; Salisbury 1969; Wilson 1995; Moe 1980). As Cigler summarizes:

> From this perspective, the development of a political group is an exchange process involving leaders offering incentives to members in return for support. Group leaders develop a package of incentives for group involvement and offer them to potential participants with distinct wants, needs and preferences.
>
> (1986, 47)

The precise constitution of this exchange is, of course, open to considerable variation. At one end of a continuum, groups may supply members with material incentives and members provide only financial support in return. At the other end, members may provide limited financial support but participate in the political life of the group in exchange for representation of their views/interests.

Exchange theory suggests that groups survive by maintaining an exchange of incentives for support with members. As such, groups are vulnerable when

'Organization' in the group literature? 23

leaders can no longer deliver selective incentives that compensate for the cost of support or where policy goals clash with the views of members. Put crudely, leaders need to sustain an incentive mix such that members keep (re)joining. This is very much a position that suggests groups survive by straightforward *continuation* of an exchange struck at formation – albeit that this may require transforming incentive mixes from a focus on political goals to selective benefit (see Wilson 1995; Moe 1980) (see the formation section above for discussion of incentive literature).

This paradigm is reliably captured in Cigler's (1986) account of the formation and stabilization of the American Agriculture Movement Inc. (AAM). He records that in the beginning,

> The organizational set-up was grass roots in form, highly democratic, with loose central coordination. The leaders flew around the country setting up local organizations, the most active of which were then asked to create a statewide organization to coordinate local activity.
>
> (1986, 50)

In its first year it had over 1,100 chapters! As Cigler puts it 'incentive theory would suggest that if AAM were to survive it would have to develop a more stable incentive base' (1986, 51). In summing up its (negative) prospect for survival in the future, Cigler says 'The group still relies on expressive and collective material benefits to attract members, and it has not developed the selective benefits incentive theorists believe essential to overcome the free-rider problem' (Cigler 1986, 66). The narrative suggests that groups that form with expressive and solidary incentives – like the AAM in its early days – risk running out of steam in the absence of selective incentives that might bind in a broad membership base once the heat goes out of the initiating issue. The dilemma they face is that shifting the organization to one structured around dispensing selective incentives might disillusion the original engaged members who were attracted by expressive incentives. The incentive theory approach diagnoses the problem of maintenance as how to develop and tweak selective incentives to overcome the ever-present collective action problem. And this has been replicated elsewhere (Jordan and Halpin 2006).

The core proposition is that after formation, the imperative driving leaders' actions becomes organizational survival rather than the original policy goals. There is a vulnerability to organizations that pursue political purposes: members may simply not all agree on goals, purposes may be unachievable or simply lose relevance over time, and purposes may simply not be enough to attract sufficient numbers of members. In the face of such vulnerabilities, the stability and survival of the group is secured by managing incentives. In passing, it is worth noting that this style of argumentation fits nicely with the predications of the so-called Michels-Weber thesis (see Rucht 1999). Namely, that as organizations get older they drift into oligarchy, bureaucracy and professionalize. Here, groups institutionalize as a function of internal processes: as groups try to establish

24 'Organization' in the group literature?

themselves on a more permanent footing, create staff roles that can be more durable (than say the exit of a influential founder), and that solidify the policy product (see discussion in Martens 2005, 22).

The biggest problem with analyses guided by such processes is that they do not in and of themselves satisfactorily capture (let alone exhaust) the diverse organizational configurations or recipes that might emerge. For instance, being 'professionalized' can mean many organizational outcomes simply because 'staff' can be from many backgrounds: in the context of environmental groups this might mean employing scientific staff, lawyers, campaign professionals, or staff with membership recruitment expertise. While one of the key planks of the oligarchy thesis is that professionalization is the enemy of member involvement, Andrews and Edwards (2004, 489) citing Staggenborg (1991) conclude that 'contrary to some expectations, professional staff increased member participation'.

Moe argues that a maintenance approach gives 'a reasonably coherent picture of the whole and of characteristics that are truly "organizational" in nature' (1980, 225–6) and 'contribute to our understanding to the extent that they are integrated into a broader perspective on the organization as a whole' (1980, 225). These claims are made on the basis that a maintenance perspective seeks to map the broader implication of the 'bases for membership' – the type of incentive that motivates membership – in any group. They claim that the different bases for membership 'induce changes throughout the organization'. For Wilson, the 'need to conserve and enhance the supply of incentives by which the membership is held in place' is the 'chief constraint on organizational leaders, [and] sets the boundaries around what is permissible and impermissible political activity' (1995, 31). Moe's own *revised perspective* integrates these two previous observations. He says of maintenance

> The key to maintenance, then, no longer simply rests with the provision of economic selective incentives, as Olson claims; nor does it solely rest, as pluralists contend, with cohesive political support. It rests instead with the continuing provision of an appropriate mix of political and nonpolitical inducements – where what is appropriate varies with constituency characteristics as well as the direction and success of leader efforts to influence them.
>
> (Moe 1980, 538)

The precise formulation may change, but it is all about incentive mixes.

This approach tends to characterize internal factors – principally the changing motivational preferences of members – as decisive in the style of organization that emerges. And the role of entrepreneurs becomes largely reactive to and constrained by established incentive preferences among supporters (often themselves shaped by environmental change). While from an influence perspective many scholars discuss the way leaders engage in quite subtle strategizing over influence settings, the exchange-based maintenance literature renders this activity subordinate to the primary exchange between supporters and leaders. But those familiar with group life will no doubt recognize that much of the work undertaken by groups and aimed at survival seems more diverse than 'maintenance' implies, noting that it is hard to persist as a group without engaging in *both* influence *and* support (Nownes and Cigler 1995).

An additional issue is the role of group entrepreneurs in maintenance. Nownes and Neeley (1996) ask 'where does a group's incentive structure come from?' They answer, from group entrepreneurs. It is true that the exchange model implies that group leaders manage the incentive mix, but we do not actually know much about 'what they do and why and how they do it' (Nownes and Neeley 1996, 120). The work of Wilson and Moe, for instance, implies that leaders are assumed to choose the 'right' mix for any given moment. But embedded in this is an assumption that *most* would-be supporters are motivated by utility-maximization: thus leaders simply act as 'relays' in formulating groups to match the basic preference structure of supporters. This inevitability means that leaders lose any strong sense of agency. However, other work suggests that leaders can manage the collective action problem, once formed, by deciding what type of group to build. For instance it has been noted that selective incentives seem to work well when the aim is build a large mail-order group, but solidary and purposive incentives seem perfectly suited to build smaller groups (see Jordan and Maloney 1997a; Jordan and Halpin 2004b, Halpin 2010). If one accepts this basic argument, then leadership cohorts have a choice about what type of group organization to build. And, in turn, this forms the basic premise around which any exchange of incentives might be constructed.

Maintenance as niche-seeking

Niche theories suggest that like-groups compete among themselves to 'find distinct membership bases, finances, and issue agendas' (Lowery and Brasher 2004, 51). As James Q. Wilson put it, 'The easiest and most prudent maintenance strategy is to develop autonomy – that is, a distinctive area of competence, a clearly demarcated and exclusively served clientele or membership, an undisputed jurisdiction over a function, service, goal, or cause' (Wilson 1995, 263). There are various approaches to niche-formation. For some, niches are built upon issue-dimensions. For instance, Browne (1990, 477) identified the propensity for groups to limit policy competition by operating in ever-narrowing issue niches. Groups compete for policy makers' attention and in this competition they differentiate from others by specializing in particular sets of issues. By contrast, Gray and Lowery draw on population ecology (PE) to establish that niches were carved out of a multidimensional resource space and not just the policy space (2000, 95). Various 'resource dimensions' – they list resources such as members, financial resources and selective benefits – are important apart from the choice of which set of policy issues to engage in. Their empirical analyses seemed to indicate that interest group niches are in fact more strongly determined by internal resource dimensions than by interaction with government (2000, 96, 108). Most recently, Heaney (2004, 2007) pursues a broader identity-based

26 'Organization' in the group literature?

interpretation of niche definition (and redefinition). The basic proposition here is that groups – existing in a highly competitive market for the attention of policy elites – consciously develop their identities in such a way as to differentiate themselves. Groups might emphasize any number of unique aspects of their organization – their representativeness, their expertise, their policy knowledge, and so on.

> By recognizing that identities reflect the needs of groups to present a public image both to members and legislators, this view provides an opportunity to unify theories of interest groups politics that currently deal separately with questions of group influence ... and group maintenance.
>
> (Heaney 2004, 621)

While I am not so sure a focus on *identity* alone will unify scholarly theories, the basic argument is sound: to better understand actual group behaviours we need, just like group leaders, to assess the relevant organizational imperatives they face in a *more* holistic manner. In the next chapter I draw on the Heaney's notion of group identity to support my claim that we ought to analyse group *organizational form*. For more detailed discussion of niche approaches see Chapter 7.

Summary

Neither of these approaches to maintenance pretends to offer a general *organizational* account of group *survival*. As Lowery and Brasher (2004, 49) correctly observe, 'Recognition of the importance of survival does not, however, make it easy to say much about it.' However, the niche-based account, and especially the identity-based version, is much closer to emphasizing the way groups organize as opposed to the processes that drive formation and survival itself. Clearly, more work needs to be done. But as they suggest, progress is by no means straightforward, and numerous methodological and conceptual challenges exist.

Group populations and mortality

An altogether different approach is to leave to one side questions about the maintenance strategies of individual groups, and to examine aggregate or population-level dynamics. The PE perspective has rightly emphasized that there are limits on the number of groups formed and that many groups do not in fact survive at all (see Gray and Lowery 2000; Lowery and Gray 1995, 2004b, 2007; Nownes 2004; Nownes and Lipinski 2005). This scholarship shifts explanations for survival *away from individual groups* to the level of *group populations*. The core contention is that like-groups can be studied as populations (what they call interest guilds), and that population levels (and by extension the survival prospects of individual groups) are largely determined by environmentally induced population-level pressures. Drawing on ecological models of population dynamics, PE scholars argue that the size/heterogeneity of a given constituency, the level of government attention, and population density (of like-groups), all feature as environmental pressures that shape group birth and death rates (the Energy-Stability-Area model).

As mentioned, this scholarship shifts analysis from individual groups to the level of group populations. It is crucial to recognize that the PE approach, in contrast to the maintenance approaches, emphasizes environmental forces *selecting out* poorly adapted groups and dampening birth rates: *group adaptation is de-emphasized as an explanation for survival*. As Nownes explains, the PE approach assumes that 'change in the organizational world is primarily a function of selection *rather than organizational adaptation*' (2004, 32 my italics). This orientation is in fact a feature of the broader approach in organizational studies on which PE draws. In his authoritative work on organizational studies, Aldrich notes

> [organizational] Ecologists tend to treat coherence of organizations as entities as relatively non-problematic, based on their assumption that organizations are relatively structurally inert. The assumption of structural inertia underlies the principle that selection, rather than adaptation, drives population level change. Populations change because of differential mortality, not because organizations live forever by adapting to each change that comes along.
>
> (1999, 45)

The PE approach explicitly privileges population level forces as crucial to survival, and not individual group traits or characteristics (Lowery and Gray 1995, 9).

The population ecology approach is important in that it problematizes group survival: the question of mortality had largely been ignored in preference to a focus on the 'event' of formation. But while PE demands scholars refocus on survival questions, which is to be applauded, the approach has limits (see Halpin and Jordan 2009). It is principally the lack of attention to the *form in which groups survive* and *to adaptive change in the pursuit of survival* that concerns this book. In PE approaches survival is appraised in terms of the dual events of group birth and death. At any point in time, PE offers a headcount of those groups that survive; but the activity that happens between the two points of birth and death for individual groups is left largely unexplored. The PE approach does not elaborate on the organizational form or configuration of these groups.[3] We know that group X survives at a given point in time, but not *how* or in what *form* it has survived. Groups are presented as though they were qualitatively the same – but surely the configuration of a particular group – even within the same 'guild' – would affect its survival prospects (and the way it adapted)? And, we might reasonably assume that the configuration of a group will be crucial in terms of shaping the 'capacity' of a given group to engage in salient activities (e.g. with respect to representation, policy implementation, provision of expert knowledge or policy-relevant data, etc.). Moreover, we do not know whether individual groups *change* forms or configurations in order to survive (or to prolong life and postpone death). The PE focus on selection rules out attention

28 'Organization' in the group literature?

to adaptation, and we are left with an account that suggests groups survive until negative population pressures pick them off.

Indeed, key proponents freely explain that the approach is not geared up to focus on variations in these individual group level features (see discussion in Gray and Lowery 2000, 59, 250).[4] While the group literature does not deny diversity in form, it does not dwell upon it nor make it the focus of study. This book sets out to make the specific ways in which groups 'choose' to organize – their organizational form – a central puzzle in group scholarship.

Group influence

Most public policy literature treats groups as 'actors' whose aim is to influence public policy. As has been observed, such studies have mostly taken for granted the existence of groups (Walker 1983, 390). Influence scholarship is a one-dimensional perspective, which tends to downplay the 'other' dimensions of group life, such as mobilization, financing, or service provision/delivery. To be sure, these activities *are* mentioned, but as background factors that hinder or enable the exercise of influence. For instance, it is relatively commonplace to suggest that the groups cannot adopt insider influence strategies in the face of calls from members for direct action – in this connection Maloney *et al.* (1994) talk of leaders walking a 'membership tightrope'. As it happens, this is increasingly becoming *the* fashionable perspective for group analysis: especially as influential scholars lament the overly dominant focus upon collective action and mobilization issues inspired by Olson's thesis (see Baumgartner and Leech 1998). I do not dispute that the collective action problem has been greedy in consuming hours of scholarly time, but I am not certain that an influence approach is necessarily *the* worthy beneficiary of a shift in attention.

For a long time the degree of *access* to state apparatus a group enjoyed has been used as an indicator or proxy for the exercise of influence. Access is generally linked to status. The literature distinguishes between several forms of status: such as 'core', 'specialist' or more 'peripheral' insider and several forms of outsider group status (Grant 1978; Maloney *et al.* 1994). The status ascribed to a group is contingent on its goals (which inform choice over strategy) and resources (see McKinney and Halpin 2007). Where a group pursues 'limited and non-controversial aims' they would pursue an 'insider' strategy, and be likely to obtain from policy makers 'insider' status (Maloney *et al.* 1994, 23). Pursuing an 'insider' strategy implies an incremental nature to a group's influence-based activities, the manner in which its demands are made and the substance of those demands. There is a basic premise that groups with 'insider' status 'will respect certain ground rules — not least of which is avoiding actions that will embarrass government' (Jordan and Maloney, 1997b, 568). Those without such aims are said to be ascribed outsider status. Of course, the exchange of (insider) status for (insider) strategy is contingent on several conditions holding (environmental variables which are subject to change). First, that the group is able to maintain and reproduce its insider

'Organization' in the group literature? 29

strategy, and, second, that the political system continues to reward insider strategies (and resists giving way to outsiderism).[5]

The second element in status is the resources a group can provide policy makers. Resources can sometimes trump strategy: a group with an outsider strategy but important resources is unlikely to be ignored. A non-exhaustive list of relevant resources would include 'the ability to organize' (the ease with which shared attitudes can be the basis for an organization), 'organizational cohesion' (the degree of member commitment to group goals with high commitment allowing leaders to speak with confidence) 'strategic location' (the control of resources required to maintain society and economy) (Maloney *et al.* 1994, 23; mostly citing Rose and Mackie, 1988). In addition, Maloney *et al.* add, 'economic significance; size (membership); knowledge (technical expertise or political sophistication); implementation power' (1994, 23).

The resource/strategy and status approach to influence has some obvious weaknesses. If one accepts, as I do, that resources and strategy are not simply 'there', then one needs to account for why settings of particular groups are as they are. This is particularly salient with respect to resources. Resource-based explanations, at least in the group literature, do not account for *how* resources are generated? Why does a group decide to develop one or other set of resources? I assert that these are critical questions, and I take them up in this volume by referring to the concept of group capacity (see Chapter 10). In addition, one might argue that strategy or tactic 'choice' is in and of itself a rather narrow gauge to assess group behaviour. Sure, these choices are important indicators of policy activity, but are we saying that they are the only – or even most – (policy) relevant? We might add to this the basic task of monitoring (see Baumgartner and Leech 2001). Even further, we might add implementation tasks and quasi-public regulatory roles. At the extreme we might see 'private' regulatory or governance activities as a – in some cases *the* – key policy activity (see Cashore 2002). It strikes me that a strategy (or even tactic) perspective defines away much that is crucial and fundamental to group policy work.

For some, analyses of choices over influence strategy or even measures of access are poor substitutes for, and indeed sidestep, the key question of influence. Of course, there are good reasons for avoiding these questions. The problem bedevilling this work is that we can never seem to find the 'smoking gun' to demonstrate that groups have been influential or exercised power in a specific instance. This has much to do with the conceptual difficulty in measuring power. However, most recently, scholars have given renewed attention to the question of group power and influence. In a recent special issue, a group of contributors seek to re-establish group influence as the subject of empirical analysis. In the lead article, Dür and Bièvre (2007) define influence as the 'control over outcomes' to be measured in the positions of public authorities and in the policies as implemented. Elsewhere, Dür (2008) suggests 'although measuring interest group influence is difficult, it is not impossible'. He identifies three methods for assessing influence as defined above: attributed influence (self- or peer-assessments by groups) preference attainment (did groups get what they set

30 *'Organization' in the group literature?*

out to achieve) and process tracing ('deep' interview and documentary case-based assessments).

The purpose here is not to evaluate the veracity of these methods to empirically identify group influence. Nor is it to pass judgement on the claim by Dür that 'the issue of influence is too important to be neglected' and that it ought to supplant talk of access or strategy/resource formulation (2008, 573). Instead, I simply want to draw attention to the fact that this discussion proceeds as though groups primarily (or only) engage in a game of policy influence, groups hold clear goals (or preferences) and that these are pursued by influence activities (mostly by some form of lobbying). Thus, group analysis proceeds to uncover how successful they have been in that endeavour. The imagery implies that influence is a product of giving evidence to congressional committees or parliamentary inquiries, or through issuing media statements. While scholars, if challenged, would admit otherwise, the influence literature proceeds *as though* all groups engage in this style of policy influence as their *dominant* or even *singular* activity. It conjures up the image of groups endogenously identifying interests and then subsequently single-mindedly pursuing these with policy makers. Like Salisbury (1984, 71) I am not convinced that the term 'lobbying' or even 'influence seeking' actually captures the majority of what groups do by way of policy work. Salisbury noted 'The word lobbying does not well convey the meaning of a presentation by a drug company representative seeking approval of a new drug from the Food and Drug Administration.' He goes on to suggest that it does not 'capture the discussions between a committee on technical standards of the Aerospace Industries Association and Pentagon procurement officials' (ibid.). One could add to this; it does not convey the way groups develop and then manage private regulatory regimes (I think here of inward-focused regulation of ethical or professional standards, or outward-directed programmes to certify the quality of products like organic food or rugs made free of child labour).

While it is easy to engage in the armchair exercise of crafting definitions of influence as controlling outcomes, the reality is that group influence is likely exercised at a multitude of stages in policy process and in ways that make tracing causality difficult to put it mildly. Beth Leech gets at the basic point when she says

> We could instead measure interim interest group success; for example, interest group success in changing the way an issue is talked about, interest group success in gaining access to members of government, interest group success in getting an issue on the agenda, or interest group success in getting members of government active on an issue.

(2011, 536)

Assessing influence as controlling outputs is to draw our analysis of group life far too narrowly. As she continues:

'Organization' in the group literature? 31

Studies that define lobbying only as attempts to pressure the legislature to change their votes are liable to measure influence incorrectly because they overlook the tactics that interest groups use that are most likely to bring success: working together with like-minded allies within government, monitoring the policy making environment, and working to build momentum for an issue to get it onto the policymaking agenda.

(Leech 2011, 545)

In this book I suggest that privileging the activity of influence has two unintended consequences. First, and paradoxically, it makes understanding the policy-orientated behaviour of groups harder to assess because it severs connections with the organizational context that both enables influence activities and gives them meaning. If the aim is to explain the pursuit of influence, the prevailing organizational structure and form of a group is no doubt crucial: both in terms of how it is pursued (strategies) and the level of success (influence).[6] As Leech explains, Berry's study of the rapid rise in US citizen group presence in both the media and in congressional testimony reflects 'that the liberal citizen groups had spent a great deal of time and effort building the capacity to conduct research and disseminate that research' (2010, 547). Second, it defines influence as the instrumental pursuit of preferences (as though they were settled matters) and seems to conjure up images of groups as organizations that *principally* engage in lobbying-style activities. A modest improvement might be to add activities like policy monitoring and networking into the mix with lobbying effort. These are no doubt precursors to lobbying activity, and not all groups are equally capable! But I plump for a more wholesale reconceptualization. I pursue the concept of group capacity as an alternative way to draw the question of influence into a broader engagement with organizational design; one that assumes groups pursue their goals via a broad range of activities apart from lobbying policy-makers.

As Leech explains

If the ability to petition government were equal regardless of means, we would have no worries about the effect of interest groups on the health of our democracy. But where alliances are forged in part because of abilities to raise campaign funds and where some interests have a much greater capacity to create and compile information, then the finding of friends and provision of information become not wholly benign. It is for this reason that research agendas that look at the *composition* of the group population and the *tactics* that different sets of groups are able to use are as important as those agendas that consider lobbying influence and policy outcomes. Who the groups in the system are and what they are able to do is critical to understanding how equal or unequal the playing field has become.

(2011, 551)

32 'Organization' in the group literature?

Identifying the gaps

As is evident above, some clear gaps exist in the classic literature. Principally, there is little *explicit* approach to the organizational character of groups. Organization does emerge within the literature, indeed it is the important wallpaper against which much activity is prosecuted, but the 'problem' of what 'form' to organize in is discussed only to a limited extent.

The formation account concerns itself with organization only to the extent that a group makes a transition to *formal* organization. Scholars may quibble over how that is achieved, but the achievement of formal organization is the end in itself. Once birth is established, then there is nothing much left to say. The characteristics of that organization are less important that its mere existence.

The maintenance approach explicitly sets out to study group organizations, but it does so with the firm conviction that organizational forms are shaped by the need to satisfy the motivational orientations of members. Thus, group organizations reflect the incentive structures leaders must develop to maintain support, and thus survive. The maintenance literature certainly countenances the idea that members, and thus group organizations, may be directed principally towards political influence. However, the general position is that such political activity generates unstable organizational forms, and most entrepreneurs tend to build group organizations that are founded on other incentives (that are less vulnerable to rapid destabilization outside of the entrepreneurs' control). This approach is useful in that it is explicitly concerned with the organizational characteristics and properties of groups. However, the insistence that the setting of the incentive system is *the* critical decision around which other characteristics are configured is less than satisfactory. It encourages scholars to generate a decontextualized set of optimal organizational adaptations, and the view that leaders will conform to one or another of these. Further, it assumes an organizational form is reached around which organizations would stabilize and thus 'rest'. In combination, this approach, while productively shifting attention to organizational characteristics, anticipates a rather narrow range of variations. It curtails any expectations of significant variations in forms within given populations, or within group careers (beyond the shift to 'safe' non-political forms over time).

The population ecology approach is important in that it problematizes group survival: the question of mortality had largely been ignored in preference to a focus on formation. However, just as with the 'formation' account, the population ecology approach is ill-equipped to answer questions around individual group organizational *evolution*. It offers a 'headcount' of those groups that survive. This does not tell us what, if any, organizational changes have been undertaken to achieve survival (or to prolong life and postpone death). The *evolution of groups* that happens between the two points of birth and death is left largely unexplored. The focus on birth and death events – and an assumption of the 'unitary character' of organizations (Aldrich 1999) – conspires to 'mask unobserved heterogeneity' (Lounsbury 2005, 93).

'Organization' in the group literature? 33

This offers a 'unitary' approach to groups as organizations. That is to say, groups are assumed to be structurally inert – largely unchanging in terms of form – and thus organizationally interchangeable and homogeneous: one group is assumed to be the equivalent of another. Thus, while it is possible to confirm fluctuations in the numbers of groups in a given 'population', little is known about whether any changes in the way groups organizations are configured has occurred during the same period. This presents groups as somewhat of a black box.

Accounts of influence have understandably tended to emphasize the primacy of changing policy and thus left organization as a prop in accounts of policy change. When the literature starts to develop exchange accounts of influence – where 'resources' are important for access – the issue of organization comes to the fore a little more. Principally, this style of account makes it clear that groups have to generate resources which are valuable to policy makers. However, organizational issues emerge here more by implication. We might be then prompted to ask 'But how able are groups to generate such resources or capabilities?': yet this is not often done in the group literature. As we will see in Chapter 10, this *is* however done more explicitly in the public policy and governance literatures.

Opening the 'black box': is there anything to find?

For the most part, the black-boxing of group organization has been a by-product of (a) methodological requirements – counting large numbers of groups makes finer judgements about qualitative variation time-consuming – and (b) analytical framework – asking questions about overcoming collective action problems does not focus on organizations but on individual calculations. But is there any evidence that opening up this black-box would yield interesting variation?

As mentioned at the outset, in the footnotes and at the edges of the group literature there is ample evidence of significant variation in group forms across the breadth of the group system. Moreover, empirical studies illustrate that groups change their organizational form throughout their life course or careers. In sum, evidence exists that a more contingent, open and malleable view on group organizational form – within populations and over individual group careers – would be well rewarded.

There is plenty of evidence that group organizations in the same general field vary significantly in their 'form'. Imig's case study of poverty action groups in the US found non-uniform responses to the same challenging operating environment. He reported that

> For one group, budget reductions forced organizational retrenchment, while for another, budget reductions led to increased fundraising and new issue domains. One group with an expanding budget shifted its policy agenda to less confrontational issues in order to maintain a stream of resources, while a second, flush with resources, employed lobbying tactics new to the social

34 *'Organization' in the group literature?*

welfare sector to pursue an agenda particularly confrontational to governmental institutions.

(1992, 517)

Such results suggest a place for group agency in accounting for survival, and, moreover, on the particular interpretations of leaders as to how survival may be achieved. The *same* 'challenging' environmental conditions prompt *different* responses. Jordan and Maloney (1997a, 17) also seem to foreshadow a focus on organizational change – they say 'organizational transformation' – among groups. Halpin and Jordan (2009) suggest that agency be attributed to groups – they both adapt and transform in face of environmental changes – and that the role (and perceptions) of leaders are crucial in explaining change.

There are few case studies of groups that pay attention to organizational form and also discuss change over time, but the studies that do exist report significant changes over time. For instance, the National Rifle Association (NRA) is in the popular consciousness a pin-up group of the US right. But, as Skocpol (2003, 157) points out, from its founding in 1871 until the 1970s it was in effect a group for marksmen. The NRA of 1891 is by no means the NRA of 2013. This case, and many others, underscores the point that it often makes more sense for activists to fight over control of existing groups than build new ones. And this, in and of itself, makes the broader point that simple headcounts of groups can underplay the dynamism of the population as a whole. A similar story can be made based on housewives' associations in Norway. The radical decline in the number of 'stay at home' housewives after the 1960s should 'following organizational ecology' mean that 'this entire organization type should lie down and die' (Wollebæk 2009, 369). But evidence shows more than half of the groups that were alive in the 1980s survive to this day: the explanation is adaptation through broadening the constituency base (housewives to women) and relabelling to Women and Housewives Associations. It is suggested that 'this fundamental reorientation *saved* this type from mass extinction resulting from a decline in the number of housewives' (Wollebæk 2009, 369).

It has been remarked by some scholars that groups seem able to persist beyond the point where environmental conditions would seem to support them. For instance, referring to Australian industry policy more broadly, it has been noted that 'government-industry relationships often survive well after the conditions upon which they were based have changed' (Wanna and Withers, 2000, 84). In the context of economic internationalization, Coleman (1997, 147) argues that peak economic groups may appear like 'the image of a dinosaur – old, lumbering, and soon to be extinct', but that they often able to 'weather the storm' using considerable adaptive capacities. The volume by Halpin (2005) largely finds national farm associations sticking – albeit with adaptive processes evident. This type of finding questions the decisiveness of environmental pressures on group survival. The population ecology approach has been drawn from a long-standing and well-developed organizational demography literature, which is focused on populations of for-profit businesses. While businesses can be driven rather easily and quickly out of business by a souring economic and trading

'Organization' in the group literature?   35

environment, there are reasons to expect interest groups to be more persistent and adaptive that businesses. As Wollebæk (2009, 369) suggests, groups have greater 'tenacity' that for profit businesses, they 'can subsist on limited resources even in the face of serious decline'. The puzzle of group survival or persistence adds weight to expectations that existing groups adapt to new circumstances.

Several tentative conclusions can be drawn which can guide the approach in this book. First, groups do respond to environmental pressures in ways that seek to undo negative impacts. Second, groups do not respond by simply 'matching' environmentally prescribed 'ideal type' forms. As Nownes and Cigler (1995, 397) argue, 'there is no *one* road to group success'. We therefore expect (or at least are open the possibility) that like-groups differ in the form of adaptation and transformation. Third, as other work emphasizes (see Voss and Sherman 2000), the experiences and assumptions of leaders are crucial to the way the group develops. How they read, diagnose and interpret challenges structures their responses, and thus the careers of group organizations.[7] Groups can borrow forms from others, adapt elements of other forms and innovate entirely new forms (Clemens and Minkoff 2004, 159). Fourth, leaders' actions to adapt to changing circumstances may also include discursive elements, such as constructing organizational frames that legitimate or make 'thinkable' new organizational forms (Clemens and Minkoff 2004).

This being said, it is also important to remind ourselves that groups structures and form are *not* simply the consequence of the 'rational' design of insightful leaders. The organizational form that emerges is likely to be heavily constrained by external pressures, the internal group politics, organizational history and the leaders' experience, assumptions and capabilities. Reflecting on his comparison of agricultural groups across several countries Halpin (2005) remarked;

> Group structures may make more sense if we assumed they were designed under a rationale of 'making do' rather than one of 'optimization'. As is apparent in many cases in this volume, while groups often seek to engage in efforts at organizational design these are often thwarted by the dictates of tradition and internal conflicts.
>
> (Halpin 2005, 231)

Nevertheless, ample evidence exists to suggest that groups do a great deal between when they are born and when they die. There is much evidence of 'adaptive' or 'transformative' intentions, discussions and often (but not always) actions. Thus, in exploring this survival-related activity, we ought to track group organizations over time and be attentive to the actions of leaders in interpreting environments and then adapting and transforming group forms.

Conclusion

The review above shows a vibrant literature. Yet it is a literature that has tended to bunch around a set of core questions. A new student to group scholarship would assume the key questions were; Are groups influential? How do groups

36 *'Organization' in the group literature?*

overcome collective action problems to form? After formation, what incentive mixes allow groups to be maintained after formation? What factors shape mortality?

The argument here is not that these questions lack merit, but that at least one very important set of considerations has been underplayed. I suggest that there has been insufficient attention to the (i) form in which organizations emerge, (ii) how organizational forms are adapted over time, (iii) the variation in organizational design within populations of like-groups, and (iv) the role of organizational form in the pursuit of policy influence. The task of this book is to enunciate these concerns, to explicate why they are important and to provide a preliminary set of concepts and approaches that might be useful in empirically researching them. In what follows, these four broad areas of conventional group scholarship are revisited through the lens of organizational form. The result is not the final word, but a provocation to scholars to more consciously weave in the organizational dimensions of group life into these areas of work.

Notes

1 In the context of sectional groups with a high proportion of a constituency, their density is often viewed as an important resource for access. This may also be the case where the group derives most of its income from members.
2 Support can be expressed in a range of observable ways that generally correlate with degrees of participation (see Richardson 1995, 76–7).
3 While PE studies *do* pursue explanations of diversity within group populations this is constrained, for instance, to the relative concentrations of groups organizing different economic sectors in a system (see Gray and Lowery 2000; Lowery and Gray 2007).
4 The notable exception would be the work of Gray and Lowery (2000). They distinguish between associations, associations of associations and institutions. Our focus here is more fine-grained, on variations among associations/interest groups. However, the Gray and Lowery work provides a neat example of the style of work that I seek to build upon.
5 See Grant (2001) who argues that interest group influence activity (at least in the UK) is in fact characterized by increasing levels of outsider activity; and that governments are giving into it, which is destabilizing orthodox patterns of insider exchange.
6 Parameters such as group resources (financing, expertise, etc.) and the types of interests they organize (diffuse or concentrated) are mentioned. But these appear as variables that fetter or embolden the execution of influence. They are not part of a discussion of the relative importance of influence to the purpose or activity of the group.
7 Of course, intra-organizational issues remain. Leaders may not have power to implement their plans, and much effort can go into keeping existing forms viable.

3   Interest groups and organizational form

Introduction: speaking the language of 'organizational form'?

How do groups settle on an organizational design at establishment? Do groups adapt and change models over their careers? Are groups – even when operating in the same environment – organized the same way? If not, how much diversity is there? What organizational models or recipes are deployed? These are important questions to the study of group life, but ones that have attracted relatively little dedicated attention. As is no doubt clear, this book sets out to (re) commence a discussion around the organizational dimensions of interest-group life. It does so by making the case for group scholars speaking the language of group 'organizational form' and pointing to how this might be translated into empirical analyses of group formation, maintenance, population dynamics and influence.

The basic premise is that the literature on interest groups underplays the issue of (variation in) group organizational form. The dominant framework inherited by contemporary scholars is focused on explaining *how* collective-action problems associated with group formation are overcome (Olson 1965; Salisbury 1969). This is transposed into the maintenance literature, where it fosters the expectation that groups producing only political 'goods' are vulnerable – members may not all agree on political goals, political goals may be unachievable or lose relevance over time, and politics may not be enough to attract sufficient numbers of supporters. In the face of such vulnerabilities, so the argument goes, the stability and survival of the group is secured by managing incentives, and typically by supplying non-political inducements by way of *selective* material incentives. While maintenance clearly is about survival, much scholarly discussion of maintenance seems to overemphasize managing incentives at the expense of more diverse considerations. One such consideration is the *organizational form* in which groups maintain themselves.

While recent work – mostly on population dynamics (see for instance Gray and Lowery 2000; Nownes 2004) and influence/lobbying (Leech *et al.* 2005; Baumgartner *et al.* 2011) – replaces the focus on individual behaviour with organizational behaviour (see Hojnacki *et al.* 2012), the dependent variable is typically a headcount of group numbers. Thus the apparent 'organizational turn'

38 *Interest groups and organizational form*

is not immediately helpful in illuminating or probing choices over organizational models. To be clear, the population dynamics and advocacy literatures do not *deny* diversity among the organizational models utilized by groups, they just do not dwell upon it nor make it the focus of study.[1] Against this backdrop, the broad argument developed in this chapter is that group scholars would do well to pay *more* attention to questions of form.

Inattention to the organizational qualities of groups is largely related to the absence of a vocabulary and conceptual scaffolding to direct attention to these issues. The foundational concept in the approach outlined in this book is *organizational form*. The term is intuitively attractive because it seems to capture nicely the idea that scholars ought to be attentive to the way organizations are put together. Applied in this general sense, the emphasis on organizational form signals a concern with the precise organizational nature of a group (and sets of related groups) at a given time, its organizational 'recipe', 'design', 'model' or 'configuration', if you like. It is an umbrella term to capture this general orientation to research.

This is not, in and of itself, novel. By happenstance, other group scholars *do* use the precise same syntax. In fact, Truman made a very early observation that groups embodied a varied range of 'organized forms' and he pondered how such forms might be arrived at, how they might change, and – salient to our task here – how one might generalize about them (1971, 115). James Q. Wilson discusses the difficulties facing US 'traditional business associations' in the 1960s, and he talks of them reconsidering 'tactics and organizational forms' (1995, xiv). By form, he refers to the unease with peak bodies, groups that speak for an entire sector, otherwise known as 'umbrella groups', and the growth of firm-based lobbying and sector specific bodies. Wilson also refers to the absence of satisfactory accounts of how civil rights movements transformed from small local groups focused on mobilizing to national bureaucratic organizations better adapted to policy implementation (1995, xv–xvi). Hayes, for instance (1986, 134) talks about the way groups resemble one or other set of organizational forms (this important contribution is returned to in Chapter 4). It is also mentioned in passing by Jordan and Maloney (1997), who settle on the term 'protest business' to identify a form of group organization that relies on high-profile influence campaigns, is funded by a mass remote supporter base and is run on clear (for-profit) business principles.[2] In their population ecology studies Gray and Lowery (2000) refer to organizational forms and use categories of firms, associations, and associations of associations, to empirically distinguish among lobbying organizations. It is more explicit in the work of Minkoff *et al.* (2008) who analyse a large data set of the structural features of social movement organizations to discern whether there exists a set of *fundamental* social movement *forms*.

While an explicit sensitivity to organizational styles and designs might be systematically lacking within group scholarship, there is evidence enough that there is no innate resistance to a concept – at least in name – like organizational form. Thus, my message here might be more accurately restated as a call to *reacquaint ourselves* with an old yet neglected thread in the literature.

Interest groups and organizational form 39

Yet, these references to organizational form do lack a systematic usage and conceptual foundation. And this is needed in order to reassure contemporary scholars that an investment in this concept will pay dividends. To firm up these helpful foundations, it is suggested that group scholars borrow from the organizational studies literature, where the concept of organizational form has been heavily discussed and deployed. In essence, the suggestion here is to effectively borrow a concept in good standing and apply it to interest group studies. Speaking the language of group organizational form can encompass a range of styles of research. That is, the approach taken to *defining* and *conceptualizing* forms can diverge considerably (see Hannan 2005 for a recent review of organizational ecological work). The purpose here is to provide a sense of the range of ways group scholars might use the concept, which will then go on to inform the specific foci taken in subsequent chapters.

This chapter makes the argument that group scholarship would benefit from rediscovering the concept of organizational form. Such a concept directs attention to the organizational architecture and models of groups (and sets of groups). The concept has been utilized heavily in organizational studies, but also in the political party literature. This chapter explores how it might be deployed to assist the study of interest-group organizations. Empirical application is left for subsequent chapters; for now, the focus is on establishing what speaking the language of organizational form entails. The purpose is not to legislate approaches, but, rather, to relate in broad brushstrokes a style of work that takes organizational design seriously and to provide various ways in which this might sensibly be taken forward. Group scholarship is a broad church, and the approach developed here attempts to speak to all members of the congregation.

Approaches to conceptualizing organizational form

In building on these formative insights scattered within the group literature, I turn to organizational social sciences: a cross-disciplinary literature encompassing political science, sociology, management and business studies disciplines.[3] Here we find several sets of concepts and methods of analysis that will assist group scholarship in pursuing organizational questions that have hitherto been left to one side (see Chapter 1).

The notion that organizational social science scholars ought to pay attention to the way specific organizations were put together started, arguably, with Arthur Stinchcombe (1965). He identified that distinctive generic types of organizations – that is, organizational forms – seemed to emerge in specific historical periods. Organizations were imprinted with something akin to an organizational date stamp. The broad idea of a form-like concept has since been a central one to social scientists engaged in research in all sorts of organizational fields – firms, public sector and not-for-profits alike – yet it is one that has evaded crisp definition. Successive reviews of this area confirm there has not been a *common* definition of the concept (Romanelli 1991; Carroll and Hannan 2000, 60; Aldrich and Ruef 2006; Fiol and Romanelli 2012). It has been suggested that 'the

40   *Interest groups and organizational form*

definition and use of organizational form has become, if anything, more elastic' over time (McKendrick and Carroll 2001, 662). This need not be a reason to avoid or abandon the term; rather, it simply calls for a good sense of varied usages and their implications. Such conceptual 'gardening' is worth the effort.

What *is* settled is that the concept speaks to a concern with the way organizations are put together: reference to terms like models, types, formats, configurations, blueprints, recipes and such-like gesture to this common sentiment. The concept is linked to the design and assembly of actual organizations. In addition, the concept denotes a concern with what we might consider as *generic* ways of organizing that might inform the way specific or *realized* entities (firms, interest groups, etc.) organize themselves. It is quite usual to discuss the 'form' of a given organizational entity (indeed, I do this throughout the book); but, used in this way, it is about assessing individual realized organizational entities. Yet, the concept of *organizational form*, in all its applications, is also about summarizing the various ways of organizing that are 'available' at a given time (as opposed to realized at a given time) as guides for how specific entities might organize. For instance, while prohibition in the US meant there were no pubs or industrial breweries in existence, the 'form' persisted and thus was able to guide re-establishment after the end of prohibition. This distinction between organizational form as a term capturing *realized* organizational entities (e.g. The Australian National University) and *generic* organizational models (e.g. the 'Research-intensive University') is an important one. While this is an important conceptual distinction, as one observer notes, the essence of the concept of organizational form is the notion that it captures the need for specific organizations to both be 'distinct' yet at the same time part of a broader set of 'similar' organizations (Romanelli 1991, 81–2). That is to say that empirically, we would expect actual realized organizations to resonate with, yet be a little different from, generic organizational forms.

This is all consistent with the broad tenor of this book; namely that speaking the language of organizational form is about being attentive to how groups (and sets of groups) design themselves as organizations. This works as a statement of intent, yet is unsatisfactory as a working definition of the concept. It is argued that there are several discernable conceptual approaches to organizational form, each of which implies different ways of empirically identifying it. Again, there is no agreed or settled narrative laying out traditions. Thus, it is argued here that two broad approaches are identifiable (with numerous variations). Awareness of these practices will serve to assist group scholars in better locating – and explaining – their particular choice of approach, thus reducing conceptual confusion and facilitating accumulation in the literature. These are not set out in order to distinguish 'good' vs. 'bad' approaches; simply to ensure that we have a language to explain our approach vis-à-vis one another. In fact, the 'horses for courses' logic is underlined by the fact that all variations are applied to some extent or other in the chapters that follow.

The various approaches to *organizational form* are set out in the sections that follow below and summarized in Table 3.1: not in order to legislate the 'right'

Table 3.1 Summary of approaches to conceptualizing organizational form

Approach	Variations	Empirical operationalization?	Defined by?
Feature-based	(a) Demographic	ISIC codes Industry directory	Objectively defined by researchers
	(b) Taxanomic	(Exhaustive) clusters of features	Objectively defined by researchers
	(c) Core features/architectures	Single or several features (core defined by theoretical purposes)	Objectively defined by researchers
	(d) Blueprints	Models used by organization leaders to guide development	Mixed
Identity-based	(a) Ecological	Identity codes	Subjectively derived from context
	(b) Categorical	Social and cultural typifications	Subjectively derived from context
	(c) Neo-institutional	Archetypes or templates	Subjectively derived from context

42 *Interest groups and organizational form*

way to proceed, but simply to show the choices, and implications of those choices. It is suggested, following Romanelli (1991) and McKendrick and Carroll (2001, 662), that one utilizes these as alternative approaches, rather than trying to integrate all approaches into a single analysis.

As will become clear this structuring of the literature is by no means settled or agreed (for a not dissimilar alternative see Aldrich and Reuf 2006, 115). It is provided as an aid to discussion and to assist scholars in pinpointing the ways they deploy the concept and the advantages and disadvantages of each. In so doing, one point to keep in mind is that there is a distinction between the ways in which one tries to operationalize organizational form/identity in empirical research. For some, these are defined a priori by the researcher: sets of core features are defined or key categories that make up identities are established. This is typical of what I refer to as a feature-based approach. For others, they belong to the actors in the context: researchers utilize the way organizations define their own identities (via missions or branding) or else establish what models real organizational leaders utilize in designing their organizations (in contrast to others). This is most usual in what I refer to as an identity-based approach. Again, these are sometimes mixed, but I have noted the norm within each approach as guidance.

Organizational form: feature-based approaches

The 'original' definition that is commonly referred to in the literature is that provided by Hannan and Freeman (1977): 'an organizational form is a blueprint for organizational action'. Just like builders constructing a new house go off a plan – its blueprint – the same is assumed to apply to organizations.[4] They suggested that these blueprints could be 'inferred' by researchers in a number of ways such as 'examining the formal structure of the organization', 'patterns of activity within the organization' and/or 'the normative order – the ways of organizing that are defined as right and proper by both members and relevant sectors of the environment' (1977, 935). By their own admission, this definition was not as precise as it may have been. This, in turn, meant that several related (yet varied) practices emerged claiming fidelity with this definition.

The *first* is popular among those who might be referred to as 'industrial or organizational demographers', whose interest rests with enumerating populations of 'forms' over time (see Carroll and Hannan 2000, 64). In this work, organizational form was conceptualized as a localized population of entities reliant on the same environmental resource base (Carroll and Hannan 2000, 64). In practice, most work relied on 'conventional industrial categories' in defining populations (and thus forms) (Hsu and Hannan 2005, 475). The concept of 'form' in this sub-literature became synonymous with industrial or market boundaries. Studies recorded and sought to explain the rise and fall of populations of fast-food outlets, Fortune 500 companies, credit unions, breweries and baseball teams.

Consistent with this approach, Hannan and Carroll state 'Organizational populations are specific time-and-space instances of organizational forms' (1995,

29). And, conversely, the existence of a population of a high-density is used to establish that an organizational form exists: the growth of the number of 'brewpubs' as opposed to regular 'pubs' and 'breweries' was sufficient for scholars to describe that as an organizational form (Carroll and Swaminathan 2000). There is a certain (acknowledged) circularity to this general approach which has proven hard to disentangle: 'form' is used to define the boundary of a population and, at the same time, if an organization is defined as part of a given population it is thus presumed to share the form of others in the population. An additional problem has been whether these populations (and thus forms) so defined are actually meaningful units of analysis. As Carroll and Hannan observe, the 'value of such research depends upon the degree to which the population studied represents an instance of a clearly bounded form' (2000, 64). Over time, there has been less conviction that industry categories are always salient in terms of identifying forms. Put simply, there is a question mark over whether such boundary lines mean anything outside scholarly convenience.

For our present purposes, the biggest problem is that this circular logic renders diversity of form difficult to assess, as it is 'baked-in' to the research question. Taken alone, the industry demographic approach generates a 'monothetic and essentialist' conception of *organizational form* 'which focuses on the average in a population and ignores the breadth of variation and the amount of diversity' (Aldrich 1999, 36). Methodologically, it means that change is assessed only in relation to a given organization's superficial 'fit' within the established boundary of a population/form definition; change in which *must* lead to its exit from the target population (and thus the organization exits from the analysis) (see Young 1988, 10). Some work does, of course, try to address this weakness. In a more focused study Hannan and Freeman (1987) examined trade union 'forms' and differentiated between two sub-forms: the craft union and the industrial union form. The former organizes individuals by skills (e.g. carpenters, bakers, etc.) the latter by workplace location. Looking for variation *within* organizations *sharing* a broad generic form requires some recourse to a more fine-grained feature-based approach to form.

Over time, work became more concerned with and attentive to the actual *features* of organizations. Here, Weber's identification of the bureaucratic 'form' is often cited as the seminal example. Several sub-approaches are evident. An initial approach was *taxonomic* in inspiration, with the aim to establish an exhaustive set of organizational types with an associated labelling system (McKelvey 1982). However, several difficulties emerge with this. For one, it is hard to see organizational entities 'fitting' so inconclusively into a single 'form' that successive researchers could be expected to reliably replicate taxonomic coding. Moreover, any taxonomy that could satisfy this condition would likely have the most tenuous of links to the 'real' world of organizing as to be of dubious value (Albert and Whetten 1985). Subsequent work tried to develop basic organizational *architectures* on which organizations might be designed. In this vein, many business-related studies have tried to pinpoint the *set* of organizational features that are *best adapted* or *optimal* to particular business operating

44   *Interest groups and organizational form*

environments: these then serve as recipes for organizational change processes that can be pushed by management consultants and the like. Perhaps the best know is the 'M-form' organization: an organization that has a set of semi-autonomous units controlled by financial targets issued and monitored from the centre (see Williamson 1975). Each of these above variations share an attempt to summarize very generic ways of organizing (applicable to any set of organizations); with one form to be distinguished from others by a single or limited set of key organizational features.

More usual was for scholars to look for 'coherent configurations' of important or salient features that exist *empirically* among some specific set of *like organizations* (Meyer *et al.* 1993). That is, to identify typologies or a small number of familiar or regularly occurring 'clusters of features' that can be given convenient shorthand labels: in turn, these *generic* forms can be compared to *realized* empirical organizational forms (i.e. actual organizational entities). This feature-based approach assumes that when organizations share the same set of features then, by definition, they share the same form. The risk here, of course, is that compiling lengthy lists of features conflates the important features with the unimportant. How to discern what features to measure, which ones matter, and in what combinations? Subsequent work counselled to avoid laundry lists in favour of identifying 'core' features that distinguished one 'form' from another: 'Organizations with the same core features belong to the same form by this view' (McKendrick and Carroll 2001, 662). But how to decide what is 'core'?

Common to each of the accounts above, is the instinct to set relevant or *core features* based on scholarly or theoretical salience or interest. Within early demographic studies and feature-based analysis, it was suggested that scholars take a flexible approach, but that the specific features of interest – the 'core' features – ought to be decided on by the scholar (Hannan and Freeman 1977, 934; 1989). Thus forms might be defined based on variations in 'core' features like the HR system, centralization of management, budget controls, and so on and so forth, depending on the research question at hand. However, subsequent work has questioned whether this approach introduces shortcomings, because it is not altogether clear that scholarly definitions of form will have any resonance with those who are participants in the context. Limitations arise when definitions of forms are divorced from the 'social world' (McKendrick and Carroll 2001, 662).

In reaction to this problem, a related approach develops definitions of form as abstract or generic *blueprints* through interviews with participants and archival material. The assumption here is that participants in a given context, just like researchers, *also* have sets of generic types or models that guide their organizational design work. An early, and perhaps mild, version of this approach is DiMaggio's study of US museums (1991). He utilized all sorts of documentary analysis to identify how two generic 'models' of museum emerged (a conventional and reform model), and how 'real' museums 'chose' between them (and the implications). Each model constituted a basic difference in mission: the former to collect and conserve, and the latter to exhibit and educate. This difference in mission then translated into target audiences, methods of internal control, key strategies and other organizational features. Baron *et al.* (1999) interviewed founders of firms to examine the blueprints they utilized in designing initial organizational structures and practices. In a similar manner, Rao (1998) examined archival material to explore the blueprints that leaders of consumer organizations worked with in deciding how they ought to be organized. The aim of this approach is to understand what blueprints organizational managers, leaders and designers have in mind when they establish and develop their organizations. This approach overlaps with the institutional *identity-based* approach which has over the past decade dominated writing on organizational form (more on this below).

Feature-based approaches define form by identifying and coding observable attributes of organizational structure. There are, however, differences. Forms are approached as (i) generic styles of organizing (e.g. M-form, bureaucratic form), (ii) a specific architecture shared by related organizations, denoted by a set of core features and identifiable by the observer (say, in the architectural style) or as (iii) cognitively held 'blueprints' that inform the way entrepreneurs develop their own real organizations. When conceptualizing form, the basic choice is between generating a list of theoretically derived off the peg forms or the individual scholar identifying models based on the blueprints recognized by those organizational entrepreneurs in the context at hand. Both are valid approaches (see Schneiberg and Clemens 2006); the key is to be clear on which one is being used.

Organizational form: identity-based approaches

While feature-based work – almost regardless of approach – utilizes 'surface attributes' or 'structural elements' to define forms (both generic and realized), the more recent literature has coalesced around an identity-based approach which explicitly defines forms as social and cultural objects (Carroll and Hannan 2000, 62; Hsu and Hannan 2005). Again, there are varied practices within this approach; yet at its core is the commitment to forms as being 'sociologically real'. That is, forms exist as social constructs and are 'real' for those participants in the context being studied. The claim is that 'the classification of organizational entities into types ... is not a process divorced from the social world', rather it involves 'social and cultural typifications' which are processes 'that build upon identities' (McKendrick and Carroll 2001, 662). In turn, this means scholars 'can rely on information provided by participants to define ... organizational forms' (Brittain and Wholey 1989, 440). That being said, differences exist as to whose perspectives on defining identities – and thus forms – matter!

Let's start at the start: what does it mean to say an organization has an identity? As a concept, organizational identity is most often traced back to the seminal work of Albert and Whetten (1985). They argue that, like individuals, organizations can be considered to have an identity. For them, a given entities organizational identity says something about its *central/core character*, what is *distinctive* and what is *enduring* about an organization.

46 Interest groups and organizational form

Of the many elements of their rich article, one particular distinction they make can help build our identity-based treatment of organizational form. Most salient is a distinction based on for and by whom an organizational identity is being constructed. On the one hand, organizations routinely ask themselves and have internal discussions about 'who are we?' or 'what do we stand for?' or 'what makes us distinctive?'. On the other hand, external audiences (who often possess valued resources) routinely evaluate organizations they confront asking something akin to 'what kind of organization is this?' Organizational forms are the currency through which these two questions are mediated. Let's take each in turn.

Organizations often ask themselves what they are for and what makes them different or unique. In this task, Albert and Whetten suggest that organizations choose salient features to describe their identity – and in so doing outline what is core, distinctive and enduring about them (Albert and Whetten 1985, 116). In turn, researchers proceed on the basis that an organizations identity is evident in its 'core features' – often encapsulated in its mission statement or key strategic orientations – and that changes in such features would change an organizations identity. In this perspective, internal organizational agents (CEOs, founders, board members) decide and set out what an organization 'is about' or 'stands for' and this becomes its organizational identity. This would lead researchers to define organizational identity as 'the shared beliefs of *members* about central, enduring and distinctive characteristics of the organization' (Golden-Biddle and Rao, 1997, italics added).

In taking this line, one need not be naive with respect to the level to which beliefs are actually shared when establishing or forming organizational self-identity. Tsoukas and Chia (2002) argue that organizational leaders have 'declarative powers' by which they can heavily shape change processes by providing 'authoritative' interpretations of how organizing should occur: that is, they are in 'a privileged position to introduce a new discursive template that will make it possible for organizational members to notice new things, make fresh distinctions, see new connections, and have novel experiences, which they will seek to accommodate' (Tsoukas and Chia 2002, 579). But this does *not* equate to the imposition of plans onto organizing itself. As they argue, 'the introduction of a new discursive template is only the beginning of the journey of change' (2002, 579). While there is a long-standing tradition in group scholarship – as in organizational studies (especially entrepreneurship and strategic management strands) – to attribute a strong role in organizational affairs to leaders or entrepreneurs,[5] it is not that leaders can *determine* the groups they wish to have. Just because one view about what legitimate form a group should take dominates does not mean the losers (or their practices) will go away. There is an important political dimension embedded in identity formation. There are likely multiple sets of (internal) expectations about what is an appropriate form for a group.

While organizations themselves seek to define their own identities, organizations are also evaluated by external audiences. Here, identity is ascribed by those evaluating an organization, and not simply a consequence of efforts by the

Interest groups and organizational form   47

organization itself (see Hannan 2005). It follows that an audience decides on the identity of a given organization, regardless of (or despite) the attempts of organizational insiders. For example, while 'oil' companies might seek to re-establish identities as 'energy' companies – thus avoiding the negative associations with the carbon economy – the success of such efforts all depends on whether key audiences (such as investors and consumers) accept this identity as somehow authentic. Here 'authenticity' refers to the resemblance of realized organizational entities with the essential features denoting the organizational form it claims to resonate with or belong to (Carroll and Wheaton 2010; Soule 2012). This judgement is likely to depend on what they expect an energy company to look like – what features are *core*, *distinctive* and *enduring* about an energy company (as a generic form) – and if said company meets these expectations. Consistent with the broad thrust of resource-dependence theories, the way external agents decide on the identity of a given organization matters because it affects the resources that flow to them (for instance from consumers/investors to firms).

In summary, then, organizations ask 'How should *we* organize?' while relevant audiences ask 'How should *they* organize?' The internal exercise of identity construction is conceptually distinct from the external process of audiences evaluating identity claims, and they might reasonably be studied empirically as separate foci. However, they are often linked simply because the ways in which organizations construct their identities often draw on the same categories that audiences would use to interpret organizational identities. Albert and Whetten argue 'Organizations define who they are by creating and invoking classification schemes and locating themselves within them' (1985, 92).[6] It is here where the concept of form – understood in its generic deployment – becomes important (indeed necessary) because it helps to distinguish 'classifications schemes' as special types of collective identities.

In this account, audiences interpret the identity claims of organizations using more general identity categories (e.g. through what Albert and Whetten call 'classification schemes'), and it is these special identity categories for which the concept organizational form is preserved. Thus, an organizational form is a special kind of *collective* organizational identity; specifically, one that is recognized as distinctive by key audiences (those possessing valued resources, i.e. customers, reviewers, donors, regulators, state officials) and to which clear expectations exist about required or core features of organizations identifying with a form (Hsu and Hannan 2005, 487; Carroll and Hannan 2000, 73). Individual organizations have identities (which they can foster, refine and amend), yet forms are cultural objects that apply to sets of organizations (Carroll and Hannan 2000, 73). Thus, a formal definition might be, 'a form is an abstract, code-like specification of organizational identities' (Carroll and Hannan 2000, 74).

Here forms are social and cultural phenomena; they are categories that audiences (whether consumers, policy makers or wine experts) use to choose, value and make sense of the world around them. In turn, organizations utilize these categories to construct their identity from. Forms emerge as audiences come to see similarities among a set of organizations such that a label or category

48 *Interest groups and organizational form*

develops with associated rules as to what key features/practices a member of such category (or an organization claiming membership of such a category) ought to exhibit (see Fiol and Romanelli 2012). Changes to these core features (as defined by audiences) in turn may cause a re-evaluation of the groups identity and thus its 'fit' with established forms. Methodologically, this means that forms can be identified from the 'perceptions and beliefs of relevant evaluators' and with reference to an 'audience [which] has significant social or material control over relevant outcomes or issues' (Hsu and Hannan 2005). As Fiol and Romanelli (2012, 597) summarize 'Organizational forms, then, represent classes of organizations that audiences understand to be similar in their core features and distinctive from other classes of organizations.' This means that identification of forms comes from 'audience members' as opposed to 'industrial or product-market distinctions', they are not about abstract 'organizational architectures' but about 'social and cultural typifications' (Negro *et al.* 2010b, 107). In summary, audiences decide what features matter for categorizing an organization as authentically 'fitting' into (wholly or partially) a given organizational form.

While mixed together in the above text, several specific approaches that exist within this broad commitment to an identity-based approach can be unpicked. Within what might be loosely called the *ecological tradition*, forms are defined as an 'externally-enforced identity' or 'external identity codes' (see Carroll and Hannan 2000, 68). This means that 'forms' exist when (i) external audiences recognize a bundle of features, product categories or even industries, as a 'code' by which they interpret and value their organizational world, and (ii) violation of key components of the 'code' has (negative) consequences. According to McKendrick and Carroll (2001, 674), 'Identity codes for organizational forms typically consist of abstract features as well as composition rules about appropriate combinations of particular features.' Codes are viewed as 'semantic objects', which means that scholars have approached identifying forms through examining texts that discuss specific sets of organizations (Hannan 2005). For instance, in a seminal article Reuf (2000) analysed the textual entries in a data base of professional medical journals (MEDLINE) to establish the range of 'forms' in the medical field. Consistent with ecological theories, the number of instances of a form – that is, population density – is often considered a key factor in establishing the existence of a form.

Those scholars who had once focused on demographic and then ecological approaches are now mostly focused on what might be labelled a *categorical approach* (Zuckerman 1999). Form is defined as 'sociologically real categories' in which 'membership matters in the sense that an audience screens organizations for conformity with standards before conferring the status of a valid member of the category' (Hsu and Hannan 2005, 487). Here the emphasis is on identifying the way categories enable audiences to interpret their organizational environment, and in turn provides organizations with the raw materials from which to construct their identities. The approach concentrates heavily on the role of 'market intermediaries' (and associated directories) – such as restaurant

Interest groups and organizational form   49

reviewers, wine guides, actor agents, film classifications, etc. – as agents of category generation (and enforcement of compliance with form). The assumption is that consumers of organizational entities require shortcuts to negotiate complex and information-rich environments. These categories aid this negotiation, and in turn organizations are wise to construct their identities from these categories in ways that appeal to audiences (and thus gather resources). Notable is the focus on the multi-valent nature of identities – the way organizations construct identities from multiple categories (they 'category span'). For instance, a restaurant might construct an identity as a 'Thai' or a 'Chinese' restaurant, or it might borrow from both to foster an 'Asian' restaurant identity. These choices both structure the way the restaurant ought to present itself – menu, table settings, imagery on the walls, waiters uniforms – and the way customers will value their offering (see Rao *et al.* 2005).

Neo-institutional analysis often focuses on the ways in which forms serve as forces for institutional convergence. For instance, Greenwood and Hinings (1988) talk about the way 'archetypes' or 'templates' for organizing exist in particular fields of activity, and that these provide specific organizations with pointers on how to organize. From this perspective, organizational forms exist as sets of ideas – external to a specific organization – about how organizations *ought* to be put together. More recently, attention has turned to institutional emergence, that is the ways in which 'new' forms are created as sets of related organizations emerge in conditions where existing strong forms are absent. Work here looks at the way entrepreneurs borrow elements from abutting fields of organizing to weave together novel organizational forms (Powell and Sandholtz 2012; Rao 1998). This broad approach is evident in Elizabeth Clemens' work on interest groups and social movements. She describes 'organizational forms' as 'templates, scripts, recipes, or models' that are formalized or institutionalized enough to be 'modular' (1997, 49).

The important thing to appreciate here is that from an identity-based approach, generic organizational forms are created by the recognition of *external audiences*. Thus, empirically, they can only be identified by looking at the ways real audiences classify the organizational word (e.g. directories, language, etc.). This approach conceives of organizational form as a 'cultural object': as 'abstract entitites – they potentially apply over space and time' (Carroll and Hannan 2000, 61, 63). From this perspective an organizational form is 'transposable' from one context to another (Clemens 1996, 1997), and it can exist even when there is no empirical case actually satisfies that identity (Carroll and Hannan 2000, 74).[7] The identity-based approach to organizational form is distinctive not because it eschews a focus on features or industry boundaries – it does not – but in that it sees the perceptions of audiences and participants are crucial in deciding what features or boundaries are 'real' in a given context.

The issue of category spanning in categorical approaches and of transposition or borrowing of generic forms, raises the issue of organizational hybridity. Scholars have long noted the likelihood that specific organizational entities manifest multiple identities (Albert and Whetten 1985; Golden-Biddle and Rao

50 *Interest groups and organizational form*

1997). This has been incorporated into the literature under the broad and fashionable theme of 'hybridity'. At its heart, hybridity refers to the combination 'of "types" that would not normally be expected to go together' (Albert and Whetten 1985). However, that being said, it is fair to say that there is considerable imprecision with respect to (i) What is the 'stuff' being combined? What makes something a 'different' type from a logical other sufficient to say their combination is genuinely a hybrid? and (ii) What object is being hybridized? Is it the specific identity of single organizational entities or is it generic identities or organizational forms? (Foreman and Whetten 2002, 621). On the first count, there is a deal of difference in the way scholars approach the dimension on which hybridization occurs. For instance, in the group and movement literature, some scholars see hybridity in terms of the policy and/or constituency mix that movement organizations seek to mix together: do groups combine unusual issues or member combinations? (Heaney and Rojas forthcoming). By contrast, others see hybridity as the combining of generic organizational forms (as demarcated by distinctive missions of service provision versus advocacy) into a new merged hybrid organizational form (Minkoff 2002). The approach worked with here is closer to the latter, whereby 'organizational hybrids' are defined as 'combinations of disparate elements – structural or institutional' whereby they 'represent a reflexive effort to borrow from two dominant models or organizing' (Minkoff 2002, 382–3). On the second count, there is uncertainty as to whether hybridization is a process evident at the level of individual organizational entities, or at a more general institutional or field level. A useful distinction – consistent with the previous discussion in this chapter – is to distinguish between the 'organizational identity' of a specific entity and 'organizational form-level identity' which applies to generic models that might be the building blocks of hybrid forms, and is a status that 'new' hybrid identities might subsequently attain (Foreman and Whetten 2002, 622).

Many authors discussed above might also readily define themselves as pursuing neo-institutional approaches. It is important to underline that these approaches have many similarities. Saliently, the most recent work explaining the formation of organizational forms themselves explains that ecological, categorical and institutional approaches 'share a view of identity as a socially constructed cognitive category with features that, at one and the same time, specify similarities among members of a category and distinguish them from the members of other social categories' (Fiol and Rommanelli 2012, 599).

Back to group scholarship

As indicated at the outset of this chapter, the claim is that group scholars *have* tacitly operated with a background sensibility to form-like concepts. In this section I briefly seek to backward-map some well-worn existing approaches onto the various conceptualizations of form discussed above.

The most obvious practice that maps onto the feature-based approach is a demographic one. Most group scholars readily utilize terms such as trade union,

Interest groups and organizational form 51

professional group, trade/business association, voluntary association and citizen group to help in identifying broad *types* of populations. Each group is allocated into its category on the basis of some rules of thumb about who the (expected) members are and/or the interests the group seeks to advocate for. Thus, workers' organizations that are engaged in bargaining their members' conditions are categorized as trade unions. Groups that have firms as members at a sectoral level (widget x or widget y) are trade associations. And so on. Is this a study of organizational form? This approach is just like the corporate demography literature where the term organizational form refers to a set of organizational entities that share a basic environment (e.g. pubs, wineries, football clubs, etc.). In the group literature this is akin to using trade association or environmental citizen group as types of organizational form. As such, it is not very helpful in and of itself where one is interested in whether individual groups among trade unions or environmental citizen groups vary in terms of 'organizational form'.

Yet, they could be utilized differently – and I think more productively – *if and only if* they are operationalized in terms of some *generic* style that guides the work of entrepreneurs and audiences. For instance, the fact that a set of interests – say secondary school teachers – organize through a union form, as opposed to a professional form, has an impact. When teachers' unions talk, they are seen as sectional interests. Contrast this with doctors who are typically organized as professionals and their commentary in policy arenas often viewed as expert opinion. How many teachers wish their collective views were seen as expert in some way – indeed the commencement of Teacher Institute structures in Australia is an attempt to find just that voice (something incongruent with a union-style form). As we will see in Chapter 5, group entrepreneurs see a trade union as a very different proposition to a trade association when trying to think through how their interests 'ought' to be organized. Where trade association is used simply as scholarly shorthand for an organization that organizes business, then it remains a demographic usage. Its other deployment might be closer to a blueprint or neo-institutional approach.

From a feature-based perspective, the most common approach is to identify what organizational characteristics are most important or core and how these ought to be labelled or even bundled up. There is an almost infinite number of ways to identify group organizational forms. A group scholar could literally identify as many distinct forms as there are group attributes. In practice, the choice of which attribute to privilege when defining form is in large part down to the type of question the student of groups has front of mind. The scholarly field is well use to operating with sets of categories or typologies that seek to capture one or another dimension of group activity, behaviour or even organizational attributes. And these might be understood as presenting a minimalist version of a core-features approach. As an illustration, let's take the two most common types of code schemes.

Many common classificatory systems focus on what might be called the 'performative' aspects of group activity. The classic one is the distinction between insider and outsider groups (see Grant 2000). Its weakness as an approach to

52 *Interest groups and organizational form*

defining organizational form, however, is that its reference point is a rather narrow and ephemeral characteristic of group behaviour. As is well recognized in the literature, both strategy and status are prone to change (even on an issue by issue basis) (see Page 1999; Binderkrantz 2006). Others, focusing on the mobilization side, pursue group type based on a distinction around the interests being organized. The most well known and used UK typology is perhaps Stewart's division between sectional and cause categories (1958). For a US audience, this translates into a distinction between public (or citizen) and economic interests. Jordan and Richardson (1987, 19) argue that the literature 'rediscovers' essentially the same binary categories. The precise measure used to decide whether a group belongs to one or other categories is hard to pin down, but terms like sectional refer to groups that pursue the interests of a section of society. By contrast, terms like cause, public or promotional all relate to groups that are generally open to those agreeing with the belief or principle being advocated. These are all perfectly reasonable labelling approaches for group acitivies, yet unhelpful in delineating form. An alternative strategy is not to treat these individual performative characteristics as a basis for defining form but as separate 'variables' (Andrews and Edwards 2004, 485). As such, we might ask whether groups of form x tend to engage in outsider or insider strategies (where strategy is a dependent variable).

These types of classification can, however, provide the raw material for a core features version of an ecological operationalization of organizational form. To provide an idea of the style of work this involves, take the excellent work undertaken on a number of groups in the UK 'poverty lobby' by Whiteley and Winyard (1987, 1988). Here the various different typologies evident in the group literature are combined to code up 'real' organizations. The aim is to then generate a set of 'forms' that are empirically evident in a specific field. Whiteley and Winyard assess the level of advocacy by each group and cross-reference that with other features, such as whether groups were 'groups of' or 'groups for'. They subsequently examine patterns in these key group characteristics and conclude that two combinations can be discerned: (i) an open membership promotional structure, acceptable to government and focuses primarily on lobbying, and (ii) a focused membership representational structure, acceptable to government and focused on service delivery (Whiteley and Winyard 1987, 33).[8] They conclude, that 'Clearly some combinations of characteristics go together whereas other combinations do not' (ibid). This might be understood as an attempt to generate a type of empirical typology, but for our purposes it is highly salient because it shows the difference between defining a group by a single dimension and combining dimensions to study organizational form.

In fact, the simplest feature-based approach is to measure a single *individual* facet of an organization's structure that might be considered subject to variation. Work on interest group organizations – mostly in the social movement literature – has focused on measuring the different primary activities they engage in (advocacy, service provision, mixed) and linking changes in this dimension with questions of survival (see Minkoff 1999). Walker *et al.* (2011) also discuss the

Interest groups and organizational form   53

composition of US advocacy populations over time, by distinguishing between membership and non-membership forms. An interest group can be considered an organizational form compared to other political organizations such as parties, or to other not-for-profit organizations such as co-operatives or foundations (Fernandez 2008). It is important to note that this *is* different to studies that try and assess the 'level' to which a set of groups have developed on a range of process orientated measures, like professionalization.[9]

As is self-evident from the above discussions, the choice of single activities such as policy strategy, or single organizational features such as mission or key aim, are by far the most frequently utilized approach to conceptualizing core-features style approaches to form. There are a few advances on that. For instance a few contributions try to pack several features up into ideal types, such as the work of Skocpol (2003) and Karpf (2012) reviewed in Chapter 1. Deciding what features to bundle together can be determined in a number of ways. Coherence can be *overlaid* by virtue of scholarly application of theoretical frameworks or synthesis, correlations and distillations of empirical findings. This generates, almost always a priori to empirical research, disembodied or decontextualized forms. This is not meant in the pejorative; such approaches are defensible; after all, establishing or mapping conformance to theoretical or best-practice ideal types is an important part of assessing institutional or environmental fit. For example, questions about the democratic nature or associative capacity of groups could be usefully explored by constructing theoretically informed forms as ideal-types – the 'democratic group' or the 'policy-capable group' – and looking at empirical conformance. This may lead to conclusions about the type of environments that foster these organizational forms or types of groups.

Another alternative is to *find* or *discover* coherence through recourse to the interpretations of actors within a context: on the basis of the 'embodied' interpretations of real organizational actors. Just as scholars construct organizational types to identify and discuss organizations they may encounter empirically – and to perhaps assess fit or match with theoretical models or environmental conditions – the actors actually engaged in running or leading organizations (indeed humans generally) deploy similar models in their everyday lives as a way of interpreting and sense-making. These organizational models are no doubt crucial in the way group leaders at least attempt to chart a response to environmental change. It informs how they interpret change, how they define challenges and the types of responses they deem appropriate. It is argued that in any field of activity leaders of organizations will no doubt recognize several possible forms as in play – as legitimate alternatives. These will be important in informing leaders' activities. This has implications for methods – implying interviews with organizational actors and detailed group biography. There is, by contrast, far less work that conforms with the identity-based family of approaches. Perhaps one exception is the work of Michael Heaney, who examines the way groups develop and shape their reputations with policy makers (2004, 2007). Here there is attention to the way groups seek to shape their self-identities, using evidence from websites and interviews. At the individual case

54 *Interest groups and organizational form*

level, there is more relevant work – such as the in-depth studies of US environmental groups that examine how their identities develop path-dependently and which use archival sources (Young 2010).

Conclusion

The argument made in this chapter is that group scholars should learn to speak the language of organizational form and to view the group landscape through the lens of form. The precise way in which organizational form is conceptualized and deployed empirically depends on the style of research being conducted. This will be self-evident in the chapters that follow.

On the one hand, if analysing a large number of cases, one might equate different group forms with one or two *core* organizational features. In Chapter 4, I use just such an approach to probe levels of diversity in form among a population of UK environment groups. At the other end of the spectrum, as evident in Chapters 5 and 6, one might operationalize the concept in an identity-based manner so as to describe and analyse changes in form *over time* in single (or very few) cases (see Halpin and Nownes 2011). I think this style of qualitative case study work, relying heavily on archival and primary interview data, is immensely valuable. The new(ish) work on categorical theories also promises a fresh approach to population-level phenomenon. In Chapter 7 this approach is used to rethink the niche-based take on groups. Then in Chapters 8 and 9 the identity-based categorical theories are used to develop a population-level account of how groups develop and define identities in new organizational fields and then how new generic forms emerge.

Notes

1 This underlines that a pursuit of organizational form is complementary and consistent to existing approaches to population ecology. A point borne out in the more recent organizational ecology literature that emphasizes (relatively stable) levels of diversity in organizational form within very narrowly drawn populations (see review by Hannan 2005).
2 They also contrast this form with an 'exaggerated' form that is voluntary, participative and internally democratic.
3 I thank Mitchell Stevens at Stanford for suggesting this formulation as a useful way to capture this field of scholarly endeavour.
4 Aldrich and Reuf (2006), as do I in Table 3.1, suggest taking organizational forms to be blueprints, which is consistent with an approach that identifies forms from within the context, mostly through the subjective constructions of organizational leaders or designers. The 'foundational' definition by Hannan and Freeman uses the same word, but at that point in time meant something different.
5 In the many orthodox maintenance theories of groups, the role of leaders – or group entrepreneurs – is deemed central (Olson 1965, Salisbury 1969 are two such seminal works). It is broadly accepted that they are best able to shape the perceptions of members and other important audiences (see Maloney *et al.* 1994). And, as the PE approach suggests, the way leaders interpret and respond to environmental population pressures is likely to be crucial to survival.

Interest groups and organizational form   55

6 Albert and Whetten (1985) use the term 'types', however their take is consistent with an identity-based approach to organizational form.

7 It may be that all organizations in a field of activity *approximate* a given archetypal form, but that none directly *replicate* it. There is a logical possibility that organizations in a field will all diverge from an organizational archetype: 'as with all ideal types ... our observations of empirical occurrences could yield nothing but deviations' (Greenwood and Hinings 1988, 300).

8 They plotted variation across group characteristics which included aims, support, status and strategies (Whiteley and Winyard 1987, 11).

9 For example, Kriesi (1996) examines changes among SMOs in terms of processes of 'formalization' (development of formal membership criteria, statutes, procedures, leadership and office structure); 'professionalization' (paid staff manage group as a career); 'internal differentiation' (internal functional division of labour and territorial subunits developed); 'integration' (horizontal coordinating mechanism to pull in subunits and functional divisions – linked to oligarchization).

4 Revisiting population-level analysis
A feature-based approach

Introduction

Interest group analysis conducted at the population level offers great promise and it is undoubtedly a growth area in the sub-field (see Halpin and Jordan 2012). There is no doubt that, as Andrews and Edwards put it, 'greater efforts to study populations of advocacy organizations will allow scholars to answer many basic questions, such as the prevalence of various organizational characteristics' (2004, 500). Yet progress beyond basic headcounts is in fact rather slow. This is probably due to the resource-intensive nature of the work, but even more so because of the absence of concepts that can be easily operationalized when dealing with large numbers of cases. In relation to mapping variation in group organizational form, the obvious up-front difficulty is in calibrating any empirical measure of difference (or sameness, for that matter). How different, and in what ways, does a group have to be from any other to be considered an alternative group form? What is the threshold test? How to separate the trivial from the important differences?

As discussed in Chapter 3, there are multiple ways in which one can work with and operationalize a concept like organizational form. The approach taken in this book is to be open and flexible with respect to this question; it is a case of horses for courses. In this chapter, a rather prescriptive approach is taken to settling on group forms, and it is one that is likely to be most readily taken up by the majority of contemporary group scholars, if for no other reason than it fits best with the current fashion for cursory coding of large-scale population-level data sets. Specifically, it might allow PE scholars to quickly incorporate sensitivity to form in their data-collection activities.[1]

In this chapter I suggest that group scholarship would benefit from developing a feature-based approach to group organizational form. As discussed in Chapter 3, such an approach directs attention to the organizational architecture of groups: bundling together core features into generic forms that have some theoretical salience for scholars and/or resonate with empirical evidence. This approach has been utilized heavily in organizational studies, but also (saliently) in the political party literature. Here I explore how it might be deployed to assist the study of interest group organizations.

Revisiting population-level analysis 57

The core of the chapter focuses on developing a set of *generic feature-based* group forms that can be used to study variation within group populations. These generic forms are defined in advance by scholars, to reflect theoretically salient key features that can be readily mapped against 'real' groups based mostly on external observations. With these sets of 'group organizational forms' in hand, I then illustrate the value of this approach by utilizing them to test the isomorphism assumption that is central to population-based organizational studies (and related group studies). Without wishing to rehash the discussion in early chapters, this analytical task is necessary for two related reasons. First, the group literature has not explicitly addressed the issue of variation in group form, and while there is a degree of agnosticism with respect to variation in *form* (at least as defined in this volume), the recent turn to population-ecology inspired work explicitly encourages an assumption of limited variation within populations of like-groups. Second, the organizational studies literature, on which the group literature is increasingly (and productively) drawing (witness population ecology work), has for a long time assumed that there will be isomorphism: a standardization of form in a given field. It is therefore crucial to tackle the assumption of limited variation in group populations early and head on.

Based on data from a population of UK environment groups, I establish that groups do embody different organizational forms or configurations at any single moment, even when they outwardly rely upon the same environmental conditions. Groups experiencing the same basic conditions survive in different forms: there is likely no single recipe to survival. This suggests scholars would benefit from a more explicit emphasis on puzzling over diversity in form.

The chapter proceeds in the following manner. To provide a more concrete sense of what a set of generic feature-based forms might look like, the first part of this chapter reviews the state of the party literature in respect of its feature-based use of organizational form. In the subsequent two parts I develop the feature-based approach with respect to groups: I address the admittedly basic (but surprisingly difficult!) challenge of identifying a set of basic group 'forms' that might guide empirical analysis. I first develop a reference *form* for interest groups, and then outline variations to this reference form. The rest of the chapter then deploys these concepts to demonstrate *one* possible empirical application: probing organizational variations among a population of like-groups (to test the isomorphism proposition).

Sketching aspirations: analysing the organizational form of political parties

Before getting to the details, I think it useful to try and set out the style of scholarship I am trying to encourage. In this respect, I have found the political party literature particularly instructive. The discussion of changes in party form offers an insight into the direction in which group scholars might – and I think should – head.

58 *Revisiting population-level analysis*

For some time the literature had discussed the 'decline' or 'failure' of party (see Lawson and Merkl 1988). The evidence of declining memberships and atrophying internal party organization led some to suggest that the party was losing its role as a linkage between civil society and state. Without disputing the analysis, others suggest the literature is really describing the *decline* of the mass-party *form*, and not the decline of parties – as a class of organization – per se (see Rose and Mackie 1988). For instance, Katz and Mair (1995, 25) argue that 'the age of party has not waned' but that the 'failure' literature utilized the mass party as the gold standard against which party practices were judged. Slippage from that form was interpreted as a failure of parties per se: that is, the failure of parties to continue to act as linkage between civil society and state – to continue as a mass party – was read as a failure of political parties themselves. This reading has been criticized because it 'fails to take account of the ways in which parties can *adapt* to ensure their own survival' (Katz and Mair 1995, 25, italics added).

Of course, the question is what 'other' forms might be evident, and how are they configured? The party literature has utilized several distinctions to designate different party forms or models: elite/cadre party, the mass party, the catch-all party and the cartel party (see Katz and Mair 1995). The precise designation of each form is not critical for my discussion, but the way in which it might be applied is instructive for my discussion of groups. These models, types or forms of party are often presented within a period-based argument – each form is succeeded by a new dominant form. However, Katz and Mair claim that in applying these to individual cases 'these models represent heuristically convenient polar types, to which individual parties may approximate more or less closely at any given time' (Katz and Mair 1995, 19). Thus, 'contemporary parties are not necessarily wholly cartel parties any more than parties in previous generations were wholly elite parties, or wholly mass parties, or wholly catch-all parties' (Katz and Mair 1995, 19). The point is that one form or other might be a dominant frame that informs party change and adaptation – it might be considered an optimally adapted *generic* form – but the extent to which it summarizes the precise *empirical* form of specific parties is an open question.

In a similar vein, Koole has suggested that rather than 'the idea that each period in time apparently necessarily has its "own" party type which best fits into the changed environment' it would be far better to develop 'a classification scheme of different contemporary party types' which would enable research to 'concentrate on the question why, and under what circumstances, a certain category of parties develop in one direction and another category in another' (Koole 1996, 520). In so doing, he suggests a distinction be made between 'defining' and 'empirical' properties: the former assist in settling whether a case belongs to one or another type, while the latter are simply features that parties in several types may share. Such a task requires that 'different types be neatly described in relation to each other' such that it is 'clear where and to what extent these types overlap' (Koole 1996, 521). The result is that, empirically, it is possible to see

Revisiting population-level analysis 59

how a given party organization might 'hesitate between two organizational modes' (Koole 1996, 521). Thus, the literature for the past two decades has been focusing on changes among party forms: the adaptation of parties to new environments.

Of course the broader question is where do organizational forms come from and, why do particular forms emerge? In their work on political parties, Blyth and Katz (2005, 34–5) refer to 'internal' (how to organize those within legislative assemblies) and 'external' (how to organize activists and supporters) and 'network' (how to knit together parliamentary and supporter groupings) problems that (a) destabilize existing forms and (b) serve to stimulate adaptations that overcome such problems, leading to (c) new forms. They argue that 'each of these dilemmas promoted a particular organizational response, while each response was itself vulnerable to another type of dilemma', and therefore they analyse 'the sequence of 'dilemma-response-dilemma' in party forms (Blyth and Katz 2005, 35). Again, this analysis does not mean that these precise *individual* dilemmas beset specific *individual* parties, but that broad changes in circumstances (societal, technological, etc.) threaten the utility of the optimally adapted *generic* form itself (i.e. catalyse dilemmas).

This chapter attempts to encourage this style of discussion about group organizational forms, changes and adaptations. Like Koole's aspirations for the party literature, my aim here is to develop ways to identify *generic* forms that can be compared for 'fit' with the *empirical* forms that specific groups manifest at points in time. This type of approach would then encourage important questions about why groups are in a given form, do they change form over their careers, why do groups borrow from one or other *generic* form and so on. As is evident in the party literature, the concern with form arose from debates about the political and representative functionalities or capabilities of parties. So it is with groups; identifying the forms in which groups survive will tell us something about *both* the specific capacities of given groups, but also – viewed in aggregate – will tell us something about the capacities of the group system itself, over time.

Before these enticing questions might be progressed, however, group scholars need to settle on some generic forms that will provide the raw conceptual material.

Developing generic interest groups forms

This chapter proceeds by generating a set of feature-based interest group forms. In order that a feature-based set of generic group organizational forms constitutes a readily useful tool, at least when deployed at a population level, it needs to evoke clear images and expectations about what characteristics a group conforming to a form ought to manifest. Borrowing from Koole (1996), we need a *set* of simple defining properties that serve to identify whether specific cases resonate with a given form, regardless of whether they differ on other empirical features.[2]

What is the 'basic' group form?

One way to start the discussion is to outline a 'basic' group form, from which alternatives might be identified. In the party literature the 'mass party' serves this type of reference function: it has been referred to as the gold standard for party form simply because it is a reference point for adjudications of decline (Katz and Mair 1995, 25). What might serve a similar function for group scholars? What image of organization is conjured up by the group term?

The sheer number of groups, compared to parties, presents obvious problems: a point observed early by Truman (1971, 115). Where party scholars are able to delimit the field by referring only to the 'major parties', no such shorthand is possible for students of interest groups. However, according to Hayes (1986) there is such a thing as a 'traditional' conception of interest group, what he calls the 'mass-membership group'. This conception rests 'on certain characteristics – in particular, an extensive formal membership and a network of local chapters permitting widespread personal contact among individual members' (1986, 134).[3] Elsewhere, this type of account is referred to as the 'extreme' group form (Jordan and Maloney 1997a). The claim by Hayes is that from Truman onwards, group theory has generally assumed that groups are the product of efforts by entrepreneurs to organize large numbers of individuals to interact to some significant degree in internal venues.

There is no question that this conception of group form has served as a central reference point in much of the literature on group (democratic) decline. It has been argued that 'old' voluntary associations – with local chapters, annual meetings and a reliance on member funding – are being replaced by 'new' groups that are less democratic and participative (see Skocpol 1999; Putnam 2000). According to Skocpol, membership associations 'hold regular local meetings', 'convened periodic assemblies of elected leaders and delegates', operated at state regional and national levels, and relied on their membership's dues for funding (1999, 465). She argues that 'Classic American association-builders took it for granted that the best way to gain national influence ... was to knit together national, state and local groups that met regularly and engaged in a degree of representative governance' (1999, 491). Some further encouragement for the designation of this form as the 'reference' case comes from the social movement literature. In their seminal work, McCarthy and Zald (1977) refer to the 'classical' movement organization, which is characterized by a reliance on the mobilization of the 'beneficiary' constituency for their resource base (see discussion in Staggenborg 1988).

A reasonable summary might be that the 'traditional group' form implies that to represent members there needs to be some way to collect *and* aggregate interests. There ought to be voice *and* exit for members and the members ought to fund and support the group. In large national groups this necessitates more than an annual meeting; it suggests local face-to-face branch structures combined with financial support from membership fees. Basic features include individual – yet restricted – membership, members enfranchised, local chapters or meetings,

Revisiting population-level analysis   61

and a reliance on member funding. As Hayes suggests, this traditional model resonates strongly with the 'group theory' assumptions that groups flow (more or less automatically) from the awakened (or realized) interests of human constituencies, and the conviction that groups would not form or survive if they did not reliably represent the interests of their constituents. The degree of criticism levelled at groups that violate this set of expectations, and the extent of effort put into coining terms to label digressions from this set of norms,[4] supports the idea that this form is a reliable (albeit often implicit) reference point (see Halpin 2010 for discussion on the roots of the 'representative' account of groups).

Variations on the traditional group form?

The contribution by Hayes also draws attention to the fact that the 'traditional' form cannot be taken for granted. What are the variations that might be constructed around this standard?

The debate over the decline of the traditional group form (previous section) has *explicitly* raised the issue of what other forms are emerging? An influential contribution from Skocpol provides hints as to possible answers. She noted that

> all sorts of new organization-building techniques encourage contemporary citizens' groups – just like trade and professional associations – to concentrate their efforts in efficiently managed headquarters located close to the federal government and the national media. Even a group claiming to speak for large numbers of Americans does not absolutely need members. And if mass adherents are recruited through the mail, why hold meetings? From a managerial point of view, interactions with groups of members may be downright inefficient.
>
> (1999, 494)

But can we be more specific about these forms? Can we package them up in neat generic bundles such that they might inform analysis?

As it happens, there is a remarkable degree of consistency on variations. When form is understood as a set of core features, the group literature tends to focus upon variations around two basic dimensions: level of membership interaction and level of centralization. Hayes, for instance, utilizes variation across the two dimensions – 'opportunity for face-to-face relations' among members and 'reliance on member financing' – in order to identify four ideal types of organizational form. Hayes argues that 'these [two] characteristics must be understood as variables that interact to produce distinct *organizational forms*' (1986, 134 italics added). Thus he identifies the traditional or '*mass membership*' and three other logical forms: a 'pure staff' group, a 'subsidized solidary' group and a 'mass group'. In their epic work on US associations, Minkoff *et al.* (2008, 533) distinguish between groups on two similar dimensions: (i) centralized/federated (do they have branches?) and (ii) members/nonmembers (do members fund them?). This framework generates four ideal types (a subsequent

62 *Revisiting population-level analysis*

cluster analysis confirms these as empirically discernable): decentralized membership (akin to Hayes's traditional concept), centralized membership, centralized nonmembership and decentralized nonmembership. Given that 'familiarity' and 'resonance' with usage in the field are both considered desirable attributes of good middle-range concepts (see Gerring 1999), this uncanny resemblance among unrelated and temporally distant attempts to identify generic group forms provides some support for considering these (at least initially) as useful conceptual building blocks.

Let me outline the additional three forms in more detail (they are summarized in Table 4.1). Unlike the party literature there are no settled labels for group forms: thus, it is worth arriving at some intuitive but clear labels at this juncture. My approach has been to take the terms used by Hayes (1986) as a start, and to modify these slightly where I feel problems of ambiguity or clarity arise.[5]

Against the 'traditional' account, the logical opposite is the *memberless* group. It has few (if any) members, relies on donors for funding and is run by a small group of professional staff. In Minkoff *et al.*'s terms, it is a centralized nonmembership group. This form is curious for what it says about formation, as much as maintenance, for it offends the long-held proposition that groups (or group entrepreneurs) would – indeed *need* – to first establish a membership base from which to recruit and form a group. This is a basic preoccupation with much earlier group theory. For instance, the formation literature has heavily (almost exclusively) focused upon the extent and nature of the collective action problems associated which such a process. But, as Hayes remarks, many groups 'have not so much overcome the free-rider problem as circumvented it by securing alternative sources of funding outside memberships' (1986, 136). As has been much discussed, donors (whether corporate, not-for-profit or state-based) are often important in the formation and sustenance of groups (Walker 1983; but see Nownes and Neeley 1996).

The next two categories have just one of the attributes of the 'traditional' form present. A *subsidized group* is one that offers face-to-face membership opportunities, yet is reliant on funding by donors (not members). Such a form can be subsidized by a multitude of sources (see above). For instance, the state in many cases subsidizes groups directly (e.g. consumer groups) or even indirectly through project-based funding (e.g. social welfare groups, minority groups). Other groups might fund a new group where they see a complementary niche unfilled. Some groups are funded by corporate sponsorship; for instance, patients' groups are often funded by support from medical and health-related firms in particular drug companies. And, of course, groups might also be able to generate income from their own activities (such as from property or from service provision).[6]

A *mass group* is one whose membership provides the bulk of funding, but the membership never meet face-to-face, nor are they enfranchised to make decisions within the group (and usually membership is open to anyone). This form is perhaps closest to the 'new' forms identified by the likes of Skocpol and Putnam: a professionalized group, funded through small donations by a large and remote

Revisiting population-level analysis 63

base of supporters that never meet. The logic for entrepreneurs deploying this template or design is laid out by Skocpol who claims

> No longer do civic entrepreneurs think of constructing vast federations and recruiting interactive citizen-members. When a new cause … arises activists envisage opening a national office and managing association-building as well as national projects from the center. Members, if any, are likely to be seen not as fellow citizens but as consumers with policy preferences.
>
> (1999, 492)

This form closely approximates the 'professional' social movement organization form, which relies on paid leaders and a broad support from 'conscience constituents' who provide money but do not otherwise get involved (see McCarthy and Zald 1977), and resonates strongly with the *centralized member* style associations identified by Minkoff *et al.* (2008).

To reiterate, these generic forms are not designed to encompass *all* organizational aspects of groups. If all possible relevant characteristics were included, then they would simply be straightforward descriptions, and thus *form* would be devoid of utility as a variable (dependent or independent) in subsequent analysis. As highlighted in the discussion of party forms, where the aim (as I pursue here) is to distil a *set* of generic forms the important thing is to focus on a few core dimensions that are non-trivial and theoretically important, rather than create 'laundry lists' of possible associated features (see Koole 1996). They are able to serve as ideal types from which specific empirical cases can be compared. This approach does not rule out analysis of sub-forms: for instance, where members of a group population all conform to a *traditional form*, one might usefully talk about 'sub-forms' that differ on one or other key dimensions (see the discussion of organizational theory generally by Carroll and Hannan 2000, Chapter 4). Similarly this approach does *not* rule out or diminish the value of other group labels.

Table 4.1 Summary of generic group forms and their characteristics

Characteristics	Traditional group*	Mass group	Subsidized group	Memberless group
Branches?	Yes	None	Yes	None
Funding source?	Affiliates	Affiliates	Donors	Donors
Style of affiliation	Membership	Supportership	Varied	NA
Limits on affiliation	Closed	Open	Varied	NA

Source: derived from sources already cited, specifically Hayes (1986) and Minkoff *et al.* (2008). See also Halpin (2010), especially Chapter 4.

Note

* This includes groups of groups, such as umbrella organizations or looser networks. This is a distinctive logic: to build a group one just adds a few existing groups together. I resist the urge to add a new form, instead taking it as a derivative of the traditional group form – given that members are just groups instead of individuals/institutions.

64 *Revisiting population-level analysis*

Just like utilizing the set of party forms – cartel, mass, elite, etc. – does not rule out the terms like populist or social-democratic parties, talking about a mass or traditional interest group does not deny the utility of existing labels like environmental group, trade union or professional group, or any others. Finally, some might argue that this set of forms is overly slanted to membership dimensions, and away from the policy dimension; the implication being that these are less useful for those asking questions on policy behaviour. I argue this is not the case. These forms reflect realistic basic choices that groups might be reasonably expected to make in order to form and maintain themselves.

One obvious omission is the impact of the debate over Internet-based groups. As highlighted in Chapter 1, the discussion of groups in relation to organizational models has extra saliency because the slow burn debate around the hollowing out of chapter-based, individual membership and democratic associations has heated up with the advent of Internet technologies and social media. It has been suggested that a transformation has occurred in the 2000s leading to a third generation of 'Internet-mediated' groups emerging. It is argued that these serve as issue-generalists – providing a platform for supporters (or donors/patrons) to develop policy agendas as they go along (so-called 'user-generated' agendas) (Karpf 2012). Supporters are expected to dip in and out of active engagement with the group depending on their aspirations, resources and interests. By implication this might be viewed as challenging the generic forms generated because it suggests 'web-mediated' based groups will likely straddle two dimensions: the *style of affiliation* and *limits on affiliation* that underpin these models. I am happy to concede that such models exist – however to date they are largely platforms for issue-based organizing. Yet, on balance, I think the more salient question is how these technologies loosen up affiliations *within* existing models of organization? This can be easily explored within the existing set of generic forms through more advanced coding schemes that apply a fuzzy-set logic as opposed to the crisp set approach pursued here (see discussion more generally on this point by Ragin 1987 and Hannan *et al.* 2007).

An empirical application: assessing group population diversity (the isomorphism thesis)

With this particular style of conceptualizing group organizational form – and a way to operationalize it at a population level – in hand, it is now possible to pose and empirically answer questions about the form in which groups are maintained. In the space available, the aim is simply to illustrate the utility of this particularly feature-based style of working with a concept like group form. To this end I test the rather straightforward 'isomorphism' proposition, that populations of like-groups will manifest the same form. Organizational isomorphism is operationalized in the organizational studies literature as 'the [degree of] similarity of a set of organizations at a given point in time' (Deephouse 1996, 1024): high isomorphism means high levels of organizational similarity. The form-based categories developed above provide a convenient (if not crude) metric to

Revisiting population-level analysis 65

test whether populations of groups – that outwardly share the same environmental conditions and confront the same general challenges – *do* embody different organizational forms or configurations at a single moment.

Why single out this research question in particular? This basic analytical task is highly salient for two related reasons.

First, as outlined in the introduction, the population-ecology inspired interest group work explicitly adopts the theoretical assumption of limited variation within populations of like-groups, namely 'isomorphism' (see Nownes 2004, 52). To be clear, PE *assumes* isomorphism as a by-product of its focus on selection mechanisms: the PE approach assumes that 'change in the organizational world is primarily a function of selection *rather than organizational adaptation*' (Nownes 2004, 32 italics added). But there is no tradition – at least in the group manifestation of the approach – to *deny* the possibility of variation in form. Indeed, a reading of Gray and Lowery (2000) might suggest they *do* anticipate this: here I am referring to their concluding section where they suggest scholars ought to go on to probe the way group leaders perceive and react to broad environmental forces and pressures (see also discussion in Halpin and Jordan 2009).

Second, the organizational studies literature, on which the group literature is increasingly (and I think productively) drawing, has long emphasized organizational *isomorphism* (or standardization) among organizations sharing a given field of activity or environment. While there is basic agreement on the outcome – the tendency towards standardization in a given field – there is less agreement on what dynamic produces this outcome. That is, there is some disagreement on the *mechanisms* that underpin isomorphism. Much neo-institutional work in organizational studies expects to find limited variation and reduced variation over time because the survival prospects of organizations rests on gaining legitimacy. The attainment of legitimacy, of resembling a legitimate form, rests with approximating generic forms that have tacit legitimacy in a given field. Those that change first to establish the next 'new' form are followed by the rump of groups that mimic the new legitimate form. Thus, organizational populations come to be isomorphic because they must adapt to dominant forms or face low levels of legitimacy, and thus threats to survival (see Deephouse 1996). Ecological work focuses upon selection forces, and assumes that organizations will *not* adapt to change. The organizational ecology strand suggests that prevailing environments generate conditions that suit one type of organization – that which is best adapted. It follows that when conditions change, the population as a whole shifts to meet the new reality.

At the level of theoretical assumptions, there is a quantum gap between an emphasis on adaptation as the mechanism that drives conformity (isomorphism) and selection. Of course, what most scholars would say is that adaptation *does* occur, but it is ineffective in the face of overwhelming forces in the environment – put simply, adaptation happens, but it is largely futile. This book will not resolve this particular tangle. However, what *is* salient for our present discussion is that isomorphism is an assumed outcome of population-level organizational dynamics.

66   *Revisiting population-level analysis*

In summary, given its centrality to group studies of organizational maintenance – and fundamental to the organizational theories drawn upon – it is appropriate to scrutinize the proposition of limited variation in group populations. The straightforward task here is to ask, 'is there a single way to organize the environmental interest?'

Study design and data

The degree of variation among populations of like-groups is examined utilizing the member groups of the Wildlife and Countryside Link (England). By its own description, the Wildlife and Countryside Link (England) 'brings together environmental voluntary organizations in the UK united by their common interest in the conservation and enjoyment of the natural and historic environment' (www.wcl. org.uk/who-we-are.asp). It is a networking body that has as members autonomous interest group organizations. The Link was formed in 1980, and has expanded year on year. In 2010, at the time of its thirtieth anniversary, it constitutes approximately 40 voluntary organizations in all (although this figure has varied year to year). Data on form was collected from official websites, group annual reports, Charity Commission[7] filings, and in some cases direct correspondence with staff members.[8] For ease of analysis, all groups that were members or at least listed as such on their website were included.[9] Each case was coded according to several dimensions listed in Table 4.1, and then allocated to one or another form.[10]

Let me briefly remark on my choice of population.[11] If I took the usual approach, I might have selected a population such as the full set of 'environment' groups in the Directory of Associations or some other established policy-relevant list (Gray and Lowery 2000; Nownes 2004).[12] The choice to examine *this* population of groups was informed by the desire provide a strong test of isomorphism. By selecting the members of the *Link* I am able to control for conditions that the organizational literature (ecological and neo-institutional) suggests are associated with variations in form.[13]

In the first instance, I utilize a population in the environmental field that *are in close proximity and exhibit high and sustained levels of interaction with one another (organizationally and interpersonally)* (see discussion in Schneiberg and Clemens 2006, 205–6). According to neo-institutional theories of organization, populations of groups that are engaged in high levels of networking and cooperation – such as the WCL case – ought to result in organizational homogeneity because it allows for the diffusion over time of well adapted organizational properties (see DiMaggio and Powell 1983; Lang *et al.* 2008, 40). If a standard model is to *diffuse*, then it should do so with a great deal of ease in my case population. From an ecological theoretical standpoint, I control for variations in the 'material and social environment'[14] available to groups by choosing a population of groups that *share the same operating and resource environment*. Thus, if poorly adapted forms were to be selected out by environmental conditions, then their disbandment ought to be rather straightforward within my population. In short, if variation can be shown to exist among this set of groups,

Revisiting population-level analysis 67

then it would provide a strong argument for variation in form more generally among interest-group populations.[15] In turn, this would support the claim that broader attention needs to be paid to the form in which groups survive, it cannot be 'black boxed' or assumed.

To summarize, the choice of a tightly drawn population is significant and purposeful. Large-scale work utilizing data, such as from Encyclopaedia of Associations or similar, has to 'assume' that these groups see the models in the broader population as somehow salient and are 'orientated to other national groups with respect to borrowing models for action' (see Minkoff 2002, 388). Here, by virtue of the sampling approach, we have a set of groups that are proven to interact regularly and recognize each other as relevant.

This research design takes some inspiration from more recent work in organizational ecology, perhaps best exemplified by the study of a set of new high-tech firms in Silicon Valley (see Baron *et al.* 1999). Their finding that firms in their closely drawn population manifested *five* basic forms was all the more persuasive precisely because they chose a set of cases that *shared* founding period, legal context, industry sector and other features usually thought to diminish diversity (support isomorphism). Any finding of diversity in the WCL population will be similarly significant (see Minkoff *et al.* 2008 for a similar discussion of research design).

Findings

It is worth recalling that the forms elaborated above are generic types; and that when I assign specific groups to these forms I do so based on which form a given case most closely approximate *at a moment in time*. As will become clear, groups do 'hesitate', as Koole put it, between forms. This hesitation in itself simply highlights the salience of adaptive change to discussions of group maintenance (which I explore in Chapter 6). It is also important to note that here I take a binary approach to coding – groups either fully resemble a generic form or not. In latter chapters I loosen this coding approach, partially in recognition of the hybridity discussion in Chapter 3.

The 'traditional' form: membership groups

While not the numerically dominant, there were however several examples of the traditional form in the case study population. The *Campaign to Protect Rural England* (CPRE) is probably the empirical case closest to approximating the 'traditional' form. It has a well-developed, and constitutionally integrated, system of branches and regions that feed into national-level policy development. Members might join centrally, but in so doing become members of a local branch. The majority of the CPRE's income is derived from its member's subscriptions. Other weaker examples of this form include the British Mountaineering Council (BMC), which represents mountaineers, and the Ramblers, which represents countryside walkers. They have local branches, but they are not necessarily linked to setting the group's agenda.

68 *Revisiting population-level analysis*

Some cases adopting this form are in fact umbrella bodies. For instance, the Association of Rivers Trusts was formed to pursue the interest of local trusts. It has a very small central office, and relies very heavily on the expertise and resources of its member trusts. These member trusts effectively run the umbrella association. The association is majority funded by members, but also receives donations and project money from government and its agencies, and by other groups (such as the WWF). Like all conceptual categories, application to specific cases reveals blurring at the edges. For instance, perhaps right on the cusp of this form is the Open Spaces Society and the The Hawk and Owl Trust. They have members and they are the major source of funds, but the local groups are more ad hoc and their influence on the group's agenda is low (or not existent).

Mass groups

The form that is perhaps most often associated with the term 'environment group' is the 'mass group'. Good examples of these in the study population are WWF, Greenpeace and Friends of the Earth. These groups don't do representation; instead centralized professional staff and key activists develop issue agendas, which they then prosecute (see Halpin 2006). Their issue agenda is broad, conceivably encompassing any issue as it relates to preserving or protecting the environment (flora and fauna and related ecosystems). The groups are funded by a large number of individual supporters, who make small contributions. However, they rarely get involved directly in the groups affairs, and are not formally enfranchised within the group's decision-making apparatus. In these groups there is generally no branch structure; if there is it is only to facilitate a small number of dedicated activists (see Greenpeace for example). A group like the Marine Conservation Society (MCS) has 'members' and they are the main source of income. But such groups do not promise to enfranchise their 'members'. The MCS says on its website '*We promise to use your donation wisely* to improve the future for our seas, shores and wildlife' (italics added). This is very different to traditional groups where members are supposed to control 'their' group. On the borderline are groups like the National Trust, that have annual meetings where they seem to debate motions, but their local branches are purely engaged in service delivery functions or some other non-policy related task.[16]

It is worth noting that some groups are 'mass' by nature, but not by scale. Groups like the Badger Trust and Bat Conservation Trust use a growing (but relatively small) supporter base (large numbers of small donors) to fund the work of activists on the ground. The organization is controlled by a growing number of professional staff, mostly from backgrounds related to the specific issue context (e.g. natural scientists).

Subsidized groups

One set of cases, at first glance, seem very ambiguous. From one perspective they look like a *memberless group* (funded by donors and reliant on staff for direction). However, they have a large number of *members organized into*

Revisiting population-level analysis   69

branches, so may appear like a *traditional group*. Yet their members do not keep the group financially viable. They are a *subsidized group*. Two styles of group case seem to approximate this form: the main difference being the order in which the group's membership emerged in relation to the founding of the group itself. That is, they manifest two different evolutionary trajectories.

Some groups seem to have emerged from the happy coincidence of, on the one hand, a set of active volunteers engaged in on-the-ground works and, on the other hand, the entrepreneurship of (expert scientific) individuals with access to external donor funding. Perhaps the best exemplar is Butterfly Conservation. It has a large number of members, 15,000 in all, and these members are organized into 31 branches. These members pay dues, but the organization is made *viable* by income from donors. Its own history makes clear that key developments – like research capacity – have been made possible by the generous contributions of donors (including Nature Conservancy Council and BP) (Annual Report 2010, http://butterfly-conservation.org/files/annual-accounts-ye310310.pdf). An independent funding source might generally be expected to enhance the role of staff and expertise vis-à-vis members. This is indeed evident in Butterfly Conservation, which says on its website 'We employ over 50 people including many highly qualified scientists, making us the world's largest research institute for butterflies and moths.' How (or if) this type of staff expertise is ultimately reconciled with the independent wishes of a substantive lay membership is an open empirical question.

Other groups, like the Council for British Archeology, had origins in amateur scientific and public education societies, but has more recently begun to develop a broader advocacy mission. This has shaped its decision to develop a member base (started in 1993), which on its website is explained in terms of 'growing influence with government'. Thus, joining the Council centrally means an individual is allocated to a regional group or branch. This member base provides some funding for the group, but almost three-quarters still comes from one-off donations and supporting organizations. As Koole suggested for political parties, some empirical cases at a single moment hesitate between generic forms: and time will tell how they settle closer to one or other form. For the most part, the cases resonating with this form seem to be in a transitory state, hesitating between other forms.

Memberless groups

In the study population this type of organizational form was for the most part adopted by a set of groups that engaged in advocacy in rather narrow policy subniches. Case examples include Buglife, Froglife and Plantlife. These groups focus their efforts on educating the public about 'their' issue, awareness-raising and implementing change on the ground with the help of policy advocacy. They rely on professional staff; but they are typically experts from the substantive field – zoologists, ecologists and the like. The group entrepreneurs here are often the staff experts: they have few, if any, professional group staff, like lobbyists,

70 *Revisiting population-level analysis*

media-relations people or professional campaigners. The funding of such groups may involve a supporter base – in fact almost all groups had some provision for 'supporters' – but the *majority* of their funding came from donors, and (very) often other groups. In one group case, a staff member from a very much larger mass group left to start one of these staff-driven groups because his particular scientific niche was slipping off the larger group's agenda. This was done with the blessing of the larger group: it was *not* defection and it did *not* undermine the larger group. This type of example underlines the complexity of population dynamics when viewed at close quarters.

Drawing conclusions about diversity?

The above analysis establishes, in a straightforward manner, that groups sharing the *same* environment and engaged in *tight* networking survive *differently*. There is no single organizational recipe or form in which English environmental groups survive. To those accustomed to examining environment groups in Britain close up, this finding of diversity will come as no surprise (see Rootes 2009, 204).[17] However, against the weight and the persuasiveness of theories of *isomorphism* in organizational studies anticipating homogeneous forms, this finding is important. If nothing else, it confirms the need to empirically explore the forms in which groups survive: we cannot take homogeneity for granted. Moreover, it perhaps encourages the group ecological literature to dwell a little more on their findings of diversity mentioned 'in passing' (see Nownes 2010). This test is a strong one, and leads to the reasonable hypothesis that if there is diversity in this population there will be diversity in *most other populations of like groups*.[18]

As discussed above, the research design can effectively control for the sorts of environmental pressures that the literature suggests – both PE and neo-institutional – ought to *drive* (whether by adaptation or selection) organizational homogeneity. But what about group-level variables? As Table 4.2 outlines, there *is* considerable variation on the types of group-level dimensions typically used to explain survival prospects; namely age and size (here measured on economic and human resource metrics) (see Hannan 2005). These provide interesting insights into heterogeneity in a population, but do not seem to correlate with form. Let me elaborate.

In this population, there is vastly *more* variation in age within forms than across forms. Traditional, mass and memberless groups all have an average age of around 60 years (but subsidized groups are generally younger, average of 17 years).[19] However, traditional groups vary between nine and 98 years of age. This defies any straightforward age affect, but what about period affects? Again, there is little evidence of a link between period of formation and prevailing form. If we examine pre- and post-1940s groups (on the presumption that this reflects a key juncture in UK political development), there is no clear relationship with form: groups in mass and traditional forms were born before and after the Second World War (and even before and after the turn of the nineteenth century). This does not mean history is irrelevant; in fact it supports

Revisiting population-level analysis 71

the fact that groups can *change* form. Truman noted that younger groups 'will frequently assume forms differing in significant detail from older groups of the same kind' (1971, 115). And the organizational studies literature has long maintained that organizations are imprinted with the logic of the time of their birth (Stinchcombe 1965). But I am analysing form at a point in time somewhat after many groups were established: the population analysed here has likely *evolved* from original forms.[20] For instance, the majority of old mass member groups originated – at least for a short time – as *subsidized groups*: well-meaning and wealthy upper-class individuals effectively bankrolled groups to achieve legislative change to protect spaces and species (Rootes 2009, 206). Cases like the RSPB and NT fit this description, but they were never *traditional groups*, and they quickly transformed into *mass groups*.[21] More recent groups – products of middle- and working-class mobilization – more directly moved to mass group forms: perhaps simply because 'their' constituency did not have financial or political power acting in small numbers (Rootes 2009, 206).

In the hands of Olson-inspired accounts of group life, size is viewed as a variable that – after a certain (largely unspecified) threshold – activates free-riding which becomes a hindrance to collective action. Applied to a discussion of form, one might anticipate that size is associated with a mass group form. That is, a mass group form is a necessary condition in order to build a large group. There is some support for this approach (but see Halpin 2010). On average, *mass groups* are larger than *traditional groups*, followed by *subsidized group* and with *memberless* groups the smallest. This holds whether measured on average spend or number of employees. Yet there is a high degree of variation *within* forms: for instance, mass group expenditures range from £396 million to just £209,000[22] and employee numbers from five to just under 5,000. Mass groups have to be made, so it is perhaps no surprise that many groups applying a mass model are not strictly 'mass' in sense of size. All this tends to support the existing work on the relationship between age and change amongst non-profit organizations which suggests that older organizations are well able to adapt and experiment (see Minkoff and Powell 2006, 607).

Taking this generic 'group form' approach further?

What type of work might follow *this specific* (yet basic) mapping exercise? An initial answer is that this might provide the basis for testing the diversity finding. Based on sociological institutional accounts of organizing, we might surmise that the field of the environment provides a somewhat more open context with respect to what is an appropriate model for group organizing, say compared to the fields of professional groups such as lawyers and doctors where states provide string incentives to adopt member-based models (in order that they be licensed to regulate professions). Thus, we could use such categories to test the thesis that fields like the environment are more organized through a more diverse population of groups than say lawyers or doctors (see Table 4.3).

Table 4.2 Summary of group cases

Name	Founding	Employees	Expenditure (£)	Form
RSPCA	1824	1,505	114,090,000	Mass group
Open Spaces Society	1865	5	208,961	Mass group
RSPB	1889	1,903	98,000,000	Mass group
The National Trust	1895	4,938	396,924,000	Mass group
The Mammal Society	1954	5	289,940	Mass group
WWF UK	1961	306	27,886,000	Mass group
FoE	1971	128	8,704,093	Mass group
Woodland Trust	1972	261	19,481,000	Mass group
International Fund for Animal Welfare	1976	8	5,400,917	Mass group
Greenpeace UK	1977	90	2,976,821	Mass group
Campaign Whale	1980	NA	NA	Mass group
Marine Conservation Society	1983	27	1,119,000	Mass group
Environmental Investigation Agency	1984	10	555,099	Mass group
World Society for the Protection of Animals	1985	100	16,500,000	Mass group
Badger Trust	1986	4	88,606	Mass group
Bat Conservation Trust	1990	28	1,304,975	Mass group
The (Royal Society of) Wildlife Trusts	1912	57	14,736,000	Traditional group
CPRE	1926	66	5,197,614	Traditional group
Ramblers	1935	81	8,132,000	Traditional group
Campaign for National Parks	1936	12	613,624	Traditional group

British Mountaineering Council	1944	26	1,923,000	Traditional group
Hawk and Owl Trust	1969	9	434,495	Traditional group
Association of River Trusts	2001	5	450,663	Traditional group
Whale and Dolphin Conservation Society	1987	42	3,915,000	Memberless group
Pondconservation	1988	12	496,476	Memberless group
Froglife	1989	11	334,643	Memberless group
Amphibian and Reptile Conservation	1989	18	820,892	Memberless group
Plantlife	1989	28	1,443,821	Memberless group
Marine Connection	1997	NA	42,743	Memberless group
The Shark Trust	1997	5	184,000	Memberless group
Buglife	2000	8	462,417	Memberless group
Grassland Trust	2002	7	289,981	Memberless group
Universities Federation for Animal Welfare	1938	8	660,000	Subsidized group
Council for British Archaeology	1944	25	1,145,271	Subsidized group
Butterfly Conservation	1968	51	2,483,879	Subsidized group
Zoological Society of London	1826	617	39,585,000	Subsidized group
Wildfowl and Wetlands Trust	1946	339	15,976,000	Subsidized group

Notes

RSPCA, Royal Society for the Prevention of Cruelty to Animals; RSPB, Royal Society for the Protection of Birds; WWF, Worldwide Fund for Nature; FoE, Friends of the Earth; CPRE, Council for the Protection of Rural England.

74 Revisiting population-level analysis

Table 4.3 Hypothesized variation on institutional field variables

Field strength	Hypothesized institutional field strength				
	High ◄——————————————————► Low				
Institutional field	Professionals	Workers	Businesses	Citizens	Non-humans
Suggested examples	Medical doctors or lawyers	Trade unions	General business groups	Blind persons, gay/lesbian or patients	Animal rights, environmental

This also opens up cross-national possibilities. The organizational diversity of populations and choice of form by individual groups are both hypothesized to be related in various ways to the national system (specifically pluralist/corporatist distinctions). In principle, corporatist systems ought to encourage group designs which emphasize encompassing and peak structures consistent with the demands of the state for policy partners (see Schmitter 1983). There ought to be more openness in pluralist systems where access channels are more open and diffuse. For instance, in corporatist countries one might assume that diversity is lower – controlling for field-level differences – because of the role of the state in both funding and licensing peak groups in functional policy areas. Alternatively, we might, for instance, move to some more explanatory analyses. Here two broad approaches seem sensible.

First, these definitions and empirical measures of organizational form might be utilized as a *dependent variable*. An initial question along this line would be, why is *group x* in a specific form (as opposed to another) at a given point in time (especially at formation)? Relevant variables might include the previous experiences of the leaders, the preferences of key audiences (donors/supporters and policy makers) and the legacy of initial forms (path-dependence). A follow-up might be, does *group x* (or *set* of groups Y) change over time? And, is there any 'typical' set of evolutionary patterns? With the use of the broad forms discussed above, we have a common language with which to argue about *if* change is happening, and in what direction. Charting evolution, using generic organizational forms as markers, might be one obvious way forward: although more inductive (field-specific) categories may be more suitable in some cases (see Halpin and Nownes 2011). These approaches are explored in Chapters 5 and 6.

Second, a concept like 'organizational form' might be used as an *independent variable* in the context of explaining both group capacity and group policy behaviour. Truman long ago observed that 'The relation between group organization and access is not ... a matter just of being organized but equally of being organized appropriately for the problem at hand' (1971, 269). As foreshadowed above, groups, even in the same narrow niche, can possess different capabilities. For instance, Culpepper's (2003) work on the varied success in the implementation of training policy in regions of France and Germany points to different group

Revisiting population-level analysis   75

capacities as a key explanatory variable, which in turn rests on different organizational structures. Indeed, he explicitly links Skocpol's evidence of a decline in traditional group forms to a loss in group capacity (2003, 196).[23] From such a perspective, the value of groups to authorities seeking to effectively govern is shaped by their capacities to, for instance, foster coordination among members: a capacity constrained by an organizations form. Even more straightforwardly, the various modes by which groups choose to engage in public policy (outright advocacy, campaigning, implementation, private regulation, etc.) and the issue agenda they cultivate (which issues do they engage in, and what don't) might be said to be shaped by organizational form.

As identified in the empirical portion of this chapter, groups do hesitate between forms. Thus, from a slightly different perspective, we might puzzle over the cost to groups of hesitating between forms. The organizational literature suggests that hesitation between legitimate forms might threaten survival: that is, 'defying classification invites penalties' (Zuckerman 1999, 1399). One might hypothesize that groups which find themselves stranded between forms will suffer a loss of status with key audiences (such as policy makers and supporters/ donors) and hence face reduced survival chances. Similarly, one might also hypothesize – based on the organizational studies literature (see Hannan 2005) – that groups changing form will also suffer reduced survival chances.

Conclusion

The departure point for this chapter was the suggestion that the group literature had learnt to overlook the organizational forms in which groups survived. I suggested that a lack of attention to the bundles of organizational features adopted by groups (and changed therein over time) represented a lacuna in the literature. We had become satisfied with the notion that groups persisted on the back of material incentive exchanges (as in the incentive-based maintenance literature) or were simply content to note that groups were just 'there' (as in the mapping work ably developed within population ecology and niche-based analysis of mortality). This chapter provides one way in which group *organization* might be 'brought back in'.[24] The broad message then of this chapter is that embracing the diversity of group organizational form would reward group scholars. Much as Hannan (2005) has recently counselled for organizational studies more generally, rather than assume homogeneity in form (and relegate any findings of diversity to footnotes) we would be better served by directly puzzling over the question 'why are groups so different?' and 'how does this variation impact on important behaviours and capacities that groups might exhibit or possess?'.

Of course, these crude feature-based forms are but one way to engage with the form concept. Given that, on their own, neither population-level environmental pressures (controlled for) or group-level factors such as age or size seem to reflect variations in form, leads one to the conclusion that the prevailing form reflects choices – and *layers* of choices – by group entrepreneurs and associated cadres. This I suggest points to the need to study the evolution of specific groups

76 *Revisiting population-level analysis*

(in populations) over time. I suggest that the prevailing heterogeneity in a given population is best explained by an *aggregate* of the specific (and often interrelated) stories of the evolution of individual groups. As discussed in the conclusions, this supports an integration of the broad concerns of population dynamics (accepting population factors are important) with a discussion of the endogenous factors driving the evolution of form. Environmental pressures are no doubt important, but they affect different groups in uneven ways, with a net affect that is comprehensible only with more in-depth analysis (see discussion in Gray and Lowery 2000).

This argument does not, in and of itself, reduce the need for a population perspective. In fact, I suggest quite the contrary. In making sense of the diversity finding, perhaps the biggest lesson is that groups engage in some rather complex identity work. As Zuckerman (1999) has stressed, organizations must address a fundamental categorical paradox: first, an organization needs to emphasize isomorphism to gain membership (as appraised by key audiences) in a recognized population – for example as an environment group – but at the same time emphasize differentiation in order to stand out from other members of the population – for example as a traditional and not donor environmental group. It follows that in order to make sense of identity work, more emphasis needs to be made on group-level deliberations over form viewed *against the prevailing populations that they seek recognition in*. This leads us in the direction of more in-depth work utilizing identity-based conceptions of form.

It is, however, also the case that the finding of heterogeneity challenges straightforward structural determinism implicit in both neo-institutional and ecological approaches. As authoritative observers of the field have remarked 'Acknowledging heterogeneity challenges conventional images of causality and pushes institutional analysis away from strong forms of structural determinism to a much greater emphasis on agency, conflict, contingency and process (Schneiberg and Clemens 2006, 214–15). The same might be observed for ecological approaches. Even though it emphasizes environmental selection forces, and as such defines away variation, there is an acceptance that a case-level analysis of interpretation of such forces is worthwhile. This opens the door for historical work on survival that seeks to explain the heterogeneity that exists in populations of like groups populating a given institutional field.

Notes

1 To some extent this style of work might be considered as a second generation of population-based scholarship. Gray and Lowery make plain that the type of data they possessed was suited to enumerating headcounts of groups, but not to the form in which groups survived *between* birth and death. Yet they encouraged follow-up work that took up the challenge.
2 It is worth (very) briefly making the point that existing labels do not readily do the job. For instance, terms like insider versus outsider, or public versus sectional, focus on single dimensions of group activity (e.g. strategy/status and interests respectively). Labels like promotional, citizen and public-interest groups are regularly counterposed

with sectional, producer and economic groups; yet these labels most often gesture to the (different) constituency being organized by a group. Thus they are not designed or utilized to convey group organizational architecture. This style of labelling is eminently sensible where the concern is with measuring variations on single attributes, but it does not provide a good basis to distinguish overall *organizational form*. See Halpin (2010) for an elaboration.

3 One might add here, that the literature also assumes a group is more or less dedicated to political advocacy (broadly understood). Groups are formed *in order to* achieve policy influence. That they subsequently move into service provision or delivery of selective goods is explained as a survival strategy to shepherd groups away from a risky policy-only focus. Thus, the traditional groups might also have a third dimension, policy-dedication.

4 I think here of terms like 'astro-turf' or 'mail-order' participation.

5 This was particularly relevant in respect of Hayes' label 'pure staff group'. This would conceivably (and erroneously) direct attention to groups that were staff-directed, which could easily be the case for groups across all ideal types.

6 A curious empirical question – raised above by Skocpol – is why groups who do not *need* members for financing would bother to have them at all? Is it a matter of inheritance, that these groups *were* once traditional groups but have shifted their funding source? Or, is it a matter of initial design? This constitutes a substantive initial puzzle for researchers, demonstrating the value of speaking the language of organizational form. As Hayes suggests, one answer is that many traditional groups start out this way, because the cost of building a branch system is so high. But is this a generalized pattern?

7 The Charity Commission regulates those organizations that claim charitable status, and thus receive tax relief. A requirement is that they submit annual accounts and a statement outlining their work for the previous year and plans going forward.

8 Some might argue that not all these groups meet the 'public policy focus' requirement of an interest group definition (see Jordan *et al.* 2004). Yet, membership of the Link is, I argue, a signal of their policy engagement (as confirmed by discussions with WCL staff). Thus, I treat *all* organizations as interest groups.

9 As at April 2008.

10 Coding proceeded as follows, (i) Branches: are affiliates allocated to a branch with possibility for face-to-face contact (yes/no); (ii) Major funding source: affiliates/donors (threshold of more than 50 per cent of income); (iii) Style of affiliation: member (voting rights and venue to discuss policy or similar), supporter (affiliate category but only superficial rights), (iv) Limits on affiliation: closed (not everyone accepted), open (everyone accepted).

11 Taking Hannan and Freeman (1988) as a point of reference, the population of the Link would certainly conform to their definition of a population: 'An organizational population is broadly defined as a set of organizations that share a '*common dependence on the material and social environment*' (op. cit. Nownes 2004, 52, italics in original). Further confirmation that our sample is appropriate comes from Gray and Lowery's (2000) use of environment groups as an 'interest guild' for testing their ESA theory.

12 The UK equivalent of the US Directory of Associations.

13 This method of controlling for the effect of independent variables is recommended in small-n studies. Matching values on independent variables holds them constant across cases, hence allowing for other independent variables to be better observed (see discussion in King, Keohane and Verba 1991, 205–6).

14 Closely related to the 'energy' and 'space' terms in Gray and Lowery's ESA formulation.

15 With this design the only thing I cannot control for is whether there is something specific to the field of organizing *environment* groups that alters the background scope

78 *Revisiting population-level analysis*

for variation. The institutional variant of the organizational studies literature refers to institutional fields as more or less open or closed (see discussion in Schneiberg and Clemens 2006, Table 2). One might hypothesize that environment groups operate in a relatively open institutional environment compared to some professional groups (like lawyers or doctors) who might be expected to operate in a highly closed or sticky environment. In this respect I share the basic weakness of similar population studies (see Nownes 2004).

16 In the NT case this relates to running historic properties, like castles, gardens and houses.

17 As it happens, these broad findings are consistent with the US. In his impressive work on the US 'major environmental organizations', Bosso (2005, 10–11) makes the following observation:

> The advocacy community examined here is composed of a broad array of organizations. Some are massive, and others relatively small, whether measured by budget or membership. A few are organized on the basis of local or state chapters and offer their members a voice in electing leaders and setting advocacy priorities; a larger number can be described as having a mass base without mass participation. Some do not have dues-paying membership, preferring to rely on foundation support of major donors. Still others – perhaps the majority today – treat *any* donor as a 'member', thus muddying the concept itself.

18 Of course, this needs to be tested against other populations, and I cannot control for any background effects from my selection of a population of environmental groups.

19 This would lend some basic level of support to the conjecture of Hayes that subsidized groups are likely to be the forms chosen to start a group, which may then go on to be a mass or traditional group form.

20 Without a full set of time-series data for all groups (including before they joined the WCL) is not possible to say if (and when) contemporary groups changed their forms. Moreover, I cannot say whether there was or is any particular hazard associated with changing form.

21 Of course Open Spaces Society is an exception.

22 Incidentally, these two groups – the National Trust and Open Spaces Society – were sister groups when founded in the late nineteenth century.

23 In this case Culpepper is concerned with the capacities for groups (he considers employers' associations) to link individual member-firms together in a dialogue that can promote non-market cooperation.

24 The notion that organizational questions have been 'black boxed' is *also* echoed in the social movement literature (see review in Clemens and Minkoff 2004).

5 Interest group 'careers' (I)

Formation

Introduction

As elaborated elsewhere, the interest group literature has been overly concerned with the event of group formation. Early scholars supposed that latent interests would be converted into organizations of like-minded persons when and where governmental activity stirred them into action or when some balance between contending interests in society was disturbed. This type of argument is associated in particular with the work of Truman (1971). In one of the classic books in the field, Mancur Olson (1965) challenged this presumption of more or less automatic group formation, suggesting that many obvious causes and sets of interests go unorganized. Refinements have been made, for instance the observation that formation may occur by virtue of the benevolence of donors (including the state) (Walker 1991). For subsequent generations of group researchers it has been more or less accepted that group formation is *both* about the coalescing of a common set of interests *and* then overcoming collective action problems. Most recently, population-based analyses suggest that 'birth' will be severely fettered by the existing population of groups. Resource constraints in environments shared by similar groups will send signals to would-be group entrepreneurs that the population is at saturation point and thus new groups ought not to be established (Gray and Lowery 2000).

These contending theoretical perspectives single out critical conditions that are necessary and/or sufficient for group establishment. There needs to be a disturbance of some kind that helps people realize a common interest. Additionally, an entrepreneur capable enough to seize the opportunity and the external financial and political resources to construct a group-joining proposition is required. Of course, population approaches might also emphasize the competitive dimension in securing resources, emphasizing the (direct or indirect) roles of either philanthropic or state resources in the task of group establishment. While the literature focuses on what one might usefully call the 'initiation recipe' – the conditions for the formation event to occur – it spends rather less time scrutinizing the *type* of group that is actually established. In sum, we know we get a group, but the qualitative nature of the group is left largely unexplored.

80 *Interest group 'careers' (I)*

This chapter rethinks the formation literature taking the lens of organizational form. There is no clear tradition in group scholarship of exploring why a group chooses to organize in one manner or another. Yet this choice is highly salient given that it represents the initial step in a group's career, and likely therefore to strongly shape future group development. I use the term 'career' deliberately, and return to this in Chapter 6.

Viewing group formation through the lens of organizational form generates several basic insights that are developed below. Key amongst them is that those engaged in the task of establishing interest groups cannot but be vitally interested in answering the fundamental question 'how should we organize?' The formation task can, therefore, be usefully conceptualized as a process whereby key agents (such as group entrepreneurs) debate, discuss and crystallize a dominant identity that shapes the *initial* design the group establishes itself in. In addition, this chapter argues that the 'birth' of interest-group organizations is not an event, it is a process. As it happens, group formation often spans a significant time period: the outcome is the crystallization of a more or less settled group organizational form. This process is critical to explaining group survival, and subsequent adaptive change, as it establishes the basic identity of the group – what it is there for – and this informs the types of strategies the group sets and the instruments it uses to implement these strategies. Lastly, case studies suggest that the early years of group life are often characterized by jousting over the basic purpose (reason for being) of a group. Group formation is tightly bound up in identity formation, which in turn is often a contentious activity. The formation process is characterized by a debate over appropriate forms – there can be no presumption of a 'natural' or 'basic' form. Choice of form, is itself fashioned by a (micro) path-dependent process centred on the positive feedback between claims about identity (made by key actors to key audiences) and tentative steps (by key actors and observed by key audiences) to act upon elements of that crystallizing identity.

The 'modal' case of group formation

The group literature approaches formation through a rather neat narrative that assumes it revolves around the creation of *de novo* organizations. This gels with the 'group theory' assumption that social or economic disturbances create conditions for collective action that result in the establishment of a group. But to what extent is this is a realistic assumption? What are the circumstances of newly established groups?

Unfortunately this question has not been the subject of systematic empirical research. However, results from the survey of Scottish interest groups provide some insight. A 2008 survey of several hundred interest groups operating in Scotland, of varying ages, and operating in a broad range of policy fields, asked 'Which of the following best characterizes how your group was formed?' (Refer to Chapter 1 for details.)

Interest group 'careers' (I) 81

Table 5.1 How was the group formed?

	N	%
Started from scratch	321	70.09
Merger of older organizations	69	15.07
Splitting from parent organization	46	10.04
None of above	22	4.80
Total	458	100.00

Source: author's data, Scottish Group Survey (2008).

The majority (70 per cent) of the organizations were founded 'from scratch' as new organizations. However, a significant minority were established either through the merger of older organizations (15 per cent) or by splitting from a parent organization (10 per cent). The results makes plain that while many groups (in this case a large minority) do not emerge from nowhere (they have some type of antecedent), the modal group is on this evidence a *de novo* group.

Some riders apply to interpreting these results. The most obvious is that the sample includes only groups that survive, and does not count those that went out of business after only a short period. This introduces the logical possibility that groups started *de novo* are disproportionately more likely to survive (thus undercounting attempts to start groups other ways). The other limitation here is that we consider Scotland, which is a subnational jurisdiction within a Westminster system. We do not know, to be frank, how this table might look if we were to consider a Scandinavian corporatist system or, on the other hand, the hyperpluralist Washington system. For now, however, there is no in-principle reason to doubt this basic finding would carry.

If the modal style of formation is the establishment of a 'new' organization, what we also know is that many of these groups were actually established some time ago. Thus, many of the groups we see in front of us have already passed through significant milestones in their careers before we, as researchers, come to notice them and give them attention. It is also highly likely that they have adapted or even transformed during this intervening period since their establishment. Yet, for most researchers, groups are approached as units of analysis in such a manner as to elide (i) their formation date and (ii) their current organizational form. For instance, the Australian Conservation Foundation (ACF) is no doubt in the popular (and research) imaginary the quintessential Australian-grown environmental campaign group (Warhurst 1994). However, it actually started life as a scientific society, only shifting its form in recent decades. In essence, scholars take what is in front of them as given, and simply proceed to look at change against that benchmark (the present manifestation becomes the effective t_0). A similar pattern is noted for key US environmental groups, like the Sierra Club (Young 2008).

This treatment of group origins does, however, have implications. For one, the rationale for dwelling on formation – and the form in which groups are established in at the 'start' of their careers – is in part a reflection of the intuitive

82 *Interest group 'careers' (I)*

strength of the basic assumptions of the path dependent account of institutional and organizational change. In his seminal text on groups, Truman makes the point that features of groups that were important in their formative period may no longer seem to resonate with contemporary conditions, 'yet their impress upon the organizational structure of the group may continue' (Truman 1971, 115). A full decade and a half later, Arthur Stinchcombe (1965) made the (more widely cited) point that organizations generally were imprinted with the logic of the time in which they were established, and thereafter found that imprint hard to shake. In later chapters I return to the ways in which initial steps may (or may not) shape change over time. For now, this debate serves to underline why clarifying the initial form in which a group is established is an important process to scrutinize.

An additional concern revolves around subsequent assessments of groups divorced from their historical trajectory. Locke and Thelen (1995) make the general point that comparative analysis generally tends to be concerned with analysing like with like – say democratic states with democratic states – but does not give due attention to the starting point of each case. Their insight is that two cases may look the same in their present condition, but they arrived there from different origins. And, while facing similar contemporary challenges, the two cases will likely react and have different opportunities to react, *because* of their different origins. Translated into a group context, one might expect the ACF to react differently to a policy challenge such as fishing in the Antarctic compared to a group such as Greenpeace Australia, which has its origins in the international environmental movement and not the local Australian scientific community. Whereas Greenpeace may seek to directly engage fishing trawlers, the ACF is more likely to push a research-based insider strategy. From the perspective of organizational form, it makes sense to ask where and how it came to be as it is, rather than assume it was born how we find it today. Indeed, Greenpeace Australia CEO explained recently 'I'm proud to lead an organisation that does not mind getting in the way of super trawlers, or sailing into nuclear test sites, or embarrassing big corporations for burning rainforests or trashing the oceans. *That's what Greenpeace does*' (Australian Financial Review 2013, italics added).[1] While this type of question may seem relevant only for group anoraks, I maintain that it is crucial for a proper appreciation of form. If we do not probe the formation *process* then we will find it difficult to understand how we get the type of groups we find in front of us, their capabilities and limits.

There is no 'natural' model!

One basic point to establish is that there can be no reliance on some default or 'natural' way for sets of interests to be organized. There are reasons why we might expect, based on first principle accounts of prospects for political representation (see Halpin 2006), that some interests are more amenable to one or other form of organization. That is, we might assume that entrepreneurs in a given area have pre-existing scripts or templates to guide them with respect to

Interest group 'careers' (I) 83

addressing the question 'how should we organize'. It may well be that entrepreneurs have scripts, but it is likely to be a set of scripts: the argument here is that there is no single natural recipe.

This general point is underlined by reference to organizing the blind in Britain. In the mid-1900s in the United Kingdom three groups dominated the organization of the interests of the blind. How did they organize themselves? The first group to emerge, the British and Foreign Blind Association (BFBA), was established at the end of the nineteenth century by independently wealthy blind persons to work for better conditions for blind persons, including developing and printing embossed literature. Saliently, it also included acceptance of donations from the non-blind, and did not seek to enfranchise them or politically represent them. It changed forms significantly thereafter (see Chapter 6), but it started out as an organization to do good works *for* blind persons.

Very soon after the BFBA was formed, a second group emerged. In 1899 the National League of the Blind and Disabled (NLBD) was established as a trade union for blind and disabled persons only (however it allowed associate membership for partially sighted workers). The advent of hiring blind persons in sheltered workshops necessitated protection of their rights as workers, and the League organized and represented them (see Phillips 2004, 306; Danieli and Wheeler 2006, 491). Much later, in the late 1940s, the National Federation of the Blind of the United Kingdom (referred to as the 'Federation') was formed as a direct membership organization for the blind and deaf-blind. Like the League, it was formed around the work life of blind persons, but was based on the interests of blind people who worked in white-collar and professional roles. While both the League and the Federation had blind persons as members, were funded by member's dues and had a branch structure, the BFBA formed on the basis of the benevolence of wealthy individuals.

In summary, we can conclude that the mission of 'improving the condition of blind persons' did not seem to recommend a particular type of organizational design. Moreover, existing models did not seem to force any conformity or mimicry. This small vignette also underlines the fact that the way scholars draw lines around populations actually matters. Some might resist the inclusion of the League as a blind group, counting it as a trade union. There is no hard and fast rule, but it seems that the interests being organized is a critical dimension to respect when understanding processes of organizing. If 'interests' are the object of efforts at organizing it makes sense to make them the unit of analysis (much as population ecology does through its concept of 'interest guild').

Formation in context: more than an 'event'?

The terms birth and death, or organizational formation and disbandment, suggest that identifying the start of a group's career – and its end – will be relatively simple. Yet, as is often the case, the conceptual scalpel resembles a blunt chisel by the time it comes up against the bedrock of empirical case material. Decades old case studies may serve to foster the self-belief of scholars that the start and

84 *Interest group 'careers' (I)*

end of a group's career *should* be easy to identify. Salisbury (1969) after all, could confidently say when the AAM went bust (see also Cigler 1986). And, in my previous examples I could tell a story including the dates on which three organizations to advocate for the blind were 'established'. It may well be easy in some cases to speak with such confidence; but the claim here is that this is probably the exception. The impulse here is to embrace the reality that formation is likely to be more complex than establishment dates imply.

Choice of methodological approach has a clear role to play in how the concept of formation is operationalized. Those working at the population level must find a single date in order to conduct calculations and engage in event-history style analyses. A close reading of the population ecology literature confirms the (perfectly defensible) compromises required to 'map' group populations in such a manner. For instance, in his work on populations of US gay and lesbian groups, Nownes freely noted

> that for the vast majority of cases, determining a founding date was easy because the date was widely known and accepted. In a handful of cases, however the *Encyclopedia of Associations* had a different founding date than newspaper, archival and historical sources.
>
> (2004, 59)

And, of course, there is the basic empirical data collection dilemma – when to count a group as 'new' and 'formed' and how to treat mergers and name changes (see discussion in Carroll and Hanan 2000). But this is trivial compared to a far more fundamental problem. What do we *mean* by formation? How do we *conceptualize* it?

The orthodoxy that formation can be understood as an event makes sense if by formation we refer to the establishment of organizational *structures* alone. We can arrive at a date for when a headquarters was purchased, a PO box established or a first meeting held. And these are useful pointers to efforts at organization. However, if one is concerned with the qualitative style of organization that is actually established, then formation makes vastly more sense when approached as a *process* during which an organization debates and then settles on an answer to the question 'how should we organize'? This question is one that all groups need to answer. Without doing so, key audiences – policy makers, donors or members/supporters, other groups – will not be able to assess them, attribute legitimacy and allocate resources. Policy makers will not be able to offer access or status, donors will not feel comfortable providing or sustaining finance, members will not know that the group is for 'them', and other groups will not know whether to cooperate or compete. In market terms, this process is about defining the group product – an obvious precursor to any discussions about whether it might be subject to free-riding (Young 2008).

Scholars have seldom problematized formation in the group literature. But, in a rare moment of reflection Imig and Berry (1996, 149) suggest that there is 'confusion between organizational formation and maintenance'. They ask

Interest group 'careers' (I) 85

whether to equate group formation with a specific date – based on a date in which it was registered or constituted – is perhaps too narrow a focus. Instead, they suggest scholars focus on 'how the organization actually operated during its *formative period*' (Imig and Berry 1996, 149 emphasis added). Their intention is that we ought to look at formation as a (perhaps lengthy) process rather than a quick event.

The insight offered by Imig and Berry (1996) finds relatively easy endorsement from the perspective of those engaged in the work of formation. Indeed, when one probes into a case in detail, the messy nature of formation as a process is often apparent. A good example is an innocent email query to a relatively new group – Pond Conservation – about formation date (which I could not find on their website). It elicited the following response:

> we have undergone several name changes reflecting our changing role. It was started as Pond Action in 1988, then became Ponds Conservation Trust, and finally renamed Pond Conservation a few years ago. Technically, therefore we started in 1988, as the key staff were on board then.

Further probing about when a clear *form* was apparent – rather than when it was born – got this response;

> It has really evolved over 22 years, as these things do, from a few people doing research and being passionate about what they do, to a proper registered credible charity with high level trustees, a director, a mission statement, and now a supporters scheme.

In agreeing with the sentiment that formation is likely a process, and not an event, I would simply note that there is little evidence it has gone on to inform subsequent research to any great extent (see Chapter 2). How might we better capitalize on the type of insight made by the likes of Imig and Berry?

We might productively ingest this style of response by scaffolding our analysis of group histories through a narrative like group careers, in which formation is the first – and critical – step from which subsequent ones depart. The concept of group careers is developed in Chapter 6. For now, what does this first initial step in a group career look like? And, how might it be conceptualized?

Conceptualizing the *formative phase* of group careers

If formation is to be conceptualized as the start of a group's career; a step that in path-dependent terms is likely to be critical in shaping future trajectories, then what goes on at this initial step in the group sequence? How might we conceptualize this activity? And how does it look empirically?

The most fundamental insight here is that formation *requires* key stakeholders in the new endeavour to answer the basic question 'how should we organize?'. This, I suggest, is an inescapable question for any group to come

86 *Interest group 'careers' (I)*

into being. The answer to this question may lie in a number of interrelated processes, which can be conceptualized by drawing on institutional and ecological threads in the identity-based approach to form within organizational social science (as reviewed in Chapter 3). The first is to view formation as a specific type of work – often engaged in by entrepreneurs – that gives rise to an initial group identity. This identity then provides the first step in a groups' organizational 'career'. Second, *de novo* group design is rarely conducted on an empty sheet of paper: existing forms in the field or generic forms provide signposts (what to replicate and what not to replicate) by which group entrepreneurs can navigate the task of group establishment and communicate desired designs to key audiences (policy makers and members/donors). Third, we might understand the process of formation as one that might span a few years or even a few decades. What we are concerned with is the first point at which a group can be said to settle upon an organizational identity and design. Last, I suggest group formation can be understood as a process of organization-building in which initial form is derived from the sum of a series of micro-steps which can be said – in the perspective of key audiences (policy makers, donors, members) – to be coherent enough to establish a clear reputation or identity. This may take some considerable time, and may take many twists and turns.

Formation as 'identity-work'

At the start of a groups' career there is by definition no pre-existing or settled organization in place. Thus, because the formation process is the first step in a sequence it must be focused on answering the question 'how should we organize?' The answer to this question is not always self-evident, and cannot be read off or assumed a priori, rather it is often a complex process of its own that requires unpacking. One valid approach is to conceptualize formation as a type of identity-work which entrepreneurs – or entrepreneurial cadres – engage in when seeking to establish an interest group *de novo*. As discussed in Chapter 3, new organizational entities confront the need to establish their own specific identity. This is an activity often conducted within a rich institutional context. There are pre-existing generic forms that provide reference points and guidance as to appropriate designs. This is not simply or only a cerebral activity, it most often is engaged with by a leadership cadre and often reflects feedback from the environment – reactions of potential supporters, donors, policy elites, and so forth.

This might sound like a largely discursive process but identity-work has clear material (and resource) implications. In common with resource-mobilization perspectives, the chief strategic consideration in identity-work is in generating acceptance and legitimacy among key audiences, such that this facilitates the flow of resources to the fledgling group. The rule of thumb here is that where emergent identities of a new entity 'fit' with existing and established generic forms, then resources will likely follow. In addition, the performance of certain identities – their implementation – has the effect of building up functional competence, which

Interest group 'careers' (I) 87

in turn provides capabilities that also have a path-dependent quality (the better you get at something, the more you do it, the better you get at it).

As discussed in Chapter 3, the notion that groups have identities is not entirely new. The work of Michael Heaney (2004, 2007) enunciated the idea that groups developed and cultivated the way they were viewed by key audiences, policy makers, members, and other groups. His account of identity seems rather tactical in the sense that groups can readily, frequently and flexibly shift their projected identity.[2] A slightly different version arises from Matt Grossman's (2012) notion of 'institutionalized pluralism' which posits that groups seek to become prominent – as viewed by key audiences – by virtue of being 'place-holders' or taken for granted advocates for key sets of interests, values or perspectives (2012). While not discussed explicitly, this account – and specifically the implied mechanism of institutionalization – suggests a less tactical understanding of identity-formation (and change). Indeed, as Engel notes, there is a sense in which identity must be 'sticky' (2007, 73); after all, if identity is about appearing unique to key audiences, then shifting their perceptions will take time. On the other hand a group appearing to have an unstable identity would likely face a problem in maintaining steady relations with such audiences. Put simply, once a group becomes known or has a reputation as something – it has a clear and well-understood identity – this is hard to change. I think this style of work has a great deal of insight to offer. And here I simply firm up this initial good work in such a way as to make it easy to digest for the field. Here organizational identity is viewed as something that takes time to accumulate – like a reputation does – and thus once settled can be expected to be hard to shift at a moments' notice or manipulate too much for various audiences.

Empirically, identity can be understood as the *self*-identity of a group: what it thinks it stands for and how it sees itself in relation to other groups. Thus, a group's identity can be empirically captured in its 'rhetoric, history, and public mission statements' (Engels 2007, 68). Similarly, Clemens suggests that group identity might be understood in terms of 'we are people who do these sorts of things in this particular way' (1997, 50). This is a different type of assumption to that of instrumental calculation or optimal fit with the environment.

Formative period as 'micro-steps'

The perspective here is that identity takes time to crystallize. It does not come pre-divined nor is it reasonable to expect that entrepreneurs approach the task with clarity of design. More plausible is that entrepreneurs come to the task with a plan, which upon implementation, is subject to positive reinforcement or negative feedback loops. This points to the way in which unfolding identities are uncertain and contingent – until institutionalized. Thus, it makes sense to conceptualize identity formation or crystallization as a (micro) path-dependent process of its own. For instance, a group that attempts multiple strategies of policy influence, yet finds early success with direct protest, might find that momentum builds among supporters for more such work, and the media covers

88   *Interest group 'careers' (I)*

the group 'as a protest group', and so the momentum builds despite the best efforts of the entrepreneurs. This is just the dynamic that is reported in the case of the Sierra Club leaders who resuscitated the group in the 1950s. As Young (2008) has elaborated, identities are built through a series of micro-steps that are often hard to predict. But, once an identity takes hold, it is rather hard to undo it (but see Chapter 6).

While identity work is about the purposeful strategies of entrepreneurs, the other side of the coin – as Young's work hints – is the way a group is perceived by external stakeholders: donors, the state, and other groups. This latter aspect raises the issue of reputation. In this respect Engels explains that

> As a given organizational identity imparts a reputation among members and within the elite political context, options for viable action become limited. Identity, thus, has a path-dependent quality. As identity is reified over time reinforced by each action a group takes, it becomes more difficult to change course or pursue strategies seemingly out of line with the organization's understood identity.
>
> (Engel 2007, 74)

Others also treat identity as a two-sided coin. As Minkoff and Powell (2006, 592) explain, 'We consider … mission as both a charter and a constraint. Mission motivates activity but also limits the menu of possible actions'. They elaborate, 'As Charter, mission serves to direct an organization toward specific combinations of ideology, organizational structure, and relations with members and sponsors. Mission also operates as a constraint with respect to how an organization responds to changes circumstances' (2006, 605). Again, this underscores the reinforcing nature of strategies and identity (a point taken up in Chapter 6).

Generic forms as 'signposts'

The historical institutional literature – and the punctuated equilibrium model specifically – implies that the start of the sequence is more or less open: anything is possible. Thereafter, change becomes incrementally more difficult to achieve. This is, of course, why we ought to pay a great deal of attention to the form of groups at birth: these will be perhaps the defining moment of the group's career. However, Thelen (2003) has cogently argued that the start of any evolutionary sequence should be conceived as more *closed* than simply 'anything goes'. There are constraints to simply 'choosing' any form. As will become evident, the case studies illustrate varying degrees of choice by groups over form during the formation process.

The initial insight developed here – and consistent with the identity-based approach to organizational form (see Chapter 3) – is that those engaged in work to establish a fledgling interest group often utilize generic forms as markers against which to solidify ideas and to debate options. It is conceptually useful to keep these two notions of form – realized and generic – distinct, but in practice, they are surely intertwined. Organizational entrepreneurs – those engaged in establishing specific empirical forms – no doubt utilize generic forms as constructs by which to make organizing thinkable. Identifying specific realized organizational forms means observing the 'horizon of possibilities' that groups have at hand, what generic forms are considered or discussed as possible, what were adopted and what were defeated (see Clemens 1997, 61). As has been mentioned elsewhere, discussions about appropriate form have a comparative quality: choices of form are made from among a virtual list of known alternatives and/or made in the face of decisions of what form they do not want to be (Clemens 1997, 61). And further, choices are often made by reflecting on *both* the forms 'usual' for a given identity and those (known) forms that are associated with other identities (Clemens 1997, 60). One can access this type of work by utilizing the deliberations of key organizational leaders: as they discuss their own group's identity they contrast their own organization with other *specific* forms, and to broader *generic* forms.

As one may imagine, identity formation is not a straightforward or rapid process, and the date of group establishment may have little resonance with the commencement or completion of the search for a clear identity. Consistent with the review in Chapter 3, debates over what style of group to establish will tend to reflect on different generic forms that are in play at a given moment. Thus, the formation process needs to capture the forms discussed, the comparisons made between forms and the choice of form made. In this sorting and sifting process, identity-formation is a key and defining activity. Answering the question 'what are we organizing for?' is crucial with respect to selecting among generic forms. But the answer takes time to emerge.

To empirics...

Formation is hard to study for the simple reason that many of the groups we are interested in are themselves many years old. Thus, for the most part empirical analysis has to rely on accounts of the formative period of groups, rather than interview or discuss formation as it happens. In 2008 a set of a dozen UK groups were chosen to be involved in a project to understand the way leaders interpreted the challenge of organizing a contemporary interest group. Several were new groups or were at pivotal points in their relatively young careers. Their perspectives are revealing about what the task of group design entails, and are drawn on in the balance of this chapter.

The 'politics' of formation

The early years of group careers are often characterized by jousting over the basic purpose and identity of a group. That is to say, group identity is not simply given, it needs to crystallize. This process is a political one, with long-standing implications. It may be over briefly, but it can drag on for years.

90   *Interest group 'careers' (I)*

The Soil Association

Let's take an example. It is easy to start the sequence at group birth, once the group is established and up and running. The Soil Association – a group organized around organic agriculture in England – was established at a meeting of like-minded individuals in 1946. It is convenient to take this date as the start of a sequence. But close inspection of this case suggests this presents problems. Scrutiny of the founding of the Soil Association reveals that three basic purposes underpinned its formation: (i) public education, (ii) scientific inquiry, and (iii) knowledge exchange among farmers. These appeared in the record of the opening meeting of the group, and might be taken at face value as a settled mission statement. However, this would be a mistake.

The report of the first annual meeting records the resignation of one founder over the crystallizing view that the group *should* be about public education and admit the broader public – not just organic farmers – into membership. The individual in question was advocating the view that the identity of the group should be founded on service to its constituent *organic farmer* members. But other founders had a different vision. As it turned out, the first president – Eve Balfour – preferred a strong public education role and she carried the day (Halpin and Daugbjerg 2013).

What were the concrete implications of this firming up of the first step in the sequence of group evolution in terms of organizational form? An identity as a union of British organic farmers would have implied local branches, negotiations with the state and closed membership. As it turns out, one might, in fact, argue that empirically 1982 was the date that the SA had established its initial – settled – form: as an agri-environmental campaigning group (Halpin and Daugbjerg 2013).

Proof of who prevailed is a tricky business to determine, and I return to this case in Chapter 6. But for now, what this establishes is that, in all cases, a choice has to be made with respect to a group's identity. This choice is often contested – there is no ready-made answer – and the openness of the start of group careers makes contestation more likely.

Additional cases

Almost uniformly, group informants interviewed for my work reported a great deal of contestation over what the 'proper' mission, purpose or aims of a given group ought to be. It seems that cohorts of group entrepreneurs can often agree that a particular gap exists in the ecology yet find it hard to agree on precisely what style of group ought to fill it.

The organization of kidney patients in the UK is one such example of contested beginnings. In the 1970s a group of individuals saw a need for action to ensure access to dialysis treatments for those with kidney failure; but in addition, others wanted to see more done on the issue of kidney transplant. The latter group went on to establish the National Kidney Foundation (NFK), while the others formed the British Kidney Patient Association. The former has developed into an umbrella group for local hospital-based kidney patient associations, while the latter has developed into a group that solicits public donations to fund individual treatments.

Formation as 'choosing a model'

Several organizations in my sample of UK groups were young. While they had formally been in existence for some time, the group had fallen into a state of disrepair and gone into hibernation, only to be reactivated by a new cohort of entrepreneurs. For such individuals, the 'original' group organizational form – understood as akin to a *blueprint* – served as a cautionary tale of what *not* to do.

Forestry Contractors' Association

In the 1980s, the UK forest contracting industry – those individuals contracted by processors to fell and cart wood to their premises – was dominated by single-person operations. Technology use was at a minimum and processors and government were keen to professionalize the sector. At this point efforts were made, successfully, to establish the Forestry Contractors Association (FCA).

According to a well-placed industry figure, 'At this point there was somewhat of a conflict between whether the FCA was a union of woodcutters or a Trade Association.' He explained that 'The idea of the FCA had a non-contracting origin. The processing sector was concerned by the unreliability of wood-cutters. Thus the idea of the FCA was pitched [by processors] to Contractors as a union.' By contrast the state was keen on a Trade Association (TA) model. 'The old TA model' was based on funds from government for industry training. However, 'When the money ran out ... the TA failed. This is a common feature of smaller TAs, and means that these groups did not fulfill their primary function of representing members.' As it happens, the initial FCA established in 1992 followed the TA model. It came to be dominated by large companies who could use it to access research and development (R&D) and training funds from government. However, several financial crises sent the organization into severe financial trouble.

Against this backdrop, the Forestry Contractors Association (FCA Membership) was formed in the late 2000s out of the ashes of the first FCA. The small group of individuals engaged in this work puzzled over organizational design carefully. The chairman recognized several models as being relevant to their design task. On the one hand, they were highly critical of the TA model that the first FCA had been established in. On the other hand, there was a determination not to appear as a trade union-style group. This again, like the SA case, highlights the politicized nature of much discussion over identity. In this instance the processing industry and the state had ideas on what type of organization was most appropriate. The task of the fledgling entrepreneurs was to tread a path

92 *Interest group 'careers' (I)*

between these. It seems that their approach was to seek out what they thought members would want.

It was apparent that there was more clarity on what model the re-launched FCA was avoiding than what it was aiming to be. The then chairman explained:

> We are not a union – even though people initially thought that was good, when we explained what that entails they were less keen. We are not a Trade Association, which is sectoral. We are not a professional body trying to maintain a contracting profession. So not clear on what model we should be pursuing, that is a key question.

They wanted to signal to the industry that they were self-employed contractors only, but also to be careful not to convey a trade union style logic to would-be members.

This identity crisis at formation has been resolved for now. Its current website explains that the 'The Forestry Contracting Association (FCA Membership Ltd) is the leading trade association within UK forestry and wood related industries. The Association focuses on those businesses and individuals who are involved or interested in the contracting sector' (www.fcauk.com/, accessed April 2013).

People Too

In a similar vein, at its formation, People Too was careful to distinguish itself from the 'orthodox' farm associations and crofting groups in Scotland. One of its founders explained:

> I had been involved with various groups, like the NFUS [National Farmers' Union of Scotland], crofting and landowning groups, but was frustrated with their approach. So I resigned from that and went on our own. I did not feel like a rogue or anything like that, there were a lot of people feeling like me. The standard pressure group wasn't waking up to the reality of modern lobbying. They were stuck in the past, sitting down with government and negotiating. We wanted a new type of lobbying, shocking, and ... going straight to the top.

Part of its *raison d'être* was to literally embody in their organizational design a critique of 'old' ways of organizing. Legitimacy is an important pressure on group populations, but its impact is a lot more complicated than just compelling groups to fit a single dominant form at any one time. As Chapter 4 established, there is remarkable diversity in form among even the closest of group 'families'.

People Too designed itself as a disciplined media savvy group. It established a very tight leadership cadre, composed of three part-time activists. None of them had direct experience in running interest groups or political lobbying. Moreover, none of them received salaries or such like from the group. Their basic model was to solicit funds from a passive membership to pay for activities consisting mostly of media-based strategies of issue (re)framing. They were dissatisfied with what they perceived as the free hand given to regulatory bodies, like the Scottish Natural Heritage (SNH), to regulate land use in remote and rural Scotland. Moreover, they objected to the support from interest groups like the Royal Society for the Protection of Birds (RSPB), which they believed were monopolizing public opinion and pressuring government for more regulation. In essence, the premise of the new group was to inject a new point of view in the public debate.

The strategy and techniques of the new group were consistent with this firming, yet still fuzzy, identity. The group established itself as a limited liability company in May 2002. It was initially funded by the three directors, with the intention to fund it by annual memberships thereafter. In the first year it had 200 or so members paying £50 per annum. The directors participated in meetings with Members of the Scottish Parliament (MSPs), gave radio and print media interviews (and wrote letters to the editors of the major Scottish newspapers), responded to government policy consultations and gave public talks and lectures. A key decision was to invest a large part of its early funds in a newsletter, 'Fresh Air'. One of the directors had a publishing background, and was made editor. According to one founder,

> The aim of the newsletter was nothing more than a piece of paper that could be circulated with alternative views and facts [from the orthodoxy]. We simply wanted to go into print, to put our necks on the line, to make it more than just chatter [socially among activists].

The group ran three annual public meetings, which included directors and other guest speakers. Financial considerations were paramount, with a founder stating that all they needed was 20 participants to 'break even', but their first meeting attracted 200 people.

However, certain tensions and contradictions emerged with this model. The commitment to a media-focused campaign led to reluctance among founders to broaden their leadership cadre. A founder explained 'The problem with expanding is we would be nervous if new people would be as cautious in public statements, based on facts. We provided a head on challenge to enemies' facts, so we had to be disciplined.' The focus on the Fresh Air newsletter also proved to be fatal financially. In all it had four editions, and then was mothballed. A director stated that 'in hindsight it was not the best use of our resources to put 50 per cent of our money into a magazine'. Like Young's observation regarding US environmental groups, positive feedback firms up fledgling identities; however, negative feedback has the reverse effect of leaving things fluid and unsettled.

Working with an 'inheritance'?

The discussion so far treats group formation as though they were all more or less blank page affairs. This *is* the modal style of formation. Yet, many groups that

94 *Interest group 'careers' (I)*

'form' or are 'born' have continuity in one way or another with previous groups. They are working off the back of some kind of institutional inheritance. In that sense, we can see one source of *endogenous* influence on the initial form that starts a sequence as some type of more or less direct inheritance. It can serve to constrain the new group, or to enable change away from the previous form.

National Landlords' Association

Some cases demonstrate the importance of established generic forms in guiding the hand of founders. The case of the National Landlords Association is instructive. The NLA is a classic case of a 'new' group being formed from an inheritance. It was first formed as the Small Landlords Association (SLA) in the 1970s. The founder placed an advertisement in the *Evening Standard* alerting others to the fact she would be protesting outside parliament and anyone else of like mind ought to join her. So overwhelmed by the turn out, she decided then and there to start a group. The term 'small' in the title was deliberately chosen to signal that it did not pursue the interests of corporate landlords. It was initially run as an unincorporated body from the founder's front room in Ealing, West London. After this flurry of early activity, the old SLA went into hibernation but 'woke up' as the NLA in 2001/2 amidst perceptions that the 'sector was again under pressure'. In addition, the need to become an incorporated body – to comply with new legislation – provided an opportunity for a new cohort of leaders to register it as the National Landlords Association (NLA).

The Housing Act 2004 was a focusing event for the re-launching of the NLA. The Act was on its way, but the new NLA simply lacked the capacity to engage in the political process. And so started a series of reforms to re-launch the group. The current president explains that he inherited an organization that had atrophied under what he called a 'craft model': 'other sectors across the country have professionalized and changed the way they do things, they moved away from the craft industry approach to a more professional approach'. But an old form is hard to shake entirely. The new chairman explains that the three objectives of the NLA are influence public policy to the benefit of private residential landlords, raise standards in the sector, and provide a range of services and benefits to assists members' businesses. He says, 'These are broadly consistent with the original SLA approach, although it may have been couched in terms like "defending the sector", it is a matter of emphasis.' The salient point here is that many group formations are in fact re-launches of atrophying groups (even though they are reported as establishments). And in such instances, the new form is often defined in terms of departures from the old. However, as this and other cases underline, departures from the old need to be argued for, and new leaders are not always simply able to have their way.

So what considerations shaped the emerging new form – the reinvention of the NLA? The first consideration was to demarcate it from the old 'craft' form. The precursor to the NLA, the Small Landlords' Association (SLA), was 'born in a different age' and according to an NLA leader was a 'craft organization'

Interest group 'careers' (I) 95

that was 'ran out of the front room' of a founders house in London. That is what it would *not* be, but what *should* it be organized like?

On the first score, the interviewee explained

> If you wanted to be taken seriously you have got to call yourself national. We said if we don't someone else will. We went through a phase where ... it is alright if you are the Royal Institute of whatever, that is a bit different, but otherwise you probably better be called national.

It was not only the Royal Institute model that served as a reference point for design efforts. A key NLA leader explained that to some extent their design work was informed by Hesseltine's 1990 work to create 'model' trade associations in the UK: the basic idea being that each sector would have a single, authoritative and well-resourced association with which to engage government. He said 'I guess that is what we are trying to do here, in the private rental sector.' One way to understand this is that the NLA set out to occupy a space as *the* representative organization for the sector. This is confirmed when interviewees talked about spending a lot of time trying to 'tidy up' the sector.

The latter focus on professionalism turned out to be the desire to be viewed as a group civil servants can work with: 'We aim to become part of the furniture', the interviewee explained. The leadership seemed to view this as being driven by a kind of positive feedback process. The brand recognition required by the NLA as a main player comes from access, but access requires brand recognition. He explains 'Brand recognition if nothing else comes from access to the minister.' He explained that the main requirement for access was good information: 'it is useful to say we talked to our members and they say "xyz". But politicians and civil servants really just want to talk to somebody, and the NLA is there to fill the gap. To be a source of information is important.' The success or otherwise of the rebirth of the NLA is explained in terms apparently close to the notion of establishing a firm identity. The interviewee explained 'There was a predecessor organization that mutated into the NLA and that brand is very well known, but this is still something we have to work at because of our youth I suspect our current group may still be not well known.'

Exogenous limits on choice

Group organizations trying to establish themselves do so against an institutional context that shapes choice. The organizational studies literature – whether ecological, resource dependence or institutional in nature – reinforces the importance of establishing legitimacy and overcoming the liability of newness. The core claim is that organizations that follow proven organizational recipes – mimic forms that are established and thus deemed legitimate – are more likely to succeed. But some fields of operation are more institutionalized than others: that is to say, the scope for deviation without sanction is far smaller.

96 *Interest group 'careers' (I)*

The evolution of Norwegian local neighbourhood associations offers a nice example. Wollebæk notes that in the 1980s and 1990s the resident or neighbourhood group was a rapidly growing form. He suggests that

> this new organizational field has not yet fully institutionalized. In some communities, such associations function as interest organizations; elsewhere they promote social activities; in some cases they manage common property.... The lack of clear outside expectations concerning what a neighborhood association is supposed to do and how it is supposed to do it increases the association's degrees of freedom and hence probability of change.
>
> (Wollebæk 2009, 370)

In mature organizational fields, norms are well established as to the legitimate ways to organize and it would thus be unwise to step outside of conventions. In others, fields are more open and innovation is less risky.

The groups I have studied in order to complete this book span a broad number of fields. The virtue of such a design is that I can look at the impact of variation in field on the way groups form.

In some areas, choosing a specific identity means that there is little room for choice in relation to how a group will be organized. The field of law is one such case. The Personal Injury Bar Association (PIBA) is interesting because, in contrast to other groups, it operates in an area of social life that is highly regulated. As professionals, lawyers are required to meet certain standards in order to maintain their registration. However, within this field, personal injury might be considered a relatively new field, and one that among the general public has a reputation for pushing boundaries. How did they establish themselves?

The founding of PIBA is set within a process of reorganization within the practice of law. Bar Associations did not get going until the 1980s, as before then they did not have a great deal of power within the Bar Council. In addition, barristers did not engage in compensation law until the late 1970s and early 1980s in the UK. In the 1980s this compensation work became 'much more scientific', and according to the president it was the point at which 'Barristers came to identify themselves as personal injury versus common law barristers.' This surfacing of a professional identity was crucial for the PIBA to emerge. However, it was not until 1995 that PIBA was established. Yet the precise design established was very predictable. According to the president, they are organized as a voluntary membership-based (and funded) organization. They serve the purposes of negotiations with the Bar Council, engaging government (through the Bar Council) and providing training and professional development to their members. Being a 'Bar Association' implies a well-established form that is hard to innovate on.

To be clear, lawyers may choose to establish advocacy organizations with a different identity which will be less constraining in terms of organizational design. For instance, British law practitioners in the personal injury field may join the Association of Personal Injury Lawyers (APIL), which organizes

Interest group 'careers' (I)   97

solicitors on the plaintiff side, or the Forum of Insurance Lawyers, which organizes those on the defendant's side. In addition, there is the Action Against Medical Accidents (AvMA), which is a campaigning group that involves solicitors and others. It is not that personal injury lawyers cannot be organized in some other manner, but PIBAs identity is established by its desire to be legitimate in the eyes of the Bar Council, which in turn makes it important for its membership. There is not so much a question over how to organize, but whether to organize as a Bar Association.

PIBA showed very little flexibility in the basic form they chose to build the group's identity at the outset, and this low level of flexibility has characterized their inability to adapt to challenges subsequently. Constraint derives from professional conventions and governmental/statutory requirements respectively. This suggests such groups are prone to a more classical model of rapid and radical change, punctuating long periods of stasis (for discussion of this thesis with respect to the Law Society of Scotland see Chapter 6).

Conclusion

If nothing else, the empirical illustrations underline that what appear with hindsight as clear early formative trajectories are, from the perspectives of those involved in formative periods within groups, often uncertain times. This chapter has offered a reworking of the way scholars understand group formation inspired by the lens of organizational form. This highlights several things about the way we might approach the question of group formation.

The first is that formation is a process, and not an event. Group scholarship has tended to see birth as an event, after which groups are (more or less) simply maintained. Yet, if we ask what style of organization is established, then we need to assess and document the process that settles such questions: a process that might well span a considerable time period. Second, because formation is the 'start' of a group's career, there is by definition no pre-existing or settled form in place. Thus, because the formation process is the first step in a sequence it must be focused on answering the question 'how should we organize?' The answer to this question is not always self-evident, and cannot be read off or assumed a priori, rather it is often a complex process of its own that requires unpacking. This perspective requires scholars going back to basics and establishing how a given set of interests can be organized (not taking for granted a group organization exists and going from there). Viewed against the idea of a sequence, it was suggested that group formation can be understood as a process of organization-building in which initial form is derived from the sum of a series of micro-steps which can be said – in the perspective of key audiences (policy makers, donors, members) – to be coherent enough to establish a clear reputation or identity. This may take some considerable time, and may take many twists and turns. As is evident, in this account form is conceptualized as a set of design constructs that entrepreneurs recognize and use to orientate the firming-up of their new group's identity.

98 *Interest group 'careers' (I)*

However, resting on some general notion of path dependence does not dispense with the question of start point entirely. The historical institutional literature also struggles with the same conundrum: when does a sequence start? Theories of path dependency imply that first steps constrain subsequent ones, but what is the logical start point, the first initial step that shapes subsequent ones? These questions are hard to answer. In fact, there is no principled answer, just the reminder that scholars ought to be attentive to the point at which they start their narratives. In the group context, it makes eminent sense to focus on formation dates – year established or similar – but in so doing accept that the gestation period for such an event, and its social milieu, are important to capture.

The next chapter addresses what happens after this formative phase of group life. Formation is conceptualized as part of an individual group's career, itself approached as an historical sequence. In this book I scaffold discussion of formation – and subsequently change or maintenance – through the concept of group careers or evolutionary sequences. In conceptualizing a group career, I draw on the historical institutional literature – from the disciplines of political science and organizational studies – to provide a basic conceptual scaffolding to probe change and adaptation among groups. It is for this reason I refer to careers as historical 'sequences'. The insight drawn here is that group formation needs to be viewed as the initial – some might say decisive – step in an organizational career.

Notes

1 www.afr.com/p/national/arts_saleroom/greenpeace_raises_its_sails_wW5kBbG-W0uMjn9pDgLwq3M) accessed 10 may 2013.
2 This scenarios seems more plausible in the case of groups that have a single dominant 'audience' that effectively dictates what it is looking for in its group partners and to which groups must quickly change. I think here of the not-for-profit sector, which is overly reliant on state funding. One could well imagine that shifts in policy frames – say from social justice to enablement in the welfare sector – could demand groups shift their identity from a rights-based advocacy (where advocacy means collective political engagement) to a service-delivery advocacy (where advocacy means case-work).

6 Interest group 'careers' (II)

Group adaptation and change over time

Introduction: the ubiquity of adaptive change

Having established in the previous chapter that *the* key task of formation can be conceptualized as establishing a firm group identity and design, this chapter focuses upon the subsequent set of questions: Can groups adapt and change form over their careers (what are the sources of constraint and enablement)? What types of change are there (and which are most disruptive)? These strike me as important empirical and conceptual questions to the study of group maintenance, but ones that have attracted relatively little dedicated attention in the group literature. This chapter addresses this gap with an explicit focus on developing an approach to describe and calibrate change in group organizational form. The aim is to encourage debate by exploring ways we might use concepts like organizational form to get a handle on the dynamic of group evolution. It presents a framework for describing organizational form, and levels of change in group form. This discussion is supported by illustrative examples from predominantly UK group cases.

The jump off point for this chapter, much like its predecessor, is that the literature on interest group 'mobilization' and 'maintenance' *underplays* the above set of questions about group organization (see Chapter 2). The lack of dedicated attention to organizational change and adaptation is all the more apparent given the fact that empirical case studies regularly observe it. For example, UK studies routinely observe groups shifting *from* an outsider *to* an insider political strategy over their careers (see Jordan and Halpin 2003). In some cases, discussion is of seemingly bold and overwhelming change within groups. Minkoff (1999) shows how women's advocacy groups adapted differently, changing their overall purpose; some reverted to protest, some engaged in service provision while others shifted towards advocacy. According to Clemens and Minkoff (2004, 165) the Consumer Union, in the US, started life as a radical organization actively seeking to regulate corporate behaviour but transformed into a more conservative scientific organization. The Australian Conservation Foundation illustrates the reverse scenario, whereby a sedate scientific group transformed into a mass-membership campaigning body (Warhurst 1994). As Nownes and Cigler (1995, 397) noted some time ago with respect to survival, 'there is no *one*

100   *Interest group 'careers' (II)*

road to group success': the question then is what roads are chosen, why, and what are the implications?

More systematic evidence of change comes from a recent survey conducted of Scottish interest groups *active* in government public consultations since 1999. To examine the *nature* of the changes that organizations might make to enhance their survival prospects, the respondents were presented with a list of ten strategies and asked to indicate which, if any, had been undertaken by their organization within the last five years (see Table 6.1).

The most frequently used strategies, cited by over half of the groups in each case, were broadening the range of issues upon which the organization focuses (54.6 per cent), and enhancing the opportunities for their members to participate in the organization's work (53.9 per cent). Almost half of the groups have changed the tactics they have been using to influence public policy (46.3 per cent) and/or have changed the services they offer (46.1 per cent). Almost one-third (32.4 per cent) have broadened the constituency they seek to represent; while a quarter (25.8 per cent) have explored mergers with like-minded organizations. Smaller proportions have added local branches to their organizational structure (13.4 per cent), narrowed the range of issues they focus on (11.1 per cent), or have changed their name (10.4 per cent). Only five (1.1 per cent) of the 469 organizations have narrowed the constituency they seek to represent.

Some further circumstantial support for this claim that many groups – even those that survive – manifest some type of organizational change can be found in US data on voluntary organizations. Data from several editions of the Encyclopedia of Associations shows that, of the groups entered in the 1970 edition that remain in the 2005 edition, a large minority of groups manifest some change (Table 6.2). Change here is defined very crudely as including name change, amalgamation or a merger: although the vast majority were simply name changes.

Table 6.1 Has your organization undertaken any of the following strategies in the past five years?

Changes to enhance survival prospects	N*	%
We have broadened the range of issues upon which we focus	452	56.6
We have narrowed the range of issues upon which we focus	451	11.5
We have broadened the constituency we claim to represent	457	33.3
We have narrowed the constituency we seek to represent	449	1.1
We have changed our name	449	10.9
We have changed the services we offer	449	48.1
We have changed the tactics we use to influence public policy	449	48.3
We have enhanced the opportunities for our members to participate in our work	444	57.0
We have added local branches to our structure	451	14.0
We have explored mergers with like organizations	452	26.8

Note
* From 469 valid responses there were some missing across each question.

Table 6.2 Type of organizational change among surviving groups (1970–2005)*

	N	%
Any change?		
No change	2,311	59
Some organizational change	1,598	41
Type of change?		
Name change	1,177	74
Amalgamation	222	14
Merger	155	10
Other	44	2
Total	**1,598**	**100**

Source: US Encyclopedia of Associations Dataset, authors own calculations www.policyagendas. org/page/datasets-codebooks.

Note

* A few groups in fact experienced multiple types of change – for example a name change and amalgamation or merger. However, given the nature of the coding scheme utilized in the online data set, this was not readily able to be counted.

This suggests that groups do attempt to manage their way around difficult circumstances. One might reasonably draw the conclusion from the above that change is ubiquitous among interest groups.

If one accepts this, it presents a twofold challenge: (i) how to define the organizational form of a group at a point in time and (ii) how to calibrate group organizational change over time. I suggest that not only do we need a framework to describe the form a group survives in at a given point in time, but we also need a way to discriminate between *types of change* we are observing. Such an approach is warranted because it is likely that changes vary in salience, they happen with varying levels of frequency, and they vary in how disruptive or hazardous they are for group survival prospects. In the absence of a settled or explicit approach to calibrating change in the group literature, in this chapter I offer one way forward based on the concept of organizational form.

Consistent with the general thrust of this book, I suggest borrowing theories and concepts from the interdisciplinary field of organizational social science to help firm-up our existing hunches. This is, I suggest, consistent with a broader rethink in the literature on the role of organizational analysis (see for instance Lowery 2007; Lang *et al.* 2008). As in Chapter 5, here the realized *organizational form* of a given group refers to the set of features (strategies and tactics) and identity it manifests at any point in time. The basic proposition is that groups, at birth and thereafter, have to confront some basic choices around 'how should we organize?' This involves broad questions such as 'what is our broad mission and purpose?', plus more practical concerns such as 'how should we engage in policy?' and 'from where and by what means should we garner financial resources?' The answers to such questions – and changes to these answers – are often times heavily interdependent and, as such, are best explored together.

102 *Interest group 'careers' (II)*

The chapter proceeds in several parts. The first introduces the idea of analysing group 'careers', which effectively involves looking at the steps of organizational evolution as a historical sequence. This is theorized utilizing a modified model of path dependency from historical institutionalism. The second outlines one particular operationalization of the organizational form concept that provides a framework to describe group form, and changes in form. It takes an identity-based approach, whereby forms are viewed as constructed by groups themselves rather than defined beforehand by scholars. However, importantly, it links identity formation to the development of 'core' identity-dependent features (strategies and settings). The subsequent section outlines some theoretical propositions about the scope and sequence of change that flow from this operationalization. The final section provides some empirical illustrations, based on UK group case histories, of how this conceptual framework might be deployed.

Conceptualizing group 'careers'

The question of group survival, I suggest, can be productively viewed less as a one-off fight against awkward selection pressures and more of a continuous process of adaptation to frequent dilemmas, challenges and unexpected crisis. A core debate within organizational studies concerns the relative value of selection versus adaptation models of group change. As has been noted, neither approach is in and of itself sufficient: selection ignores agency and is overly deterministic, while adaptation is too focused on the agency of individuals and ignores structures (Galaskiewicz and Bielefeld 1998, 20). There has been somewhat of a rapprochement between these two positions, but empirical work has not yet tended to bridge approaches because of methodological and data demands (see Lewin and Volberda 2003). The expectations I pursue in this volume *are* clearly consistent with what might be called a 'relaxed' adaptation model. Moreover, we should be as interested in the way – the qualitative *organizational form* – in which groups survive as we are in conducting head counts of their persistence. As noted above, group scholarship has not established a tradition of analysing group evolution or adaptive change.[1] Yet this is something PE scholars suggest could be a worthy line of inquiry. Below, I outline one way to organize and conceptualize group evolution.

Group 'careers' as evolutionary sequences

The initial conundrum in working with group histories is how to organize and conceptualize them? The approach I take is to look at sequences of group evolution. A risk in taking an historical perspective on individual group evolution is that any account simply becomes a descriptive statement of one change 'event' after another. To support analysis we need an *analytical* account of group change over time. So from where could group scholarship take its cue?

Group careers consist of strings of changes in organizational form and together constitute adaptive sequences. This is not an unusual approach to

Interest group 'careers' (II) 103

political organizations generally. Long-standing observers of political parties talk of a need to focus on party 'careers' (Rose and Mackie 1988). In so doing, they suggest that attention be paid to the way parties persist by changing form: for instance, the way a mass party transforms itself into a cartel party. The party approach to careers is also evident in the social movement literature where scholars document the 'natural history' of a social movement (Curtis and Zurcher 1974). Here I explore group historical evolution through a lens provided by new institutionalism: historical institutionalism in particular and to a lesser extent the institutional organizational studies literature. This approach provides one way to engage in a narrative of group survival that is less about one-off events – birth and death – and more about adaptive change. In particular, it draws attention to the factors that shape adaptation and what propels groups along their career pathways.

Resting on some basic path-dependent framework – such as that common in historical institutional accounts – is hardly radical. In fact, as outlined in the previous chapter, it is largely consistent with the basic underlying perspective of some of the seminal works in group theory (Truman 1971). However, it is true that such an *explicit* approach is not common in group scholarship (but see Engels 2007; Young 2010; Halpin and Daugbjerg 2013). While not the case for groups, there is a tradition of deploying new institutional analyses to organizations (see Stinchcombe 1965; March and Olsen 1984; DiMaggio and Powell 1991; Erakovic and Powell 2006). But even though assessing organizations as institutions is not novel, this may seem like an unlikely source of inspiration given that historical institutionalism is principally associated with explaining *inertia and stasis*. In that sense, deploying an historic institutional approach would seem to provide little advantage to the PE emphasis on stasis and environmentally induced selection processes. Indeed, a central feature of historical institutionalism is its emphasis on path dependence, with its 'punctuated equilibrium model'. In path-dependent models historical flows of events, or *sequences*, are 'punctuated' by 'critical junctures' which mark break points where developments take a new path (Hall and Taylor 1996, 942).[2] Thus, one criticism of the literature on path-dependence is that it offers just two stark images: institutions 'persist and become increasingly entrenched or are abandoned' (Thelen 2003, 212–13). As is evident in Powell's account of organizational change, path dependency also implies that the initial step in a sequence constrains subsequent prospects for change: 'Organizational procedure and forms may persevere because of path-dependent patterns of development in which initial choices preclude future options' (Powell 1991, 192–3). At face value, this does not really seem to provide much purchase on institutional *change*. Indeed, it offers two opposite accounts: (*i*) *institutional reproduction* (where any change is very minor in nature, continuous and common – sustaining the original form) and (*ii*) *institutional innovation* (where change is major in nature, rapid, and infrequent and changes the original form) (Thelen 2003, 213; Streeck and Thelen 2005, 6).

However, a new thread in the historical institutional literature focuses explicitly on *institutional change*. And it is this thread I draw upon. The sheer

104 *Interest group 'careers' (II)*

implausibility that institutions or organizations can persist – be simply reproduced – for long periods of time without also changing to adapt to new circumstances has prompted a shift in focus from institutional reproduction mechanisms to change. The point here is that the survival and persistence of institutions over long periods implies *some type* of change; yet, conversely, institutions seemingly survive rather large exogenous shocks without any *radical* change. This is particularly so for interest groups, many of which have very long careers. It is hard to imagine that groups formed in the late 1880s, for instance, have survived without making any concession to changing times and conditions. Change – albeit of an *incremental but not insignificant nature* – surely must underpin persistence: survival implies adaptation and transformation (Thelen 2003, 211). This argument has generated accounts of 'gradual transformation' in which 'institutional discontinuity' is a product 'incremental, 'creeping' change': the emphasis is on '*incremental change with transformative results*' (Streeck and Thelen 2005, 9). As Thelen puts it, 'institutional survival is often strongly laced with elements of institutional *transformation* to bring institutions into line with changing social, political, and economic conditions' (2003, 211). This sounds just like the sort of approach to adaptive change that PE de-emphasized (but did not discount); thus it provides a helpful steer to a pursuit of an adaptive account of group survival.

If accounts of institutional persistence over extended periods require some element (albeit subtle and ongoing) of evolution or change, then this implies a shift in how models of path dependence are deployed and how sequences of organizational evolution are appraised. In this regard, Thelen says

> This amounts to a call for introducing somewhat more structure at the 'front end' of the analysis of institutional development than most path dependence arguments do – by attending to the way in which historically evolved structure limit the options of political actors even at critical choice points. It also calls for injecting somewhat more agency and strategy at the 'back end' of such arguments – by emphasizing the way in which institutions operate not just as constraints but as strategic resources for actors as they respond to changes in the political and economic contexts that present new opportunities or throw up new challenges.
>
> (2003, 213)[3]

This thread in the literature seeks to surface 'institutional continuities through apparent break points, as well as "subterranean" but highly significant changes in periods of apparent institutional stability' (Thelen 2003, 233).

So what does this mean for analysing group evolutionary sequences? In making sense of group evolution and adaptive survival, the core questions for group analysts are; (i) how much constraint is evident in the establishment of a groups initial form?, and (ii) how much choice can be said to exist in subsequent adaptive changes to initial group form? The approach elaborated here affirms the importance of group agency at critical choice points in sequences, but also highlights the sometimes sticky institutional context that structures initial choices at the start of sequences (as discussed in Chapter 5). Figure 6.1 provides a representation of these considerations.

Leadership and agency

Talk about choice and group adaptation implies groups exercising agency; rather than being passive victims of souring environmental conditions. This sounds straightforward, but of course groups are organizations, so who expresses group agency?

There is a long-standing tradition in group scholarship to attribute a strong – even dominant – role in group affairs to leaders or entrepreneurs.[4] I take a similar line. However, it is not that leaders can *determine* the groups they wish to have. As with any organizational change, leaders are only able to shape direction. Tsoukas and Chia (2002) argue that organizational leaders have 'declarative powers' by which they can heavily shape change processes by providing 'authoritative' interpretations of how organizing should occur: that is, they are in 'a privileged position to introduce a new discursive template that will make it possible for organizational members to notice new things, make fresh distinctions, see new connections, and have novel experiences, which they will seek to accommodate' (Tsoukas and Chia 2002, 579). But this does *not* equate to the imposition of plans onto organizing itself. As they argue, 'the introduction of a new discursive template is only the beginning of the journey of change' (2002, 579).

Just because one view about what legitimate form a group should take dominates does not mean the losers (or their practices) will go away. There is an

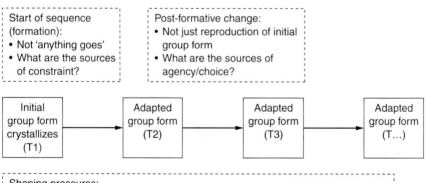

Figure 6.1 Interest group evolutionary sequences.

106 *Interest group 'careers' (II)*

important political dimension to be recognized here. There are multiple sets of expectations about what is an appropriate form for a group, and leaders need to negotiate these. Change is not bloodless, rather it is often an overtly political contest; but leaders are in a better position than most to influence it. Change needs to be argued for to be won. Following Clemens and Cook, we can view leaders as involved in the *selection* and then persuasion, argumentation or contestation required to implement selected group forms (1999, 446). The actions of leaders in identifying changes in the environment (both challenges and opportunities) – and then convincing the group of the need for change – are crucial in accounting for group evolutionary pathways. Leaders may deploy 'embedded analogies' (Clemens and Cook 1999, 457): historical lessons that have a tacit 'taken for granted-ness' may be hugely influential in persuading supporters of the need for change to a given group form, and in attracting legitimacy. This type of process links past steps in a sequence of group evolution with contemporary considerations regarding organizational next steps. Several of the group cases below provide an insight into the role of leaders in deploying the past to legitimate adaptive change.

Group organizational form and change

A key assertion made here is that groups do not simply persist, waiting to be picked off by souring environmental pressures. They seek to adapt and change to improve survival chances (whether adaptation actually improves survival changes or not). Yet, to adequately make sense of change and adaptation – to study it empirically – we need a way to describe and plot the organizational manifestation of groups at points in time, and changes over time. It is easy enough to say groups 'change' group form as they travel along their adaptive evolutionary sequences. But what is meant by group form? Moreover what about the *magnitude of change* in form? It would be safe to assume that not all group change will be equally significant. Thus, one of the key dilemmas in embarking on analysis of group adaptive change and evolution is how to get a handle on the magnitude or order of group change. When is change fundamental and when is it simply routine? Put more formally, if we want to have organizational change as a dependent variable, then we need some way to calibrate the degree or scope of change: we need to know what change (and types of change) looks like. Inattention to the organizational (and adaptive) qualities of groups is, I suggest, largely related to the absence of a vocabulary and conceptual scaffolding to direct attention to these issues.

How might this understanding of form in the organizational studies literature assist us to make sense of interest group organizations? Borrowing from this literature, I deploy an identity-based approach to organizational form, whereby realized forms are viewed as constructed by groups themselves rather than defined beforehand by scholars. However, importantly, and consistent with the organizational studies literature, it links identity formation to the development of 'core' identity-dependent *features* (strategies and settings) (see Chapter 3). Thus, I suggest a group's organizational form at any moment manifests three broad components/layers: (1) organizational identity, (2) organizational strategies, and (3) technical settings. Not only is this a way to describe a group's form at a given moment, but it also provides a language to describe changes over time. These components constitute levels at which group adaptive change can occur. Thus, change can be assessed over time both in terms of alterations to individual components and in the cumulative impact of these changes on overall group organizational form. Table 6.3 summarizes the general approach to identifying form, and thus levels of change in form. Let me briefly elaborate on each.

It is helpful to think of an interest group as having a broad identity that reflects its core purpose, its *raison d'être*. It has been argued that groups aspire to, and proactively cultivate, their own unique identity (Heaney 2004, 616).[5] Here I utilize the term in a similar manner, to indicate what the group stands for, its mission. Clemens suggests that organizational identity might be understood in terms of 'we are people who do these sorts of things in this particular way' (1997, 50). Identities are important for organizations, as they are central to how key audiences understand them. For groups, an identity is central to whether policy makers and supporters see them as relevant or credible and thus supply them with resources. Identity is transmitted (and thus can be assessed) through public communications: such as websites, logos, publications and promotional or policy material (see Heaney 2004; Engel 2007). Here I restrict identity to what the *leadership* of the group *wants* or *claims* it to be (not the views or interpretations of others, such as policy makers or members).

Identity is likely to be an enduring feature of a group's form. That is to say, it cannot be changed tactically. Organizational identities solidify as key audiences (internal and external) *come to* recognize that a given entity stands for one thing or another. Audiences need to be able to 'read' a particular organizational form as legitimate and authentic against known (and valued) generic forms (Zuckerman 1999; Deephouse 1999). This has implications for the actual *features* that organizations possess. Building organizational identities through connecting to generic forms implies the development of certain core features considered inherent to such generic forms. Without these features organizations appear as lacking authenticity with the generic model. In turn, variation too far from a recognizable form will be punished by loss of legitimacy (and thus resources). It is most likely that the realized identity of a given organization is slow to establish: a product of repeated (consistent) performance that confirms initial assessments by audiences. Some group scholarship has plausibly argued that without positive feedback, key audiences would have no basis to 'read' the actions of groups (identity would be confused) (Young 2008). The point is that it takes repeated successful interactions for a group identity to be established, and thus it stands to reason that such reinforcement embeds identities firmly in the consciousness of audiences which in turn makes shifts in identity hard (Engels 2007, 74). It also follows that a decline in legitimacy of a group's identity with key audiences, like policy makers or donors, could also represent an organizational crisis for a group. Such identity crises are of course problematic for groups, but this is a question I confront under discussion of organizational change (see below).

Table 6.3 Group organizational form and change

Organizational component (level of change)	Description	Examples of change
Technical settings (first order)	• Settings for organizational features • Technical approaches to implementing features • Means to achieve strategic purposes	• Development of telemarketing programme to recruit members • Development of website • Development of relationship marketing programme • Changing annual general meeting format • Recruiting new staff expertise
Organizational strategies (second order)	• Policy strategy • Resource acquisition strategy • Formal organizational structures	• Change from 'outsider' to 'insider' lobbying strategy • Change from small member support to large donor support • Expand constituency coverage • Narrow policy area of interest
Organizational identity (third order)	• Aim(s) • Mission	• Change from advocacy to service delivery • Change from representative-based focus to issue focus

Source: Adapted from Halpin and Nownes (2011).

Interest group 'careers' (II) 109

The next two components – referred to in the organizational literature as 'features' – are strategies and techniques. I distinguish between strategic features that are enduring or have what might be considered global to the groups personality (they touch all aspects of the group) and tactical/technical settings which are small changes that simply adjust existing strategies.

Strategies refers to the how a group organizes itself to achieve the overall identity. While it is unlikely that groups – or any organization for that matter – will have complete alignment between identity and strategies, we expect that strategies articulate with broad mission. Groups have an almost infinite number of strategies (to recruit staff, to communicate, etc.), but some strategies are more crucial to how groups are formed than others. Interest groups, by definition, engage in two core tasks – mobilizing support and resources, and engaging in policy advocacy or influence activities (Jordan *et al.* 2004). Therefore, the strategic features of a group we are most concerned with include decisions about whether to have members or donors, an overall policy strategy (e.g. 'outside' or 'inside'), and choice of policy domain(s).

Technical features are about settings for implementing strategies. We are concerned here with the means by which strategies are pursued, what tools and techniques. Settings in these dimensions might include, for example, who to affiliate to the group (members, of which type, and how openly?). It may also extend to what tactics to pursue the policy strategy with: ought a group to engage in litigation or try and mobilize a grass roots consumer boycott on a given issue, and what specific policy issues to cover (selection of which issues within a domain, etc).

In summary, the concept of organizational form outlined here focuses our attention on the way groups develop identities and how this fits with the features a group manifests at any single point in time. As such, it is more flexible and nuanced than the approach adopted in Chapter 4, which derives fixed forms based on theoretical salience of core features. It serves two purposes. With this concept comes language we can use to start describing individual group organizational form at a single point in time, and also to assess the extent of change over time. In short, and for present purposes, this ought to be a useful tool to provide a more nuanced account of group change.

What style of work would this heuristic support? It is envisaged that this conceptual framework would be used to inform two basic approaches to empirical research, both relying mostly on (comparative) case-based methods. The first is in making sense of change in *individual group case histories*. That is, using these categories to explain the adaptation and change within specific groups over time. The second is using these categories to examine diversity in organizational form within *middle-n-sized populations of like groups*. While these research approaches are at some variance from the trajectory of most recent group scholarship, which has tended to emphasize large-n analysis of lobbying or influence (see summary by Baumgartner and Leech 1998, Lowery and Gray 2004a), in my view they are important to make sense of organizational change and adaptation (a point made by Gray and Lowery [2000] in their discussion of how to formulate a more nuanced account of group survival).

110 *Interest group 'careers' (II)*

Calibrating changes in organizational form: some propositions

I suggest that this framework can also help us to *calibrate group adaptive change*. The conceptualization of form elaborated above provides a framework to talk about levels of change and to explore the significance/salience of changes for overall form. This framework provides a language to distinguish between change in identity, strategic settings or features, and technical settings. This can help generate useful hypotheses and analyses of the scope (how all-pervasive it is) and path of change (the sequence/order of change). In this section I simply draw these out and make them explicit.

Scope of change?

The organizational social science literature has long made a distinction between core and peripheral organizational change (see Hannan and Freeman 1984, Scott 1995; Greenwood and Hinings 1996; Rao *et al.* 2000, 240). We might therefore conclude that in terms of scope of change, there are two types of change: radical and routine.[6] Referring to the framework in Table 6.3, the former entails a change of group identity while the latter is a change in strategy or technical settings. From this broad approach, we might surmise that most changes in form are minor in nature – that is, they involve variations in strategies and/or technical settings (consistent with prevailing identity). Changes in identity are more infrequent. As for changes in these three components of organizational form, we might hypothesize that identity is the hardest to change. This is summarized in Table 6.4.

Sequence of radical change?

The framework also provides some hints as to possible sequences of radical change. These are revealed by the relationship between these 'levels'. Read from one direction, overall group organizational identity is important for setting the group's strategy and technical settings (its organizational 'features'). As Carrol and Hannan (2000, 68) explain, 'identity constrains what an organization can do and what is expected and not expected of it'. In a group context, therefore, the choice of identity is crucial because it will shape the test applied by others in assessing its value. For example, a group that claims a representative identity needs to be deemed to actually represent its members if it is to be valued. If it is viewed as a

Table 6.4 Scope of change

Type of change	Frequency	Description	Level of disruption
Radical	Low	Change in overall identity	High
Routine	High	Change to strategies or technical settings	Low

Interest group 'careers' (II) 111

glorified insurance business or social club, it may lose its legitimacy and resources. Read from the reverse perspective, some features of an organization are 'identity-dependent', which means that 'an organization cannot change the value of that feature without giving up its identity' (Carroll and Hannan 2000, 69). Thus, discussions over changes to features (strategies or technical settings) might in some circumstances be crucial to sustaining (or undermining) a given identity.

This discussion reveals two basic pathways to *changes* in organizational form by a given group. First, elites might agree to change identity, and then changes in core identity-dependent features will follow. Second, changes in identity-dependent (variously referred to in the literature as 'core features' or 'indispensible properties') organizational features may start the process of identity change from below. Change these features and the identity (and thus form) of the specific group has changed. For instance, Polletta and Jesper (2001, 293) note that if Clamshell (an anti nuclear power group that identified itself with values of anti-domination) decided to jettison its consensus decision making model, it would 'destroy the group's identity'. In sum, changes in overall identity will shape identity-dependent features, and, likewise, small changes in identity-dependent features may accumulate into an overall change in a group's identity. These are summarized in Table 6.5.

The balance of this chapter will provide some opportunistic examples from UK group practice as a way to illustrate how this framework and associated propositions might help us make sense of adaptive change among groups.

Some illustrative applications of the framework

In this section I provide some illustrations as to how this framework, and its associated propositions about change (scope and style), can be used to understand group organizational change. The first example illustrates how the

Table 6.5 Ideal type style of radical change

Style of radical change	Description	Change dynamic	Level of disruption
Identity-led	• Identity crisis • Critical juncture offers opportunity for internal activists to reset focus • Often relies on de-legitimacy of existing identity from key audiences (state or members)	Rapid	High
Feature-led	• Change to strategies or technical settings accumulate • Especially changes to identity dependent features • Tipping point reached where identity shifts	Cumulative	Limited

112 *Interest group 'careers' (II)*

framework can be used to sort out the level or scope of change, and that this analytical task has some valuable pay-offs in terms of identifying the driver of identifiable group change. The second and third cases focus on exemplifying two styles of radical change: feature-led and identity-led.

Calibrating scope of change: radical or routine?

The framework above is useful in gaining purchase on more controversial debates over the character of change among groups. A very brief example will help highlight the value of these distinctions when discussing group change.

A largely US debate has discussed the assertion that 'nowadays' groups manifest only weak links with grass-roots members, often have no branch structures, and are run by group professionals. Key authors make the claim that group entrepreneurs no longer 'build' groups with local branches and active members (see Skocpol 1999). This has been disputed, with some identifying that there is no such period effect: both new and old groups are based on organizational models including branches and active members (Walker *et al.* 2011; Minkoff *et al.* 2008; McCarthy 2005). In the UK, the excellent work of Jordan and Maloney (1997, 2007) has drawn attention to the idea that some UK environmental/conservation groups – perhaps the larger better-known ones – have developed organizations that are similarly devoid of branches or active membership, and are instead run by professional staff funded from cheque-book supporters. Their term 'protest business' further emphasizes the role of business techniques (specifically membership marketing using direct mail and relationship marketing) (see Bosso 2005 for a US equivalent). No one disputes the accuracy of their analysis. And no one disputes that from the 1990s onwards such groups have grown large on the back of such techniques. The question is whether such a 'change' is a radical or a routine change? This is highly salient, because if it is radical it is likely a product of our times, as new practices replace old ones. By contrast, if it is a modernizing of an existing model, then it is unlikely to be a generational effect.

Examining the historical organizational development of some groups that outwardly conform to the protest business tag is illustrative. Three groups – the Royal Society for the Protection of Birds (RSPB), Oxfam and the National Trust (NT) – are more than 60 years of age (1889, 1942 and 1895 respectively) but currently broadly fit a 'protest business' model or *form* of group organization (Jordan and Maloney 1997). They are engaged in 'insider' form of policy advocacy, utilize expertise and science to support their case, and are funded by a large and relatively remote/passive mass-membership. These groups have come to scholarly attention because of their rapid post-1990s growth in membership numbers: the RSPB for instance has over one million members. Research has attributed this growth to the *recent* deployment of *modern* membership marketing techniques and aggressive selling of joining opportunities to an ideologically predisposed general public. Techniques such as 'direct debit' payment methods, direct-mail solicitation, professional performance-paid recruiters, and canvassing of 'warm' leads through database mining, are all identified as explanations for

Interest group 'careers' (II)   113

the rise of group size – and, of course, financial resources. But what are we to make of these changes? On the one hand, scholars seem to imply that these democratically hollowed out groups are new contemporary forms (see Skocpol 1999; Putnam 2000). While our groups may not be new, the implication would be that they have evolved from more democratically virtuous origins. Analysis of case study histories suggests otherwise; which, in turn, has important implications for the level of pessimism one has regarding the contemporary state of groups as democratic agents.

Each of these groups did indeed have a small formative period where they were the subject of the intense participative efforts of a small number of group entrepreneurs. For instance, the RSPB was formed by a small band of women who objected to the use of plumage from rare birds in women's hats (Basset 1980). Oxfam started amidst the Second World War as the Oxford Committee for Famine Relief and (like many similar committees of its time) was run by a handful of local notables (church leaders and academics). The National Trust was formed by a small number of upper-class social elites who, for a small while, were resistant to any mass membership whatsoever (Fedden 1968). Yet in a short time they soon crystallized into what could be described as early protest businesses. For example, by the 1920s the NT decided to solicit mass membership, and it formed a membership department in the 1940s. Oxfam, by the 1950s (five years after formation) was employing business techniques to fundraise (selling gifts through a shop-front), soliciting support through media campaigns, and by the 1960s the 'pledged gift' system was underway (whereby people were cold-canvassed at their doors to pledge support for Oxfam and provide a donation) (Black 1992). By the 1940s, the RSPB was offering their member's rewards for recruiting new members, and soon after implemented an RSPB shopping catalogue for members to purchase merchandise.

While it is true that, for instance, Oxfam and the RSPB both started to deploy paid recruiters as a strategy to increase members (strategic change) and direct-debit instruments to maintain member numbers (technical innovation) in the early 1990s, this change was consistent with the long-established (at least pre-1940s) identity of both groups as mass-supportership groups. They were growth-orientated and applied business methods at a time where such ideas were foreign to the voluntary sector (Black 1992). The more recent changes in the 1990s were *extensions* – modern innovations – on *long-standing commitments to a particular form of organization.*

The conclusion here is that each of these three groups was committed to a protest business identity *very early on*. Thus, the contemporary changes noted by Jordan and Maloney (1997), and normatively criticised by Putnam (2000) and Skocpol (1999), are simply an extension of a long-standing commitment to this group identity. They are *first-* and *second*-order changes, technical updates and strategic reorientations. These groups would surely have used direct debits and advanced data base management linked to mail-shots in their earliest days, were they around to be utilized. The proof that they have not changed overall form is that they utilized the *equivalent member marketing technologies of their day.*

114　*Interest group 'careers' (II)*

Thus, survival for these groups has been about low-order change – updating techniques or settings – and upholding initial choice of identity and form.

The *continuation* of the initial group identity has been achieved by successive leadership cohorts restating long-established organizational mantra (see Engel 2007 for a similar discussion of identity-shaped path-dependence). For instance, in 1903 the fledgling RSPB decided to go into debt for the first time; it says 'increase in finances unfortunately lags far behind the opportunities for work and usefulness which are constantly presenting themselves. It has been felt impossible to refuse to do urgent work' (RSPB 1903, 11). This moment established an ethos that guided the RSPB thereafter: to aggressively grow its financial base given that the resources needed to protect birds are infinite – there will never be enough money! In the 2006/7 Annual Report, the Marketing Director says 'There is never enough money in conservation: for us, more income simply means more work for birds' (RSPB, 2006/7, 34, www.rspb.org.uk/Images/annu-alreview0607_tcm9-174726.pdf). This is a legacy from the earliest days of the RSPB, where supporter growth to meet the inexhaustible needs of birds was a mantra. The difference is that the RSPB just got *very good* at growing support after the Second World War.

Styles of radical change?

Two UK cases I have researched provide good illustrations of the two ideal-type styles of radical change: the first is identity-led and the second is feature-based.

Identity-led change (UK Soil Association)

The UK Soil Association – the premier group advocating for the organic farming sector – started in 1946 as an organization dedicated to scientific research, public communication and education. Today, it resembles a campaign-style group, engaged in a media-based strategy targeting consumers' views on organic food. How did it get from there to here?

Scholarly accounts of the Soil Association suggest quite a clear cut difference between the pre and post 1980's (Reed 2004; Tomlinson 2007).[7] The organization's early emphasis on the development of farming methods through its own on-farm research and associated education activities to disseminate these to other farmers changed under 'new management'. An internal coup took place that saw a switch from the emphasis on scientific research, which aided farmers, to that of education for consumers and broad public policy influence. A new leadership cadre took over, motivated by their desire – and the previous incumbents' reluctance – to engage in trade and market based issues *and* to adopt a more campaigning stance. Tomlinson observes of this period 'At the beginning of the 1980s the organic movement began to diversify away from its previous scientific preoccupations, not least with a focus on the marketing aspects of organics' (2007, 151). Reed goes further, noting that the aim 'to co-ordinate research and provide information on Organic Farming' had been eclipsed by 'a more

Interest group 'careers' (II)   115

aggressive and outward facing policy' (2004, 255). The new leadership were largely from non-farming backgrounds and met in and around non-farm campaigning events (Reed 2004, 254). According to Reed, a key facet of the new agenda was its promotion of 'consumer power' (2004, 257).

The transformation of the SA reached a critical juncture in the Extraordinary Meeting of 1982, but key actors explain that is was a process that took around five years of strategizing to achieve. At interview with the author, Patrick Holden explains that Peter Seggar initiated change;

> He got elected to Council in 1976 and he started stirring it up on the Council and fell out with Trustees and had a struggle with Eve. Then over following years more of us got on Council.... Eventually we had five of us young Turks on the Council, and we had a bloodless coup. There was a very major polarization of view on the Council between the young people who joined the Council who wanted to make organic farming a commercial reality, so we were very interested in standards and development of production systems, etc. And the old guard who were hanging on to the philosophical truths, the holism.... We took them on and eventually they gave way to us, it was the new organic movement.

The extent of this strategizing lends weight to the idea that the SA was a prize worth winning. Organic farm-sector development could not be progressed without the SA being the prime mover. It could not be worked around; it had to be pressed into the service of industry revitalization.

A key focusing event was the fact that Haughley Farms (a property donated by the founder Eve Balfour and used to conduct organic farm trials) had almost financially ruined the Soil Association. It provided an opportunity for the new breed of savvy leaders to reinterpret the founding mission and the way it was put into practice. This new cohort of leaders argued that the long-standing education and research 'mission' of the Soil Association ought to be taken forward by an even more explicit focus on *direct* engagement with consumers – in fact mobilizing them into supporting the Association, and using them to drive political and commercial actors to develop an organic market. The report of the Extraordinary Council Meeting of 1982, where this change was brought about, confirms that financial considerations were a key factor in bringing on a leadership coup. To confirm the change of emphasis towards campaigning, 1983 saw the appointment of a campaign director.[8] The SA pursued a consumer campaign in 1983–4 ('Eat Organic Message'). It took a view that demand creation was crucial given the power of consumers – if demand were there (if it could be demonstrated) then government would have to listen to them and support the sector.[9]

The most salient point is that the Soil Association has changed. That the group has always been called the Soil Association belies a transformation from a group about amateur-science for 'new' organic farmers to a campaign group educating the mass public about food systems and the environmental cost of modern farming techniques. This is a story of how a group with a unique identity

116 *Interest group 'careers' (II)*

can change over relatively short time and in so doing how its transformation reflects struggles for definition and purpose. Activists positioned themselves within the organization and took advantage of a focusing event – an impending financial crisis – to effectively transform the organizational form (identity, strategies and techniques) of the SA. Change was rapid and radical (see Halpin and Daugbjerg, 2013).

Feature-led change (RNIB)[10]

The Royal National Institute of Blind People (RNIB) is a current UK interest group that pursues the interests of the blind. It was founded in 1868 as the British and Foreign Society for Improving Embossed Literature for the Blind, which was established by a group of wealthy blind men as a benevolent organization primarily developing written materials and offering rehabilitation services for the blind.[11] Appraised from a contemporary viewpoint, the group has undergone a rather significant change from its initial form at birth.[12] The RNIB has changed – or evolved – its overall form from a provider of services to the blind in the tradition of philanthropic benevolence, to a group organizing and politically representing the blind. It has undergone a third-order change in its overall identity. In mapping its trajectory, the question is whether it was the result of a single moment of rapid and radical change or a continual process of adaptive change? How was change enabled and constrained? And how do overall changes in group identity interact with lower-level changes in strategies and settings (in which direction do they work)?

In 2002, the RNIB announced a series of organizational changes to affiliate the blind into direct membership. It was now offering 'full membership' to those who are blind and partially sighted. By its own account,

> The new structure means that RNIB will become an organization 'of' the blind and partially sighted people, i.e. one whose constitution ensures that a majority of its governing body, and a majority of any membership, are blind or partially sighted.
>
> (RNIB 2001)

This is a significant change from its origins, and would be expected to have significant impacts on other organizational features. As the group itself explains, the 'RNIB is a *membership organisation which radically affects how we govern ourselves*' (http://www.rnib.org.uk/aboutus/Pages/about_us.aspx, italics added). This is consistent with a third-order change, a change in overall group identity, and suggests significant change in terms of strategy and settings.

Close inspection of the case history suggests change was *not* the result of a single moment of rapid and radical change. It is accurate to say that in 2001 such changes were passed by the governing body of the group – and formalized in its Royal Charter and by-laws – but the claim that this is the result of a short period of rapid, and comprehensive, change is erroneous. The change of name provides the

Interest group 'careers' (II) 117

symbolic cherry on the cake in terms of demarcating change for the group. The historical record suggests change was the accretion of decades of change, and was made possible by precedents and decisions made half a century beforehand (without which contemporary change may have proved considerably harder to achieve).

A convenient empirical indicator of the extent to which third-order change has been realized in RNIB practice is the percentage of blind persons in the main decision making organ of the group. Fortunately, access to the RNIB *Annual Reports* provides data to track how this measure has evolved. This provides a proxy measure of the distance travelled between the two points: the extent to which the new *representational* organizational identity has been realized.

As background, it is important to know a few historical facts about the basic governance of the RNIB. Prior to the 1920s, for almost 60 years, the RNIB was run by a group of mostly blind men (Thomas 1957, 44). It was a purely voluntary endeavour. The roots of the contemporary reforms to the RNIB regarding blind representation can be traced back to developments in 1925/6, 1931 and 1937. These successive and tightly bound waves of reform altered the composition and thus the internal politics of governing the RNIB. The essential point to know here is that as government started to take over care for the blind (early 1900s), the RNIB was under pressure to share its substantial fundraising wealth with local charitable organizations and local government. The government proposed a national body be established to achieve coordination, and it suggested the RNIB take over this mantle. It did so, but in return had to allocate representation on its council to member organizations from local government and other organizations 'of' and 'for' the blind. In essence, the National Institute for the Blind (NIB), as it was then, became a group of groups.

The reforms led to a NIB Council (the governing body) that was 'predominantly a representative body directly elected by organisations for and of the blind throughout the country' (NIB *Annual Report 1930–1*, 8). To achieve this 'representation', the NIB Council was constituted by five broad groupings; Group A (representatives of the counties associations for the blind), Group B (representatives of national bodies), Group C (representatives of public authorities), Group D (national members) and Group E (representatives of workshops and other voluntary organizations). Groups of the blind were a sub-category of Group B. The NIB constitution at the time stated that of the 24 'national members' (Group D), not less than one-third should be blind. The groupings – but not the specific allocations/entitlements – established in 1937 were later recorded in the Royal Charter (1949), and remained in place until 2001 (these are reflected in the categories listed in Table 6.5). This change in internal governing structure *did not* change overall identity; it remained a group delivering services for the blind.

Returning to group evolution, the share of blind persons in this governing body provides an indicator of the distance travelled from its initial form as a benevolent group to its current form as a group representing blind persons directly. As Table 6.6 illustrates, the percentage of blind persons within the council has varied over time, but it has grown incrementally over the past half century. The major outcome of the latest 2001 reform process was a

118 *Interest group 'careers' (II)*

Table 6.6 Composition of executive council of RNIB 1966–2001, selected years*

Group	Details	1966	1971	1975	1980	1986	1996	2001
A	Regional bodies	35	34	30	30	20	10	10
B	Local government bodies	23	21	20	18	10	8	8
C	Agencies for the blind and national bodies	14	14	15	14	10	28	30
D	Organizations of blind persons	6	12	30	30	30	44	48
E	National group	22	24	25	23	23	21	21
Total		**100**	**105**	**120**	**115**	**93**	**111**	**117**
% blind[†]		20	26	40	45	58	65	65

Source: Halpin (2010).

Notes

* These figures do not include honorary officers and Standing Committee chairmen which seems to be a category intermittently reported, and is thus omitted.

† All trustees who are blind, across groups.

constitutional guarantee that governance structures would have a blind majority. However, the actual number of blind persons has been a majority since the 1980s.

The details for 1975, compared to 1971, show a large jump in the percentage of blind persons in the RNIB, which can be attributed directly to reforms that increased the number of Group D places from 12 to 30. Two points are salient. First, the establishment of Group D in 1937, even with a very small allocation of seats, established the practice of allocating dedicated places for groups of the blind in governance structures. Actors within the RNIB were thus able to argue for an increase in numbers, rather than reassert the general principle of having groups of the blind present. However, at the start of the 1970s, almost four decades had passed since the establishment of Group D, the allocation had hardly budged. Thus, second, the 1970s was the start of a conscious campaign for blind presence in the RNIB. This change is the starting point for the 'new' reforms heralded in the early and mid-2000s. But how did this come about?

Interviews with former leaders reveal that blind persons *within* the organization sought (and won) successive reallocations from other groups to Group D, and used the election of blind persons to Group E, as mechanisms to convert the RNIB into an *unofficial* representative group of the blind. They reveal that while the 1930s reforms *did not* guarantee a large number of places for the blind, they did establish two important principles: (i) that the presence of blind persons' in the RNIB could be regulated by the (re)allocation of seats between groups on the Council, and (ii) that blind persons should be given special status within the NIB. Since then, blind persons *within the RNIB* have used these principles as devices to argue for blind representation, and thus to nudge the group further along the evolutionary path towards a representational group identity. Interviews with activists within the RNIB from the time suggest that they used these historical precedents as levers to advocate for more change in the same direction.

Interest group 'careers' (II) 119

These efforts were aided by the changing social mood that saw a need to promote disability rights; this was an important legitimating factor in pressuring the RNIB to work more closely with groups like blind persons.

In short, to take the 2001 reforms and name change as *the* critical juncture in the evolution of the RNIB would be to miss a great deal. It is also worth keeping in mind that a great deal of first- and second-order change went on *without* immediately undermining or directly challenging the RNIB's philanthropic form. Change was slow, adaptive, yet significant: and it *added up to transformative change in identity*.

What about non-adaptation?

In the cases covered in some depth above, change in group form seems relatively open. Several vignettes illustrate that there is considerable variation with respect to the degree of adaptation groups can engage in, even where leaders read the souring environment, and could imagine ways they might respond.

At one end of the spectrum, the most obvious case of barriers to adaptation was the Law Society of Scotland (LSS). Its statutory base means that even though leaders can identify a need to adapt, they cannot do so effectively. The LSS is charged with a dual responsibility; looking after the interests of the legal profession in Scotland but also of the public in their dealings with the profession. According to key staff, its chief challenge was retaining its relevance to legal practitioners given that most new legal work is now in 'reserved' areas where registration is not necessary (Interview 2008). The net effect is that *individual legal practitioners* have no need to register with the LSS directly for their work. The respondent explained 'Some may opt out of it thereby not having to pay the Commission fee ... it is a challenge for the Law Society, because we are so dependent on the practicing certificate fee as our main source of income.' So what about responses? Obvious responses would include re-formulating the award of membership, changing the types of practitioners they register (expanding membership) or offering other selective incentives. But there are severe limits on the types of responses the LSS can make without changing the Act of parliament that governs its work. At interview they said 'we really need to market what else we do better. But there are things in the Act saying these are things we can never do.' The LSS case shows that groups attempt to exercise what agency they have to work through challenging conditions, but sometimes the room to move is small. It is this type of case, where agency is heavily constrained, that most closely approximate the PE account whereby groups facing a souring environment are mostly left to wait for selection forces to end their organizational career.

In other cases, group leaders indicated a desire to change the organizational settings but were unable to do so for various reasons. The leaders of the Forestry Contractor's Association (FCA) explained that they were constrained by the past in terms of revitalizing their group's financial footing. In classic path dependent terms, the new Chairman explained

120   *Interest group 'careers' (II)*

> We are trapped by the group we inherited. The old group expanded its membership base, which included trainers in the forestry area. Therefore, when the new group decided to increase income by providing subsidized training, the training members objected, they do not want it.

The FCA could not follow its instinct to raise revenue by offering training services, because the previous group had decided to allow trainers into the group as members (which had the unforeseen consequence of precluding their provision of training services). Future adaptive options are closed off by decisions made in the formative era.

So what can we conclude from these cases? Some groups are simply operating in a very 'thick' institutional setting, which provides strict limits on change. The Law Society of Scotland recognizes its vulnerability to a loss of members, and knows what it *would like to do* to respond; yet it can do very little without violating the scope of its operation as set out in the statute that established it and governs it. In others, the form struck at establishment casts a long shadow, cutting off what are in principle good adaptive options.

Conclusions

Group scholarship has given relatively little attention to the question of group survival. Survival has tended to be addressed under the label of maintenance studies where it was subsumed by discussion of keeping collective action problems at bay. The population ecology (PE) approach has been a welcome addition to the literature in that it has explicitly approached the issue of group mortality. Yet it does not directly engage in analysis of the *adaptive* changes that groups may engage in to survive. This emphasis is acknowledged by PE scholars themselves. This chapter has been concerned with exploring one way to fill this gap in the analytical repertoire of group scholars.

This chapter puts forward another way to work with organizational form. Where Chapter 4 pursued a feature-based approach, this chapter pursued an identity-based account. To summarize, I suggest that at any one moment, a group organization will manifest a dominant group identity. This identity will be accompanied by a set of strategic and technical features. These three components could be thought of as a realized organizational form. Changes in overall identity imply changes in strategic and technical features such that the overall configuration is broadly consistent with general, and legitimate, organizational forms (lest the groups' value to key audiences, and hence survival prospects, decline). By contrast, changes to technical features and strategies are not necessarily going to contribute to a change in overall identity: as long as they are non *identity-dependent* features. In so far as this provides an overview of group organizational configurations, it fits with calls by group scholars for a more holistic analysis of group organizations (see Nownes 2004; Heaney 2004; Halpin and Jordan 2009).

Utilizing results from a broader research programme documenting histories of UK interest groups, I have demonstrated how this approach to adaptive change in group form may be applied. This work suggests that most groups are likely to manifest changes in strategies and settings consistent with their identity. However, through the RNIB and SA cases, I did establish that it is possible for groups to change overall identity too. There are no doubt other ways to elaborate on group adaptive change and survival, but the modest aim here is simply to establish that this approach is valuable in describing and calibrating the scope of change in groups over time.

Notes

1 Of course the seminal scholars *have* often noted the varied and puzzling survival stories of some groups (see Olson 1965; Salisbury 1969). And the varied life courses of groups have been the subject of specific organizational histories.

2 Bulmer and Burch (1998) refer to *critical moments* which they define as moments whereby debate and discussion over change is undertaken, but from which change may (or may not) ensue.

3 This is echoed by Colin Hay (2006, 60) who argues that historical institutionalism 'has tended to be characterized by an emphasis upon institutional genesis at the expense of an adequate account of post-formative institutional change'.

4 In the many orthodox maintenance theories of groups, the role of leaders – or group entrepreneurs – is deemed central (Olson 1965, Salisbury 1969 are two such seminal works). It is broadly accepted that they are best able to shape the perceptions of members and other important audiences (see Maloney *et al.* 1994). And, as the PE approach suggests, the way leaders interpret and respond to environmental population pressures is likely to be crucial to survival.

5 Heaney notes that many groups may speak about identity in terms of 'mission', 'brand' or 'branding' (2004, 624).

6 Greenwood and Hinings (1996, 1026) distinguish between radical change – where a shift in archetype is present – and convergent change – where change occurs consistent with the existing archetype.

7 And interviews (early 2008) conducted by the authors with Soil Association staff confirm this broad analysis.

8 *Quarterly Review*, 1983, Summer, p. 27.

9 *Quarterly Review*, 1982–3, Winter, pp. 8–9.

10 See Halpin (2010) for further case details.

11 They were responsible for championing the use of the Braille system in printed materials.

12 The case can be treated as one single group organizational sequence, or career, because (i) all named groups share a consistent focus with the interests of blind persons, and (ii) they share an unbroken chain with the constitutional origins of the 1886 group.

7 Niche theories

Differentiation *through* 'form'?

Introduction

The group literature has long shown an interest in how it is that groups position themselves vis-à-vis one another. While this might be subsumed into a general discussion of population dynamics or maintenance, a particular facet of this general topic has proven irresistible to scholars, namely niche theory. Population-based theories, as applied to groups, rest on the basic idea that competition for scarce resources exists within the environment (which is conceived of as a closed system). At some point a population density level is reached where finite resources are stretched beyond what can sustain the existing population, and something has to give. It is at this point that population-based arguments turn to niche theory. In anticipation of competition, groups partition the resource space by creating a realized niche that avoids reliance on the same set of resources as other groups. When pushed up against case material the expectations are pretty clear: groups ought to be different. But can this broad expectation be fine-tuned or nuanced any further?

In this chapter I suggest there is more that can be done to further develop this intuitively attractive and delightfully simple insight. Three highly related additions are presented here, generated by adopting a lens of organizational form to the issue of niche-building strategies. The perspective developed here is simply, following what seems an irresistible tendency for scholars, to resort to the idea of group identity to get at the issue of niche-building.

The first concerns recalibrating assumptions that make sense in aggregate population work but seem unhelpful in the case of comparative case analysis. While existing approaches see niches as a by-product of outright competition for the same set of resources among 'substitutable' group forms, the core insight developed here is that niches emerge (and resources are partitioned) through the creation of '*non*-substitutable' forms. While it is convenient (and defensible) in large-n aggregate analysis to adopt the working assumption that groups are substitutable, up close we see they incorporate partitioning *through* their organizational designs: it is already 'baked in'. This is not to say that groups can't shift settings to alter resource niches: for instance, by broadening membership scope or adding a lobby tactic (see Table 6.3 in Chapter 6). But this subtle adjustment is modest compared to fundamental choices of group design.

This insight supports a second argument around the way the 'environment' that groups operate in and draw resources from is conceptualized. Rather than view the environment as an n-dimensional resource space, it is suggested that it could be productively viewed as an organizational identity-space. The virtue of this approach is that it connects niche building more closely to the act of organization building by group entrepreneurs.

Third, it is suggested that progress in the niche approach means engaging with qualitative variations among populations of related groups. But to do so, better scaffolding is required to make sense of the *strategic* choices of groups regarding positioning within such populations. Here I explore one such approach. This chapter explores how the 'average' group in a resource-rich environment might be expected to strategize over niche-seeking. While it is expected that groups would seek to differentiate themselves, it is important to also accept (and acknowledge) that there is an imperative to demonstrate conformance or sameness. It is suggested that groups would rationally seek out to be as 'different as legitimate'.

Before proceeding to these three propositions, this chapter first sets out the current state of niche theory deployed in interest group studies.

Niche theory in interest group studies

The notion that groups secure their survival by maintaining a viable niche has been an enduring one in group scholarship. At least part of the attraction might be that it promises to draw together – in one conceptual gaze – the activities of organizational maintenance and formation, on the one hand, with lobbying and influence directed activities, on the other (Gray and Lowery 2000, 91). Indeed, scholars concerned with group 'survival' or 'maintenance' seem irresistibly drawn to the niche concept. The idea has been deployed in various ways for at least three decades. Central to the niche idea is that groups rely on finite resources from their environment and that there is competition among groups for those resources. Importantly, competition occurs among like-groups and not among policy competitors: for example, among environment groups as opposed to between business and environment groups. Thus, like-groups are well advised to operate in a way that limits competition for key resources: that is, by occupying a quiet niche. However, precisely *which* resource dimensions niches might be built around, and how groups might strategize in seeking out such niches, is the subject of some discussion (and disagreement) (see summary in Table 7.1).

The initial focus for accounts of niche-building was on policy space. In the face of competition for the attention of policy makers groups react by specializing. It is better for a group – in terms of survival prospects – to ignore most of what's going on in government (even when it may be relevant to the 'interests' they advocate for) and concentrate resources and attention towards an *issue* niche. Moreover, policy makers would prefer to 'transact' with agents that have a reputation for some type of policy expertise (or other policy

124 *Niche theories*

good). This is more easily generated and demonstrated where the group specializes in a policy niche. Browne argues that 'Organized interests define themselves in terms of carefully constructed issue niches' (1990, 477). Groups compete for policy makers' attention and in this competition they differentiate from others by specializing in particular sets of issues. The mechanism driving narrow issue identities is a transactional one: Browne suggests that 'organized interests develop issue identities – indeed are compelled to do so – because their representatives must have something recognizable to market within one or more relevant networks of decision making' (1990, 500). Following transaction cost approaches, groups invest in narrow sets of resources that give them an advantage in getting access in narrow policy niches, and thereafter success in such niches drives further positive investment and specialization – moreover, upfront costs into new areas are costly, and benefits uncertain (see Williamson 1985). A group 'gains a recognizable identity by defining a highly specific issue niche for itself and fixing its political assets (i.e. recognition and other resources) within that niche' (Browne 1990, 502). The key metric here is how many issue niches groups span. According to Browne: 'Only a few organizations, usually the least influential, focus on encompassing or sectorwide issues or become large scale coalition players' (1990, 477). Such an assessment naturally curtailed much optimism about the likelihood of an active hyper-pluralism, given that incentives were strong for groups to avoid straying into policy territory outside their specialism. Indeed, recent work in the UK context supports the basic pattern of issue specialization, whereby groups generally stick to narrow issue domains (Halpin and Binderkrantz 2011).

While Browne focused on policy niches, Gray and Lowery drew on their broader population ecology approach in arguing that 'an organization's niche is defined by a multidimensional space, not simply its place of interface with the policy-making process' (2000, 95). It is salient to note that this approach draws on Hutchinson's (1957) conceptualization (based in ecological theory from the natural sciences), which had been borrowed and deployed in various ways by early organizational ecologists (see Hannan and Freeman 1997; Hannan and Carrol 1992). Various 'resource dimensions' – Gray and Lowery list resources such as members, financial resources and selective benefits – are said to be important aside from the choice of which set of policy issues to engage in (or which issue-set to develop expertise in). Importantly, they include resource dimensions that straddle *both* the internal and external environment (by which they mean policy and membership audiences). Yet, according to Gray and Lowery's empirical work, interest group niches are in fact more strongly determined by *internal* resource dimensions than by interaction with government (2000, 96, 108). It is the focus on competition among groups within the 'membership environment' (as opposed to the policy environment) that most clearly distinguishes their work from that of Browne.

Interestingly, like Browne, Gray and Lowery utilize the term 'identity' to refer to how groups establish a niche. They say

Niche theories 125

Identity can be located within any portion of the resource dimensions defining an organization's fundamental niche providing the minimum requirements for survival. The particular identity that an organization establishes – its realized niche – will be specified through how partitioning occurs of critical dimensions of the fundamental niche shared with competitors.

(2000, 95)

This is a highly salient footnote to their work, on which I seek to capitalize.

Yet many questions remained under explored: How do groups set nichewidth, and why? Do groups recognize competition? And if so, what do they do about it? Gray and Lowery (2000) make plain that they see their work on niches as a work in progress. In their seminal work, they identify several challenges to making progress on the deployment of the niche concept. One of these was the need to be clearer on the way specific sets of resources were made the subject of partitioning by groups. At the end of their empirical examination of niche building among lobbying communities in the US states, Gray and Lowery (2000, 197–8) explain;

An even more basic type of research must address resource dimensions. Our enumeration of the resources potentially important to niche design was drawn from prior research, none of which was intended to provide a comprehensive list of the things interest organizations need to survive and prosper. In short, our list has a necessarily ad hoc flavour. Additional research informed more explicitly by the niche concept … should generate a list of resource dimensions about which we can be more confident.

Work sympathetic to this approach has shown that groups do recognize these *internal* resource issues as highly salient for survival, yet suggests that group leaders actively engage in efforts to ameliorate them (Halpin and Jordan 2009).

Most recently, work has addressed the question of niche-seeking and formation by looking *directly* at the question of identity: and specifically distinguishing (issue) niche formation from identity formation (Heaney 2004, 2007). As discussed above, both Browne and Gray and Lowery utilize the term organizational identity to gesture respectively to (a) the way groups have a profile as either a policy specialist or (b) the set of resources a group taps in a realized niche. The work by Heaney takes this a step further by directly arguing that the way groups build niches is by fashioning a multi-dimensional identity with policy makers. Like Gray and Lowery, Heaney has suggested that groups 'specialize' along multiple dimensions. Yet, where Gray and Lowery focus on group internal dimensions, Heaney nuances the idea of niche construction further by distinguishing between different aspects of group identity *in relation to the political process*. This approach explores the public statements of groups, and from that discerns the complexity of their identities (and changes therein over time). Heaney suggests that 'Whereas some interest groups indeed identify themselves closely with issues, others look more to representation, ideology, or advocacy methods to

126 *Niche theories*

separate their organizations from the crowd' (2004, 612–13). Following this reasoning groups 'should pursue issue niches only in proportion to the degree to which they depend on issues in building their identities' (Heaney 2004, 635). And, he finds that many groups *do not* see issue choice as a central component of their identity: they see other facets of their identity, such as whether they are representative, as crucial (2004, 639–40). Like Browne he suggests that groups care about and work hard to shape their identities, but unlike Browne he argues these identities need not revolve around issues at all. Like Gray and Lowery, he suggests that any niche-building/seeking is likely to be established on multiple dimensions, only one of which revolves around policy selection or specialization. While Heaney's explicit focus is on the way groups explain and project their unique profile to *policy makers*, there is no reason it might not be deployed more generally. Indeed, this is what I attempt below.

To summarize, niche theory suggests that differentiation is a critical feature of populations: and pushed to its logical conclusion one ought to expect groups to survive only where they sit in unique niches. A niche is achieved by finding and securing access to a set of unique resources. For groups, these resources are typically understood as both constituency/financial and policy-based. Tracing back to James Q. Wilson and William Browne, the literature has assumed that a niche meant dominating a set of issues as a specialist. Of course, a niche might be more than a policy monopoly, and it has been expanded to include access to a sufficiently large constituency or to financial resources (say from donors) (Gray and Lowery 2000). Thus, we might expect that the way in which other like-groups are constituted will be important in shaping the way that a 'new' group might form. As Browne identified, it has long been appreciated that 'organized interests do worry about their own identities and how others see their group' (1990, 499): yet the challenge is to come up with a framework upon which to hang observations of this 'identity work' and to do so in a manner that acknowledges this is mostly a comparative exercise (groups construct identities with reference to others they might be confused with).

Framed in the terms of the existing literature, the task of this chapter is to develop a niche account that works from the Gray and Lowery resource-based niche position towards the identity-based niche account developed by Heaney, but to do so in a manner that does not leave talk of resources behind.

Niche theory and group *difference*

When niche theories are discussed the emphasis is on difference among groups. The key point to appreciate here is that *finite* resources define a *fundamental* niche within which like-groups compete: it follows that survival strategies entail *partitioning* this resource space into viable *realized* niches (Lowery and Gray 2004). What does this lead us to expect empirically?

The following extract from Lowery and Brasher (2004) provides a useful illustration of the way niche expectations are borne out in scholarly empirical analysis. They take the case of well-known animal welfare organizations in the US.

Table 7.1 Deployment of niche concept in group literature, summary

Approach	Policy-niche	Organizational resource-niche	Identity-niche
Key text(s)	Browne (1990)	Gray and Lowery (2000)	Heaney (2004, 2007)
What drives niche-building?	Access to/influence on policy makers	Organizational survival	Uniqueness to key policy audiences
Dimensions for niche-building?	External policy dimensions (i.e. policy attention/identity)	Internal and external resource dimensions (i.e. policy attention, constituency resources)	Internal and external dimensions (multiple)
Theoretical inspiration	Transactional theory – reduce costs of exchanges with policy makers	Population ecology theory – increase survival chances caused by population pressures	Transactional theory – provide assets that policy makers demand
Expectations	Groups strive for narrow non-competitive issue niches to maximize influence and reduce costs of transactions with policy makers	Groups seek to partition multidimensional set of resources from competitors to survive	Groups shape complex and unique identities in order to demonstrate they possess assets demanded (in transactions) by policy makers and supporters

128 *Niche theories*

Niche theory accounts for many stark differences between the ASPCA and PETA. Their memberships are markedly different, with the former's typically older and wealthier. They lobby on different issue agendas. PETA espouses a set of issues associated with animal rights, while ASPCA focuses on animal protection. Their finances differ. PETA depends on membership dues, while ASPCA receives substantial corporate funding. And they employ different lobbying strategies ... in terms of critical resources each needs to survive, the ASPCA and PETA have partitioned their overlapping fundamental niche so as to produce two distinct, but so far viable realized niches.

(2004, 53)

Thus, Lowery and Brasher (2004, 58) helpfully summarize the basic expectations of niche theory as follows: 'niche theory suggests that the major response of most organizations to competition over shared niche space is partitioning so that they have an exclusive set of members, funds, issues, or modes of access to the political process'.[1]

Anecdotally, there can be little doubt that groups operating in the same field routinely vary from one another. In the international human rights field the two strong and high-profile groups are Human Rights Watch (HRW) and Amnesty International (AI). Both share the same broad purpose – to advocate for human rights – yet they adopt different organizational models. While neither organization claims to 'represent' their members – they are both solidary-style groups (Halpin 1996, 2010) – they differ in the way they utilize individuals in their advocacy. HRW has a very different advocacy methodology. It employs over 200 staff around the world to research the human rights records of governments. According to its website it publishes over 100 reports annually to distil and communicate findings. These results are published in such a manner as to maximize media coverage, the result of which is often that HRW is able to meet with policy makers and world leaders to push its policy agenda. It is the accuracy and depth of the HRW research that provides it with policy resources: this is valued and trusted by policy makers. AI draws most of its funds from a large number of smaller contributors, its supporter base, but HRW is funded by fewer larger donors. AI is composed of national member organizations, while HRW is highly centralized.

One does not have to take my word for it, this difference is explicitly spelt put by the groups themselves! On its website, HRW asks 'How is Human Rights Watch different from Amnesty International?', it answers

We put pressure on governments by exposing abuses through the media, and by convincing powerful leaders or stakeholders to use their influence on behalf of human rights. Amnesty International also investigates and reports on abuses and derives its real strength from being a mass membership organization.

(Human Rights Watch 2013)

Groups within populations recognize distinctions among their own, a point returned to later in this chapter.

A website for individuals interested in invertebrates in the UK sets out the distinctions between groups organizing the field. It lists 'invertebrate' interest organizations in the UK based on distinctions between those focused on 'conservation of invertebrates', 'the study of invertebrates' or 'those conserving other forms of wildlife but are also devoting resources to insect conservation'.[2] The first set of groups includes organizations like Buglife and Butterfly Conservation, while the Royal Entomological Society is a good example of the second category. This category of groups is composed mostly of amateur and professional societies of enthusiasts, who typically focus on disseminating research findings, holding meetings and seminars. The policy work of such groups is likely restricted to giving expert evidence to inquiries or the media. The last category is a field-spanning group – a generalist that is engaged in several fields, one of which is invertebrates: the Royal Society for the Protection of Birds is a good exemplar. Thus, it is clear that in the group world the idea of differentiation has currency and can be recognized readily.

It is easy to conclude then, that groups implicitly recognize niche-theory edicts to both build and foster difference. One of the difficulties in such an approach is that while it supports ready diagnosis of differences, it does not provide a lot of guidance for empirical analyses. We just expect each group to be different, somehow. And, as it turns out, this is not hard to do if one looks closely enough. If the value of niche theory is simply pointing out we get difference, then job done! However, it is suggested this might be built upon further. In what follows I try to develop a novel take on niche-building that develops from a form-based perspective.

The (non)substitutability imperative

An initial modification that recommends itself from an organizational form perspective is a challenge to the assumption of substitutability. This assumption is necessary to support large-n population-level analysis. Yet, I suggest, this assumption is a hindrance to contemporary efforts at understanding how specific sets of groups in small and middle-n work create and sustain niches. Let me elaborate.

The dominant understanding of niches in group studies is probably closest to Gray and Lowery's resource-niche approach. This perspective draws from – and is bundled up into – a population ecology theory which has as its primary explanatory concern the density of organizational populations (in this case lobbying organizations). The niche approach it elaborates comes imbued with the implication that groups are all substitutable.[3] That is, in principle, and in what might be thought of as their natural *non-partitioned* state, groups that share a fundamental resource niche by definition compete with one another for that set of resources. As it happens, this assumption is shared by the broader ecological approach in organizational studies. Authorities in the field, for example, point out that 'Ecologists

130 *Niche theories*

tend to treat the coherence of organizations as entities as relatively non-problematic, based on their assumption that organizations are relatively structurally inert' (Aldrich 1999, 45). An assumption is made of the 'unitary character' of organizations, which in turn serves to mask heterogeneity (Lounsbury 2005, 93). Put simply, groups are taken to be functionally equivalent.

Such an assumption seems reasonable when viewed against the broader population ecology model with its focus on explaining aggregate density. However, when one is concerned with small sets of actual groups, as with the Lowery and Brasher example, this assumption seems hard to sustain and unhelpful. The problem here is that real groups are anything but substitutable. While population headcounts foster the notion that 'a group is a group', we all know that if we were to peer inside and unpack the black box of environmental, business or consumer groups there would be untold and *non-trivial* organizational diversity. While we reasonably treat the American Phytopathological Society (a group of plant scientists) and the Sierra Club (an advocacy group supporting nature) as 'environment groups' (see Baumgartner and Jones 1993), neither would be expected to directly compete for resources: they are at the *outset* highly differentiated 'products'.

So what, you ask? The salience of this insight is that the populations of groups that are assumed to be equally able to 'survive' in any part of the fundamental niche, actually *arrive* into the population with their realized niche baked-in so to speak. In relation to niche theories, I suggest it is more helpful – and closer to the way the issue is viewed by group leaders themselves – that we assume *the imperative of groups is to establish from the outset a non-substitutable form*. Take the example of agricultural groups in the UK. The National Farmers' Union (NFU) is a general farmers' union, which organizes farmers as small business people and participants in rural communities. By contrast, there are a plethora of smaller sector-based groups, such as the National Sheep Association and National Pig Association, each of which address issues that pertain solely – or at least heavily – to their own members. There is a well-worn division of labour between associations and the generalist NFU, which means, in effect, the type of policy niche-building described by Browne seems apparent in the patterns of policy engagement. The point is that these sector-based groups are not in any sense substitutable for the generalists. Their basic decision to take on the *form* of a sector-based group means that they only barely compete in a resource sense, and that they rarely get in one another's way in a policy sense. The real resource pinch comes not from competitors eating up their territory, but from natural processes of industry shrinkage that make the viability of a stand-alone generalist group model marginal. It is this that tends to drive group aggregation, at least in the agricultural sector (see Halpin 2005).

It is at this point that the question of identity comes in. Because groups are established with an identity, and that identity brings with it inherent limitations as to its potential market, its fundamental resource niche is significantly smaller than one might suppose it to be when considered in abstract. This means that most groups are *not in fact ever in competition for the same resource niche,*

Niche theories 131

because their identity at the outset is likely to be sufficiently different enough to avoid it. Indeed, in general terms, successful formation relies on groups finding an identity niche, and then establishing that there are sufficient resources attached to that identity niche position. Moreover, the temptation for other groups to shift niches is constrained by identities – groups can't suddenly reinvent themselves, because it takes time for a new reputation to be established among those with actual resources (members and policy makers) (a point that can be inferred from the discussion in Chapter 5). Indeed, where formation fails it is not often due to a crowded niche so much as the resources attached to various resource positions turns out to be insufficient. The case of People Too! in Chapter 5 illustrated the absence of a market for their style of group product: they were not going head to head with existing groups so much as putting forward a substantially different group offering.

This general style of analysis around non-substitutability is not just an artefact of scholarly analysis, but also evident in the public reportage of established groups. The occasion of the fortieth and fiftieth anniversaries of the WWF and Greenpeace provided cause for reflection on how each organization compared as brands. An observer explains

> The types of people who are attracted to them are totally different. If environmental problems make you really pissed off and you want to get out there and stick it to the man, you go to Greenpeace. If they make you sad, and you want to sit in your room with a cuddly toy and look at pictures of cute animals, you would go to the WWF [and] there is room for both, of course, but I don't think there's a lot of overlap in the personality types.

An insider is quoted as saying 'Some of the people who work for WWF are probably quite similar to those in other NGOs like Greenpeace, but the people who support them are very different'.[4] What is salient here is that the partitioning is not on the basis of subdividing a large pool of potential members by some set of sociodemographic features. Rather, each group has a distinctive lobbying product and it is this reputation or identity that then attracts – and discourages – a set of individuals to support it (or not). Potential members are in effect 'lost' by virtue of the group's identity, it is a design decision that then impacts on the level of potential resources (by reducing the market).

At the heart of niche theory, as applied to groups, is competition for scarce resources within a closed system. As some density point is reached, finite resources are stretched beyond what can sustain the existing population, and something has to give. In anticipation of this, groups partition the resource space, thus avoiding reliance on the same set of resources. However, what we often see is not outright competition for the same set of resources among 'substitutable' forms, but rather partitioning *through* differentiated realized organizational forms/identities.

The role of identity in shaping population relations is also detectable in the way group leaders explain existing partitioning and the prospects for changes to

132 *Niche theories*

that partitioning. Here the case of the National Kidney Foundation (NKF) in the UK is instructive. The NKF explains that the core of its identity is 'Run by Kidney Patients for Kidney Patients'. This is an identity that is most clear when compared to the other group in the field. For instance, the NKF contrasts itself with the British Kidney Patients Association (BKPA) which 'in fact acts as a clearing house for donations to assist individuals with financial needs'. But competition is not the predominant dynamic. The CEO explains 'The NKF in fact will pass on cases to the BKPA from its helpline.' In previous work, I have discussed the ways in which groups in the Scottish rural agricultural scene have related with one another – reacting to expansions and contractions in the resource base (of policy attention and member constituency) by seeking to cooperate over resource challenges while preserving identity-based differences (Halpin and Jordan 2009). This same commitment to cooperative niche partitioning is evident in many groups examined. Groups themselves engaged in close relations seem more likely to explain relationships in terms closer to cooperation: or at least in terms that make clear that they view any actions of straightforward opportunistic resource competition as unwise.

This angle suggests a reinterpretation of the puzzle within Gray and Lowery's PE theory, namely that many groups reported they experienced little or no competition from peers for resources. Their solution was to explain this as 'passive' competition – suggesting that even if group leaders were unaware of resource constraints, the broader population-level ecological processes driving density were no doubt in operation. By contrast, from the perspective developed here, one could argue that this finding is because there is *little* actual niche overlap. Given that our approach assumed that groups first position themselves by establishing a reputation – 'We are the group that does xyz!' – and that resources then flow from that positioning; post hoc analysis of populations of like-groups is almost certainly going to be mapping what are largely *already* well partitioned spaces. That is, the partitioning will likely already be stabilized, because (i) it is a by-product of identity establishment and (ii) identities are hard to establish but once they are it is difficult to shift either tactically or unilaterally by leaders.

What type of 'space' is being partitioned?

One of the key implications from the discussion above is that resource partitioning – or niche creation – occurs *via* organizational design, or the creation and maintenance of a group's specific realized *identity*. This is consistent with some early threads in the group literature. As discussed at the outset, work by Heaney argues that identity formation is the mechanism by which groups foster uniqueness in the eyes of key audiences, and that this (in turn) shapes resource availability and even policy access (2004, 2007). Recent work also suggests that groups actively interpret, strategize over and respond to environmental pressures; and, that this is facilitated by the 'manipulation of group identity' (Halpin and Jordan 2009, 265). Here I take this a step further. It is argued here that it makes more sense to also rethink the way the space being partitioned is conceptualized. Rather than start from the assumption that niche-building occurs among potentially substitutable entities competing over the same fundamental *resource space*, an alternative is to conceptualize it as *identity space* within which groups position themselves: the implication being that identity positioning has a knock-on effect in resource terms.

Without wanting to get lost in a very technical literature, it is important to appreciate the way the environment or space being partitioned is conceptualized from a resource perspective. For this we go back to the foundational organizational literature.

Early ecological work saw organizational niches as the area within a resource space that an organization could survive or thrive (versus those areas of resource space that they could not, or would struggle). Drawing on ecological theories, the basic idea was that species occupy distinctive locations in a multidimensional resource space, despite often having the *same* values on these dimensions. For instance, different bird species occupy different niches owing to the time they eat or the type of tree they breed in. Put in an organizational context, McPherson (1983) drew the analogy that the resources human organizations competed for were in fact members. He suggested that human organizations – his focus was voluntary organizations – competed with one another for 'niches' within a multidimensional social space defined by sociodemographic characteristics (age, gender, education, etc.). Thus he argues 'The key insight of our conception is that organizations which have overlapping niches are recruiting from the same pool of potential members' (McPherson 1983, 522). For instance, he notes that the niche overlap between elderly organizations and all others (such as professional or union organizations) is low because 'organizations for the elderly occupy a distinctive niche in social space, since their age overlap with other organizations is minimal' (McPherson 1983, 525). The environment being partitioned – conceptualized as a multidimensional social space – is not necessarily evenly distributed with individuals (and thus resources). For instance, the preponderance of relatively high-income and well-educated individuals means that organizations are likely to crowd that space; or thought of in the inverse, this niche within the space is better able to support a denser population (it has a higher carrying capacity). This account is strikingly similar to Gray and Lowery's observation that groups compete mostly on the membership resource dimension.

An alternative view is to see the space within which organizations seek to form niches as a *categorical* space (Hsu 2006; Hsu *et al.* 2009; Negro *et al.* 2010a). From this perspective, organizations choose to engage to varying degrees with categorical positions within their environment: these positions are socially constructed (or 'sociologically real' categories) and thus able to be shaped by organizations as well as by broader economic and social processes. For example, producers of movies develop their product to speak to categorical positions represented by movie genres, wine producers develop products that speak to existing 'varieties' and 'domains of origin', and chefs develop identities for their restaurants that speak to established cuisine

134 *Niche theories*

categories. The pattern of this engagement represents their identity niche (see Hsu *et al.* 2009). Put more simply, the proposition is that organizations choose to identify themselves with one or more organizational categories and that this (fuzzy-set) category profile constitutes their identity. Categories represent set positions in identity space (including tastes, preferences and expectations of audiences) and organizational conformance with these positions taps discrete sets of resources. It a recent review the point was made that institutional and ecological approaches both seem to agree on basics, namely that identities are socially constructed categories that define what makes organizations similar to one another yet different from organizations in other social categories (Fiol and Romanelli 2012). The notion that identity-space be deployed in organizational studies has been repeated by key authors within the related social movement literature (see Soule 2012).

In the group context we find that despite a basic commitment to a resource-space conceptualization, there is a practice of accepting a looser identity-based approach. For instance, Lowery *et al.* (2013, 390) state that 'resource space can be the political space spun by issue-axes' whereby the 'scarce resource for organizations is their audience's demand for services'. One way to think about this approach is to view the space being partitioned as arrayed with different established group generic categories/forms: they are points in an organization's environment at which audiences are willing to engage with (and ultimately resource) a type of group 'product'. For example, the group of individuals concerned with the environment, and thus predisposed to joining or supporting environmental groups, can be conceptualized as aligning with a range of nominal identity positions. So, for instance, those interested in birds can join a recreational group, a campaigning group, an amateur ornithological society, or an animal rights organization, to name a few. These positions have impacts on the way said groups then go about actively building their group identities because they need to appeal to one or more of these positions to extract resources. Thus, if the recreational group starts lobbying overtly, then those who find a recreational identity appealing, and not a political one, will likely exercise voice or exit. The identity positions with which a group establishes itself therefore has implications for resources it attracts.

This type of identity-positioning dynamic is best detected empirically where potential 'breaches' occur. Take the case of the National Trust in England. It has a long-standing reputation among the public as a group that avoids engaging in political debate. While it actively engages in policy work around conservation of the built environment, it does not overtly campaign for policy change and certainly does not seek to get its members to engage in campaigning directly. However, in 2011 the Trust wrote to all its close to four million members asking them to sign a petition opposing the UK government's planning reforms. The Director General explained 'I am taking this unusual step because ... we believe that these changes, which are supposedly in the public interest, come at far too high a price.' In a media interview again she outlined that the Trust 'isn't a campaigning organisation'. However she went on to explain that

Niche theories 135

> [Campaigning] is dependent on the issue.... I would not expect us to be doing it all the time. If we became rentaquote, that wouldn't be right. We reserve our voice for something that is really important, absolutely at the heart of our core purpose and touches what we stand for and where we make a difference. This felt like the single most important issue in the time I have been here. I think we should campaign on issues that are central to what we do and I suspect it would be rare, but when we make a contribution it matters. I think this is what this has shown.[5]

In addition, for the first time, it reportedly lobbied all three UK party political conferences.[6] That this step of overt campaigning had to be carefully explained to supporters hints at the extent to which it rubs against the grain of existing identity positioning. And, as is self-evident, the Trust has had to explain this new move in terms of preserving the existing identity of the group – to preserve its identity-niche and thus resource base. This type of dynamic might be usefully understood in terms of *authenticity*: the NT is under pressure to illustrate that it continues to fit with expectations of the behaviour and image of an authentic group of its type (see Soule 2012, for good summary of this idea applied to social movements).

In explaining the niche-structure among a gaggle of related groups, we find recourse to identity-based population management as opposed to brute resource competition. The Australian university sector is relatively small by international standards – especially compared to the UK and US. However, it has a rather complex set of representative groups: a situation no doubt given impetus by the recent surge of reforms which allow for more competition over a key resource – namely government-funded undergraduate student places. The various groups include Universities Australia, the Australian Technology Network, Innovative Research Universities, the Regional Universities Network and the Group of Eight. Universities Australia is the peak body for all universities. Its president, in response to his address to the Australian National Press Club, was asked whether this proliferation of umbrella bodies amounted to 'Balkanisation'. His answer provides some insight into niche partitioning processes viewed from the perspective of group leaders. He responded, 'It's not Balkanisation but a wonderful diversity.' He suggested it was similar to any industry sector,

> If we were the oil and gas industry there would be the oil sub-group and the petroleum sub-group and so on, but they would come together under a peak body.... We are behaving in exactly the same way and for the same completely rational reasons.

Asked whether he thought the existence of these competitor groups would hurt Universities Australia, the president responded, 'It benefits rather than hurts UA [Universities Australia] to have these groupings. They look after particular interests. In a sense they encourage diversification, because they encourage their members to cluster around shared concerns.' This ecology did not emerge by

136 *Niche theories*

virtue of aggregate environmental resource shifts. Rather, it reflects a recognition that real identity positions (with resource implications) were evident and at a point group entrepreneurs sought to fill that position with a newly established group organization, while at the same time related groups could not (or chose not to) try and cover that same 'empty' identity position.

In Scotland, analysis of the rural turn in agricultural policy, which saw the emergence of several rebel groups to challenge the NFUS (see Halpin and Jordan 2009), surfaced similar instances of what might be called mutualism. This concept refers to the population dynamic whereby the development and legitimization of one sub-form in a population – say womens' service delivery organizations – promotes (rather than impedes) the growth in legitimacy and density of a related population – say womens' advocacy organizations (see Minkoff 1999; Walker *et al.* 2011). Such an approach turns on its head the idea that like-groups partition space directly through changes to the style of advocacy, breadth of recruitment or such like: what I referred to earlier as strategic adaptations or technical updates (see Chapter 6). Instead, it shows that like-organizations actually partition space through selection (and development) of their overall realized organizational form.

To be clear, the argument here is *not* that resources are irrelevant or somehow not partitioned, but rather that when viewed close-up groups do not actually directly 'partition resources', but engage *in a range of other actions that have the effect of partitioning resources*. Progressing niche theory further is not just a matter of specifying the set of resource dimensions better, but also specifying the activities that have the effect of constructing niches and most importantly studying those processes *directly*. Here the argument is that the core activity groups engage in that has resource implications is establishing an identity position within identity space. This is not a rejection of ecological accounts, but rather an embrace of the constant reference by Browne, then Gray and Lowery, and, more recently, by Heaney, to the way group identities are critical to niche construction.

Defining the modal niche-building strategy: *same but different…*

In this final section, the aim is to pull the above discussion together and derive from it some insights about the strategies that a group might be expected to take in niche-building. While these are only afforded the most superficial of empirical tests here, the intention is to provide clear targets for the empirical efforts of others. So far I have argued that (i) groups enter populations with the aim of achieving non-substitutability and (ii) (in so far as they succeed) do so by positioning themselves in a niche within identity space that in turn attracts sufficient resources. In building on the above points, one concrete way forward is to offer better scaffolding to make sense of the strategic choices of groups regarding positioning within populations of like groups. But how might we translate that into a concrete strategy?

The start point for the discussion is the recognition that two apparently opposing imperatives deemed important for survival strategies are in fact two sides of the same coin. On the one hand, the literature assumes that organizations need to conform to established modes of practice or forms in order to extract legitimacy. This emphasis on isomorphism is an element of both ecological and institutional approaches. On the other hand, there is the well-established notion that differentiation enables organizations to avoid resource competition (principally by avoiding competition for customers).

The organizational social science literature has started to take this seriously and tried to better capture the twin – perhaps even contradictory – imperatives for organizations to conform to standards to attract legitimacy, but also to differentiate from peers to avoid competition. In a highly influential article Zuckerman (1999) develops the proposition that organizations (he focuses specifically on firms) confront audiences in a two-stage process. In the first, the audience filters out claims for legitimacy that do not fit established categories; and hence, in this phase, organizations are guided by the imperative to demonstrate conformance (or isomorphism). In the second phase, organizations try to illustrate that while fitting the legitimate form, they are somehow unique among those organizations or firms also considered legitimate. Here the imperative is differentiation. He concludes that 'Gaining the favour of an audience requires *conformity* with the audience's minimal criteria for what offers should look like and *differentiation* from all other *legitimate* offers' (Zuckerman 1999, 1402 italics added). Put another way, he suggests that 'differentiation works hand in hand with isomorphism' (1999, 1402).

The work of Deephouse (1999) is also salient here. He observes that 'firms face pressures to be different and to be the same' and develops an argument that, to optimize *both* performance and survival prospects, organizations 'should be as different as legitimately possible' (1999, 148). The resolution offered by Deephouse (1999, 154–5, 162) is highly suggestive for group scholars. He suggests a 'balance' model, whereby the optimal strategy is a medium similarity path – to accept the costs of a small increase in legitimacy challenge arising from incomplete conformance to field standards, but gain the benefit of less competition by differentiating strategies.

His work seems useful translated into the group context (he focused on firms in the US banking sector). One could usefully propose that entrepreneurs engaged in establishing (and adapting) the organizational design of their groups – which might be conceptualized as their mission, strategies for mobilization and influence, and techniques for implementing them (see Chapter 6) – are subject to competing and contradictory pressures: difference (catalysed by the imperative to avoid competition over scarce resources) and sameness (catalysed by the imperative to attract legitimacy from key audiences who control key resources). It is suggested that groups engage in strategies to survive organizationally that adopt two related but seemingly contradictory logics. First, an organization needs to emphasize isomorphism to gain membership (as appraised by key audiences) in a recognized population – for example as an environment group – but

138 *Niche theories*

at the same time emphasize differentiation in order to stand out from other members of the population – for example as a 'traditional' and not 'donor' environmental group form (thus partitioning key resources).

In terms of survival, groups may do well to adapt their identity through differentiating themselves from others in their field to avoid competition for finite sets of resources; but if they differentiate by adapting too far away from field norms they risk losing legitimacy from those very audiences with whom groups exchange resources. That is, policy makers, supporters or donors will have trouble understanding what the group stands for and why it should be supported. Stated from the reverse direction, groups seeking to survive may do well to develop their organizations in ways that reflect field standards so as to enhance legitimacy with key audiences that grant resources, yet if they conform too closely to others in the field, they risk competing for precisely the same set of resources. Put back into the words of group scholarship, such a strategy combines niche theories concern with capturing resources, and identity-based niche theories concern with avoiding an identity crisis whereby key audiences misunderstand group mission, and thus perhaps overlook group relevance (see Heaney 2004).

Table 7.2 represents various ideal type strategies available to groups in order to manage contradictory pressures of conformance and differentiation. Each group will experience varying levels of (i) competition for resources and (ii) challenge to their legitimacy, based on whether its realized 'form' varies from the field norm of its competitors.[7] Let's review these strategies briefly.

The *replication strategy* is one whereby new groups in a field are established (or existing groups adapted or transformed) into forms that resemble the field norm. The expectations are that such new groups would be easily recognizable and gain easy acceptance, however they would also be positioning themselves in such a way as to occupy the very same realized resource niche. For instance, a new national general farm group in Scotland modelled on the NFUS would be a straightforward replication strategy.

At the other end of the spectrum is the *innovation* strategy. Here a group develops an entirely unique form, one that is hard for key audiences to read and to accept (readily). This might be because a group imports forms or organizations from other fields: say a doctor's group imports a campaigning model from the environmental field. In principle this choice to adopt a novel form for the field, means that there is no overlap of realized resource niches with existing groups. But the absence of resource overlaps does not tell us whether there is in fact sufficient resources associated with the innovation strategy, simply that there ought to be no head to head competition for resources as a consequence of adopting it. In Chapter 5, People Too engaged in such a strategy.

In the middle, the rational strategy is to pursue *differentiation*. This means being as different as is legitimate, to reiterate the point made by Deephouse above. Again, the fact that I anticipate the average group going for a differentiation strategy explains why most populations at any one time appear to us as well partitioned in terms of identity-niches. Take the area of groups representing

Table 7.2 Ideal-type identity niche positioning

Strategy	Legitimacy challenges?	Resource competition?	Prospects?
Innovation	High	Low	Sensitive to highly regulated or well-established fields
Differentiation	Medium	Medium	Optimal in most fields
Replication	Low	High	Sensitive to resource limitations and densely populated fields

Source: based on discussion by Deephouse (1999).

the Australian retail sector. Two organizations are key at the national level. The Australian Retailers Association (ARA) was founded at the start of the twentieth century, and developed largely on a base of existing state-level organizations. The other group is the Australian National Retailers Association (ANRA), formed in 2006. It presents itself as 'representing the country's leading retailers', and membership is by invitation only. It has large national retail chains as its members, including Coles, Woolworths, Bunnings and David Jones, and the CEOs or equivalent from these organizations sit on the group's board. As one might expect, the ARA legitimizes its work by recourse to history, membership numbers and national coverage – 'Promoting and protecting retailers for over 100 years', while the ANRA talks about the number of employees members have and financial clout – 'ANRA members employ more than 450,000 people and account for $100 billion in retail turnover'. There is no sensible way to predict in advance levels of diversity, but with such a set of ideal-type strategies in hand it is possible to see post hoc how survival is (or is not) underpinned by choice of a differentiation strategy.

The insight is simply that identity differentiation is a strategy that involves both difference and sameness. Competition over resources might be seen to drive a strategy of difference, but this is likely to be moderated by a desire for acceptance by important audiences for whom sameness (or familiarity) is crucial. Groups, therefore, would be expected to moderate strategies of differentiation designed to tap a unique resource niche, with strategies of sameness or likeness to aid audience familiarity and acceptance.

If the differentiation strategy really is the prototypical rational response to building niches, we would expect to see groups consciously talking about identity as a limit on expansion that would, to the outsider, seem to be a logical way to expand the resource base. By their very nature, reflections on identity-based positioning strategies are often kept internal to groups, either captured in internal reports or discussed within boardrooms walls. However, some of the UK groups interviewed provided nice illustrations of how their niche-building (and maintenance) strategies operated through identity-shaping efforts and the knock-on effect for resources (Halpin and Jordan 2009).

140 *Niche theories*

Partitioning of resources, mediated by identities, is evident in the discussion within the National Kidney Foundation (NKF) of survival prospects going forward. The NKF is financed predominantly by pharmaceutical companies. However, the donor income from companies is at its limit, while demands from patients expand. The CEO canvassed options as follows:

> It cannot go direct to the public for donations, as the individual Kidney Patients Associations (KPAs) [the constituent members of the NKF] do that – they rattle tins outside hospitals and run raffles – and it would cut across their funding stream. Moreover, the BKPA asks the public for donations and legacies.

Two points are salient here. First, the NKF decided not to take resources from allied groups in the field even though this was in principle a viable option. Second, it retained a *differentiated* strategy even though a *replication* strategy would likely see it accumulate resources from groups in more viable identity positions.

The CEO continued that an alternative option was to expand 'coverage' from end-stage renal patients – principally those on dialysis – to chronic kidney disease (CKD) patients – which is an ever expanding group estimated to be around 2–5 million persons in the UK. They say 'representing CKD is difficult, we cannot cover 36,000 GP surgeries … we can provide leaflets to surgeries and they can talk to our helpline. We can only respond to them, we do not seek to represent them'. However, the NKF explained that it did not want to grow into this space yet, because it would transform the group radically away from its original mission and identity as being about services for end stage renal failure patients. This underlines the basic argument of this chapter, namely that resources *follow* chosen identities (not vice versa). By its own admission, the NKF is at a critical juncture. As is evident, the logic of expanding the niche to encompass multitudes of more 'members' – and thus resources – butts up against the existing identity of the group. To expand the niche would risk legitimacy and status with existing members and donors.

This is a point worth underlining. Of course, groups can shift technical settings or strategies marginally to shape resource access within existing identity constraints. And, as evident in the survey evidence from Chapter 6, many groups make adjustments that marginally increase the resource base. This is the focus of the exchange-based maintenance literature – how to maximize membership within an existing set-up. But at some critical threshold the issue of expanding identity-based niches means risking an identity crisis. In the case of the NKF, at this juncture in time, the risk was deemed too great.

These identity-based niche strategies are also evident when group leaders consider pressure for mergers within their field. The Association of Optometrists (AOP) explained that they have been in merger talks with several allied groups in the field. Asked why merger is so desirable the interviewee answered, 'The core reason is external image. External shop front is the imperative in mergers. We already present common positions, but there is a recognition we need a single voice.' He said

Niche theories 141

We currently pay for a Head of Public Affairs to run the Eye Health Alliance ... it is a cuddly name, and means we are not seen as pursuing interests of just optometrists – our members – but we also include patients.

Asked if it was necessary to compete over members he replied

As yet we do not really compete for members, as this would reduce our relationship.... At this point we work very close with them on political issues and they are important to us. To be honest, the power and influence that we get from working with them is worth hundreds of its members.

Here the automatic response, assumed by population ecology, to directly challenge the partitioning of resources through merger (or takeover) is mediated by the need to gain acceptance from allies and government. The impulse to maintain partitions for resource reasons seems trumped by identity-based niche preservation.

Finally, the case of the British Health Trade Association (BHTA) is also revealing. At interview, the CEO explained that

We're constantly under pressure as a trade association to be as one.... Pressure from our political masters is that you would do better if you were one voice.... We can't be one voice, because there are variations in marketplaces and the way in which issues hit you.

Their approach to this is a variation on the more orthodox accommodation, namely to give each subsection its own internal committee or division. The head of BHTA explains that they incorporate 13 different sectors under the umbrella:

What I found when I got this job is that we weren't identified. So as part of identifying ourselves sectorally ... I've said well actually all together you are this, so that gives you an identity to government. And underneath that, you have your identities as mini-associations, basically. Which allows us to be vertical, but very horizontal when we have to be. The trick in the secretariat is to identify the horizontal issues as opposed to just going with vertical issues.

Further he explains 'All we are saying is that we are giving you a brand, we are giving you administration, we are allowing you to meet.' This case is evidence of the ways in which groups themselves – especially those that Bosso (2005) called 'keystone' groups – actively partition space by managing the identity formation and positioning processes of related groups.

Conclusion

At its most straightforward, the approach here suggests that groups first set out to establish a reputation with key audiences and firm up an identity. When I refer to group identity, I mean an organizational identity, not simply a policy identity – although that is no doubt likely to be a relevant sub-component in

142 *Niche theories*

many group cases. This identity – 'we are the people who stand for or do xyz' – will by virtue of its appeal determine resource levels. The idea then of identity space is to focus on the fact that those who have resources – policy makers, donors and supporters – can choose products via perceived identity and those who want them – group entrepreneur – can shape products via group identity. Abstract resource space makes sense as an expression of the niche game in aggregate, but individual groups partition via shaping their offer to the market, and this offer is shaped by identity. For example, in passing, Jacobson (2011, 997) makes the observation that US unions, by choosing between craft and industry organizations, define their constituency, and in so doing redefine the resource space of their groups. I am suggesting we simply take this one step forward and accept that groups make decisions on basic blueprints and designs, convert these into realized identities and that this act is how resources are then partitioned. Niches are identity-based.

So what does this do to the resource-based conception of niche-building? As Lowery and Brasher (2004) note, PETA and ASPCA are unique on many dimensions, yet their difference is *only* of interest to scholars precisely *because* they are also in some way like-groups (somehow the same). The term like-groups is utilized in the population ecology framework as a convenient shorthand to refer to the concept of 'interest-guilds'. Accordingly, Gray and Lowery (2000, 61) explain that 'Groups of interest organizations that are similar to each other in terms of relying on common resources are identified as members of guilds.' The concept provides the boundary around which to analyse niche-partitioning behaviour by groups, simply because this is a population that shares the same fundamental niche (in this case constituency resources). The approach developed above retains a focus on resources, but views it as connected to identity-based strategies of niche-building.

This entire approach highlights a certain amount of circularity in the ecological account of resource partitioning that needs to be acknowledged. Organizations within populations must partition to survive, yet survival itself is taken as evidence of successful partitioning (Deephouse 1999). For our purposes, what this highlights is that resource niches are actually created by baked-in features of organizational designs or identities. With this insight in hand, it is possible to develop a different form-based account of niche formation. The struggle isn't to show the dynamism in niche partitioning or formation, but to puzzle over its relative stability. Conceived in a broadly path-dependent manner (Stinchcombe 1965), identities, as with organizational forms generally, are slow to establish and then relatively hazardous to change. When we find settled populations the fact is that they are already well partitioned. Thus, we would not expect to find overt signs of competition, however interviews with those at the helm of related group organizations – and the review documents they write – reveal the border skirmishes and partitioning behaviours that belie such apparent order.

Notes

1 This basic position is repeated in the social movement literature. Reflecting on the experiences of many well-known social movement organizations in the US, two leading authors in the social movement literature reaffirm the expectation that difference (*aka* niche-seeking) is the key to survival: 'Diversification and differentiation – of issues, activities, and resources – were central to successful adaptation, survival and growth' (Minkoff and Powell 2006, 604).

2 See discussion at www.amentsoc.org/insects/conservation/insect.html.

3 This is not to say that Gray and Lowery are not attentive to the notion of form or identity. They use both terms, and engage in analysis based on recognizing three types of form: institutions, associations, and associations of associations.

4 Harvey, F. (2011) 'Greenpeace and WWF anniversaries highlight wildly different tactics', *Guardian*, accessed September 2011.

5 www.guardian.co.uk/theguardian/2011/oct/29/fiona-reynolds-planning-reform-interview.

6 www.economist.com/blogs/bagehot/2011/09/national-trust accessed 29 May 2013.

7 Deephouse defines strategic similarity among banks in terms of their decisions regarding pattern of investments in different asset classes. He measures the distance of each banks practices from the population average as the level of 'strategic similarity'.

8 Assembling group identities in nascent fields
Revisiting a population-level perspective

Introduction

While the population-ecology literature has helpfully pointed out that aggregate population dynamics shape the net survival prospects of groups, the approach does not set out to probe specific design choices of groups or issues of organizational diversity. A core focus for this volume is developing such sensitivity within the existing population research genre. As discussed in Chapter 3, this might be achieved in a range of acceptable, yet different, ways. This is contingent on how one conceptualizes organizational form in the first instance. In Chapter 4, a feature-based approach to exploring variations in form was developed. This, I suspect, might be the least challenging and thus most easily digestible approach to incorporating concerns with form into population perspectives. However, in the next two chapters, this book explores the way population-level dynamics might be developed from explicitly identity-based approaches. The next chapter adopts a firmly *categorical* conceptualization of organizational form, whereby groups assemble their identities from generic forms which manifest themselves as group categories set by and developed through the work of 'market' intermediaries. This present chapter adopts a closely related approach (mixing institutional, categorical and ecological approaches),[1] asking how generic forms emerge in contexts where no clear or legitimate forms are apparent.

What set of attributes do groups utilize in constructing their unique identity? Where do these building blocks come from? And are some 'recipes' more stable than others? This chapter addresses these questions *at the population level*. It examines the way that sets of related groups – in this case environmental groups in England – build their more or less unique identities from the combination of attributes available to them from relevant fields of organizing. We look at how these contemporary members of the modern English environmental movement draw on different attributes associated with three distinctive contexts – conservation, science and political activism/campaigning. The approach adopted in this analysis provides one way of investigating how 'new' and innovative models of organizing are drawn from generic 'sources'. That is, how novel generic forms or models emerge from the creative combination of *other* generic forms in related fields.

Assembling group identities in nascent fields   145

As it happens, probing such questions is best done with a particular focus on organizational emergence in 'nascent fields'. This is because in such fields of endeavour generic forms are not yet settled, which means that entrepreneurs must grope around to develop viable recipes. It is thus an ideal context to examine how generic forms themselves emerge. This is a challenging area of research. Organizational social science – both institutionally and ecologically minded – has somewhat of a weak spot with respect to how forms emerge. And there is consensus among leading scholars in organizational social science that there has been insufficient attention to the origins of organizational forms (Padgett and Powell 2012; Fiol and Romanelli 2012). Thus, this chapter contributes to the specific problem facing group scholars, while also speaking to broader conceptual challenges in organizational studies. Theories of institutional innovation and entrepreneurship are used to explore how agents create new or composite forms in nascent fields from the fragments of abutting or even remote fields of practice.

In what follows, this gap is addressed through an effort at deconstructing and reconstructing organizational variation within a discrete population of interest groups. For reasons mostly of convenience, the setting for this analysis is, again, the set of UK environmental groups belonging to the Wildlife and Countryside Link (WCL) (the same population as examined in Chapter 4). Attention is paid to how elements or building blocks from diverse fields of endeavour are assembled over time to comprise the set of forms that we can see these groups manifest today. Both aggregate and individual cases are examined to come closer to an understanding of how (diverse) forms evolve. New models emerge from the (unique) engagement of ideas from different fields of activity as much as the innate creativity of individual agents.

Organization-building and the origins of 'new' organizational forms

As discussed in Chapter 3, organizational form can be operationalized in many and varied ways. First-generation studies focused upon generating – sometimes empirical – taxonomies based on measuring all possible features of organizations (see Romanelli 1991). Subsequent work tended to avoid laundry lists, recognizing that some features were core to a specific organizations resonance with some broader or fundamental set of forms. This so-called feature-based approach operated on the basis that 'Organizations with the same core features belong to the same form' (McKendrick *et al.* 2003, 63). Most recently, the emphasis has been to integrate form with questions of organizational identity. That is, the definition of form should not be divorced from everyday social and cultural processes of classification and category (re) formation. Thus, the research focus becomes locating forms through practices of 'real world' categorization, as embodied in directories, formal statements of organizational mission/purpose or in consumer/user typologies (McKendrick *et al.* 2003, 63–4).

146 *Assembling group identities in nascent fields*

There is no singularly 'better' way, but choice of approach will partly depend on the number of cases being compared and the research question at hand. The approach adopted here takes inspiration from a thread in organizational social science literature – mostly working on the organization of firms – that probes the emergence and change in organizational form at a field or sectoral level using middle-n historical studies, and that empirically explores forms as they are realized in specific contexts utilizing a mix of qualitative and quantitative methods (see Powell and Sandholtz 2012; Greenwood and Hinings 1993; Baron *et al.* 1999). In so doing, a distinction is made between generic and realized forms. This reflects a distinction between 'the existence of institutionally prescribed archetypes' on the one hand and 'their empirically assessable appearance in individual organizations within an institutional sector' (Greenwood and Hinings 1993, 1058).

Consistent with this thread, the approach proceeds in two broad stages: the first establishes the generic archetypes, blueprints or forms that are in play within the field, and the second proceeds to examine how these are manifest in realized forms or identities (in real organizations) within the same field. Considered in this way, these generic 'blueprints' provide a guide as to the core features or identity-dependent features that are essential for a specific realized organization to fit (see Hannan and Freeman 1989). It is argued that such features are those that 'critically shapes its ability to mobilize support from members, sponsors and authorities' (Minkoff 2002, 381). Thus, it is hypothesized that there are costs inherent – mostly in terms of a loss of legitimacy and thus resources from key audiences – in real organizations departing from established forms. It follows that the realized forms in a field ought to manifest some significant level of form-coherence. As discussed above, audiences need to be able to 'read' a form as legitimate and authentic against known (and valued) generic forms (Zuckerman 1999; Deephouse 1999).[2]

For present purposes, what is salient is that the choices from among these various generic forms are enacted by key agents: in our case group entrepreneurs. Their job is to combine organizational artefacts supplied from existing generic forms into new realized organizations[3] and subsequently, to sell this design as authentic to the set of interests it is to be pressed into service to serve. There is a rich vein of work in sociology that points to the task of leaders in the art of organizational bricolage: those 'who reassemble familiar forms of organization' (Clemens 1996, 206). Leaders or political entrepreneurs are sketched in to a role in organizational change, but there are diverse considerations when 'choosing' organizational forms (see Clemens and Cook 1999, 459). As outlined in the previous chapter, on the one hand, they face incentives to mimic where possible existing and accepted (legitimate) organizational forms; perhaps even 'cloaking' new claims in traditional forms. On the other hand, leaders may also utilize long accepted models of organization in unique ways. Alternatively, leaders may pursue utterly unique forms of organization, but establishing them faces a liability of newness problem. Empirically, bricolage can be identified in, for instance, the (re)combination of organizational elements/categories in new

Assembling group identities in nascent fields 147

and interesting ways. Close to the empirical matter of this book, some talk about the combination of protest and service delivery mission among voluntary associations – the production of so-called hybrid forms (Minkoff 1999).

Of course, an altogether more difficult question is where new organizational forms come from in the first instance? And this is the focus in the present chapter. This has been a blindspot in neo-institutional theories for some time. It is also an issue for sociologically derived variants applied to organizational form, where scholars have typically assumed there is a single dominant model for organizing in play in a given field without always being clear on where this generic blueprint came from (see Baron *et al.* 1999, 542).[4] It is also a problem for ecological approaches because the methods of coding suited to large-n population-level analysis make it difficult to assess where legitimacy comes from, and its direct affect on choices of form. We are asked to assume that accelerated growth in a population is a consequence of a form being established – but it is rare to actually investigate what mechanisms underpin such legitimation. And indeed, studies demonstrate that even though a certain type of product category grows in density, this does not guarantee that this category will achieve the status of form – that is, density itself is no guarantee that audiences will interpret it as a form-like category (with all the incumbent trappings of legitimacy-conferring and sanctioning dynamics) (McKendrick *et al.* 2003). It is therefore no surprise that the organizational social science literature has dedicated much recent attention to the exploring the origins of organizational forms (see Scott 1995, 147; Padgett and Powell 2012).

The question of where forms come from is more acute – and perhaps better accessed empirically – in so-called nascent fields where the rules of the game that might attract legitimacy are less well established (or not immediately self-evident to key actors). Studying the way general organizational forms crystallize in nascent fields – and thence how specific organizations come to occupy specific forms – can be instructive for broader questions of institution-building in organizational social science. However, for our more immediate purposes, it promises to shed light on the processes that underpin the range of organizational forms that are realized by groups we confront every day. In such new fields, resource spaces open up but the style of organization that emerges to populate it is uncertain.

Recent work explores just this question. For example, Rao (1998) addresses the crystallization of the 'consumer watchdog organization' (CWO) form in the US. He shows how increased household consumption coupled with increased product choice, high levels of consumer advertising and lax consumer laws combined to create a 'resource space' for CWOs. But how would organizations filling this space design themselves? Where does the inspiration come from? To be more specific, what might a CWO end up looking like as a style of group organization? His case studies show how two broad variations of a CWO emerged in the field, each drawing on different sources for organizational design (different precursor organizations): the Consumers Union sourced experience

148   *Assembling group identities in nascent fields*

from trade unions, while Consumers Research adopted approaches from standard-setting bodies and the practices of retailers. He argues that 'new forms *do not arise automatically in resource spaces* but have to be constructed from prevalent cultural materials' (Rao 1998, 916, italics added). This resonates very much with the empirical examples of formation presented in Chapter 5.

A similar approach is adopted in analysis of the emergence of 'dedicated biotech firms' in the US. As Powell and Sandholtz (2010, 8) explain, while technological innovation – a series of findings within elite universities – created the conditions for new firms to take up the insights of basic research, design applications and bring them to market, 'they did not determine the path of its development, most notably the organizational form in which this new research would be conducted'. They argue that the 'choice' regarding form – or more accurately two basic forms (and four specific variations) that emerged empirically – were highly contingent: with the emerging form of individual firms 'the result of innumerable social and political choice points, each of which could have radically altered the field's trajectory' (2010, 8). This is not a case of anything goes: organizational entities that are constructed from fragments that span too many fields will cause confusion among key audiences, and hence reduce their capacity to attract resources and legitimacy (see Zuckerman 1999). In the case of biotech start-ups, entrepreneur's approached the question of organizing new firms with expectations established in their past lives in science (university professors) and finance fields (venture capitalists). Over time, the source forms from these two fields merged and produced four new hybrid forms among dedicated biotech firms: the form of specific firms was chiefly informed by the 'prior experiences' of founders (Powell and Sandholtz 2010, 29). Their study identifies the distinctive features of generic forms that operated in the field of early dedicated biotech firms and how real firms borrowed and mixed from them.

As with organization-building generally, in this line of work a key mechanism bringing diversity about is the role of institutional entrepreneurs who try to legitimate ways of organizing by combining existing (and familiar) 'cultural material': this is often referred to as *bricolage* (see Clemens 1996 for a discussion in the context of US groups). Work has pointed to the role of the pre-existing experiences of entrepreneurs as they enter nascent fields, and how these are carried in blueprints or recipes of how an organization ought to be established (see Baron *et al.* 1999). Further work has shown that the where no formal blueprint exists, that entrepreneurs 'carried tacit blueprints from the domains they knew well' (Powell and Sandholz 2010, 13–14; see also Oliver and Montgomery 2000).[5] As Powell and Sandholtz argue,

> when established routines for conducting everyday affairs prove limiting, people begin to search and experiment. In so doing, they draw on their stock of existing knowledge, both formal and tacit, and look around their social worlds for cues about appropriate steps.
>
> (2010, 12)

Assembling group identities in nascent fields 149

This work directs us to several elements in the recipe for organizing in nascent fields: (i) environmental change that opens up space for a new organizational field, (ii) entrepreneurs with experiences that make organizing cognitively accessible, (iii) precursor organizations (and related) fields which are sources of 'material' to organization builders. Each of these provide mechanisms for the (re)combination of fragments of generic forms into new novel realized organizations – which in turn, and over time, may foster new generic forms in their own right.

As we will see, the birth of the UK environmental movement involved the engagement of various fields of endeavour, which created both uncertainty and the seeds for institutional innovation. The movement emerged at the intersection of (at the very least) campaign, conservation, and scientific fields, the engagement between which provided the seeds for unique organizational models, but at the same time made settling on appropriate ways of organizing difficult. The question is how this raw material for organization-building came to be utilized and embodied by contemporary environmental groups. To be clear, the suggestion that the constituent organizational members of the environmental movement are a combination of various models or organizing is not, in itself, unique (see Rawcliffe 1998, 17). However, here this observation is taken a step further by looking at what impact different building blocks have made to specific groups in the sector.

Approach

This chapter reviews the state of the current environmental groups in England, but with an eye to spotting the extent to which they (still) draw on or are influenced by divergent organizing models present in the early years of movement formation. The emphasis here is on family resemblances between current organizations and broad ways of organizing that are taken for granted in fields associated with the establishment of the UK environment movement. As mentioned above, this is a different approach to that applied in Chapter 4, where the emphasis was on identifying a finite number of generic forms – based on a set of predefined and theoretically salient features – and the coding of real groups into a single category. In this chapter key features belong to core generic forms, but we are interested in how these are assembled into new patterns. Moreover, we examine the extent to which borrowing occurs and seek to establish whether new generic forms emerge in this nascent field of the UK environment movement.

Case context

The sample for this chapter is drawn from the contemporary membership of the UK Wildlife and Conservation Link (WCL). More details of this population are available in Chapter 4. Suffice to say that this population provides a convenient microcosm of the modern UK environment movement. Given that the network is self-identifying as an advocacy community, there ought to be little doubt that all

150 *Assembling group identities in nascent fields*

members' have policy aspirations, however indirect or modest they may be. As discussed in Chapter 4, it is in some way a strong test for our method, as it ought to be more prone to isomorphism of organizational form by virtue of its highly integrated and networked nature.

A unique database was compiled utilizing all 37 member organizations as cases. The census year of 2008 was chosen for research convenience – but note, membership of the WCL does change from time to time. Information on each group was gleaned from a range of public sources, including websites, newspaper coverage and press releases. In select cases email or phone correspondence was used to clarify features of specific groups. In addition, several interviews with the then WCL executive officer were undertaken to assist in providing context to specific cases and the network as a whole. The results of this material were synthesized into a database such that each case was comparable along the same set of features.

Coding approach

The basic insight of this conceptual approach is that groups (indeed, organizations generally) possess sets of features or attributes, only some of which are core to the generic form/category that audiences use to filter and assess populations. Moreover, in nascent fields, the salient core attributes are themselves unclear. Thus, we expect group entrepreneurs to borrow and mix elements from other fields which then serve as the raw material for the building of new organizations. Their activities often involve combining elements within a context that is uncertain with respect to what will be acceptable and without a clear sense of implications; thus, change over time is assumed (as information and feedback loops make themselves felt). The first task is, therefore, to identify (i) those fields from which entrepreneurs might borrow and (ii) those features of the generic forms that epitomize each field.

Based on interviews with individuals active in the WCL – and perusal of the literature on the UK environment movement (see overviews by Rawcliffe 1998; Rootes 2009) – it is possible to identify three general fields that are relevant to contemporary environmental group organizing and their related generic forms. These are (a) campaign group, (b) conservation society, and (c) (amateur) scientific society. Table 8.1 sets out the three generic forms and the core features of these forms that serve as the building blocks for the emergence of new or hybrid forms in the environmental advocacy field in the UK. Campaign groups are characterized as engaged in outsider policy activity with the explicit aim of changing public policy. The implicit rationale for this generic model is that policy action is the best way to make change for the environment. By contrast, conservation groups are characterized by on the ground work – directly acting to conserve habitats, buildings or species. The very earliest antecedents in the late 1800s often had the aim of preserving specific sites of environmental or conservation value through direct purchase with funds elicited from elites. Finally, there is a long tradition in Britain of amateur science or natural history societies, whereby

Table 8.1 Generic forms and their core features

Generic forms	Core organizing constructs	Organizational logic	Identifiable features
Campaign group	Political activism	Political change is required to effect on the ground change and use mass membership to leverage political attention	Recruit broadly (open membership) 'Star' media-friendly president Full-time paid leaders Challenging policy strategy Member-funded
Conservation group	Elite benevolence/charity	Preserve biodiversity and the built environment for future generations	Purchase property Volunteer-led Reliance on donor funding Establishment president Royal charter
(Amateur) scientific society	Scientific norms	To directly build and share knowledge in a scholarly manner	Journal to report findings Programme to record field data/trials Organize regular scientific symposia Scientific or academic president In-house paid scientific staff

152 *Assembling group identities in nascent fields*

individuals went on study trips and collected specimens or made observations. The Victorians were well disposed to natural history, which has arguably legitimated a genre of hands-on amateur scientific organizing (separate from learned societies and such like).

Following Powell and Sandholz (2012) I take an inductive approach to identifying the set of features that epitomise these generic forms. The key here is to focus on non-trivial features, those that can be considered core or identity-dependent for each generic form. I first generated a long list of many possible features and then tested whether these were at all evident in the cases and how they resonated with the academic literature. Initial ideas were tested with key informants in the case context to ensure they were as sociologically real as possible (that is, that they meant to participants what I as a researcher assumed them to mean). Having said that, no doubt one could find other features or argue that additional fields are or were relevant. I think the data is of value, and leads to interesting findings in its own right. But even if one has concerns over the data itself, one should focus most on the approach and methods which provide fresh ideas on engaging with the concept of organizational form through population-level work.

The analytical aim here is to plot the ways in which group leaders utilize the organizational material from these several adjacent and potentially relevant fields to develop *real* organizations in a nascent field. Thus, having identified a series of features that resonate with basic sources of form that were evident in our cases I then coded each group in the sample with respect to the features it shared with generic forms.

Analysis

The prevalence of each attribute within the population, along with the criteria for coding, is presented in Table 8.2. As is evident, the process requires a list of attributes that can be coded in a binary manner, and that are easily evident from the viewpoint of a somewhat informed observer. This latter requirement is entirely consistent with the theoretical position which assumes that these categories – to be 'sociologically real' – need to be accessible to the average group audience member (in this case it would include policy makers, other groups, donors and supporters). Here I borrow the coding method that has been used elsewhere to study the emergence of organizational forms (Ruef 2000) and more saliently by Powell and Sandholtz (2012) in their study of form emergence among biotech start-ups in Silicon Valley. The absence (coded 0) or presence (coded 1) of each feature was assessed in each of the 37 group cases and a 'group-attribute' matrix created. The column labelled 'Source' notes the generic group form from which the feature originates. So, 'Member-funded' is from the campaign group form, hence it is labelled C. The next column provides details of how each feature was operationalized in the data collection phase. This is provided in as simple a way as possible to allow ease of replication. The last two columns report the number of groups with each feature, and the percentage total.

Assembling group identities in nascent fields 153

A salient observation at this juncture is the variability by which such properties manifest themselves across our cases. For instance, almost all groups manifest some basic core properties, namely a full-time leadership and the practice of recruiting openly. At the other end of the spectrum, only a handful of groups have a scientific journal or run field trials or similar scientific activities. Reflecting on the 'source code' for each property, we might make the early observation that the most common features derive from the campaign group form. By contrast, the features of the amateur scientific society seem to resonate less across our cases. However, the relative frequency with which specific features are evident in aggregate across our cases is of less salience than the way these are combined within single group organizations.

Table 8.3 provides statistics for correlations among the set of group attributes. While such statistics are rightly to be treated with caution given the low number of observations, they nevertheless point to some obvious relationships that will be salient when we consider clusters of group cases in a moment.[6] For instance, 'organizing scientific symposia' and 'scientific president' are both highly and positively correlated with having a 'journal to report scientific findings'. This at face value suggests a strong coherence between features that all 'belong' to the same 'amateur scientific society' source code. By contrast having 'in-house scientific staff' is significantly and positively correlated with 'field trials' and 'purchasing property': yet the latter belongs to the Conservation source code, suggesting some borrowing is likely. This exercise is also revealing for another reason. Namely, it highlights areas where categories end being mutually exclusive. The statistic of $r=-1.00$ for 'donor-funded' and 'member-funded' highlights that these are mutually exclusive categories. No actual group is majority-member and donor-funded.

Let's move this to an analysis of the groups themselves. Table 8.4 shows the percentage of features each case study group 'borrowed' from each generic source. The aim here is to identify the diverse sources apparent in organization-building by environmental groups in the UK. To this end, I started by exploring the extent to which groups in the sample shared features sourced from the three fields of political activism, conservation and science.

The first column provides a count of the number of overall features each group manifests, regardless of source. Apart from the final column, which I will come to in a moment, the rest of the analysis is broken down by generic form. In each subsection, the number of features each group exhibits from that specific generic form is noted. The *ratio* column reports the number of features each group manifest for each source, divided by the total possible number of features (there are five sets of features for each source). That is, ratio is calculated as $ratio=n/5$. This is akin to similar measures used to assess group of membership of a given case in a specific 'set' (see discussion in Negro *et al.* 2010b).[7]

The final column provides a figure for each case, and the table is sorted from highest to lowest according to this score. The *Herfindahl index* is a standard measure of diversity utilized in the social sciences. The HHI score is widely used in the field of economics and business to describe levels of competition in

Table 8.2 Frequency of features amongst population

	Features	Source	Operationalization	N	%
1	Recruit broadly (open membership)	C	Joining the group is not restricted	35	0.95
2	Full-time paid leadership staff	C	A group's day-to-day activities are organized by a full-time paid staff member	33	0.89
3	Member-funded	C	A majority of the group's funding comes from member subscriptions	23	0.62
4	In-house paid scientific staff	S	A group employs professional full-time paid scientific staff	17	0.46
5	Program to record field data/trials	S	The group organizes a data-collection programme involving members	16	0.43
6	Donor-funded	K	A majority of the groups funding comes from a donor (not including supporters annual donations)	14	0.38
7	Purchase property	K	A group has purchased or has been gifted property relevant to conservation activities (not including things like office space)	13	0.35
8	'Star' media-friendly president	C	The president is a well-known public personality (profile predates group role)	8	0.22
9	Challenging policy strategy	C	Engaged in at least one protest event	7	0.19
10	Volunteer-led	K	A groups day-to-day activities are organized by unpaid volunteers	6	0.16
11	High social status – 'establishment' – president	K	Group appoints noted establishment figure as president (e.g. royal family member)	6	0.16
12	'Scientific' or 'academic' president	S	Group appoints established scientist as president	5	0.14
13	Royal charter	K	The group is awarded a royal charter	5	0.14
14	Organize regular scientific symposia	S	The group organizes an annual scientific meeting where academic-style papers are given	4	0.11
15	Journal to report findings	S	A publication along the lines of an academic journal is published under the auspices of the group	3	0.08

Note
C, Campaign; K, Conservation; S, Scientific society.

Table 8.3 Correlations among group features, WCL members

Variable	1	2	3	4	5	6	7	8	9	10	11	12	13	14	15
Recruit broadly (open membership)	1														
Full-time paid leadership staff	−0.083	1													
Member-funded	0.060	0.267	1												
In-house paid scientific staff	−0.259	0.321	−0.511†	1											
Programme to record field data/trials	−0.033	0.128	−0.331*	0.509†	1										
Donor-funded	−0.060	−0.267	−1.00†	0.511†	0.331*	1									
Purchase property	−0.325*	0.256	−0.243	0.571†	0.386*	0.243	1								
'Star' media-friendly president	0.126	−0.029	0.004	0.043	0.204	−0.004	0.026	1							
Challenging policy strategy	0.115	−0.054	0.235	−0.445†	−0.422†	−0.235	−0.356*	−0.254	1						
Volunteer-led	0.105	−0.791†	−0.110	−0.406*	−0.088	0.110	−0.324	−0.053	−0.025	1					
High social status – 'establishment' – president	−0.219	0.153	0.192	0.183	−0.236	−0.192	0.137	−0.231	−0.025	−0.194	1				
'Scientific' or 'academic' president	0.094	−0.117	−0.344*	0.111	0.134	0.344*	0.040	−0.208	−0.191	0.255	−0.174	1			
Royal charter	−0.255	0.138	0.145	0.429†	−0.026	−0.145	0.537†	−0.016	−0.191	−0.174	0.470†	0.075	1		
Organize regular scientific symposia	0.083	−0.159	−0.267	0.028	0.047	0.267	−0.074	0.029	−0.168	0.319	−0.153	0.626†	−0.138	1	
Journal to report findings	0.071	−0.215	−0.177	−0.075	−0.059	0.177	−0.219	−0.156	−0.143	0.407*	−0.131	0.751†	−0.117	0.853†	1

Notes
* Correlation is significant at the 0.05 level (two-tailed).
† Correlation is significant at the 0.01 level (two-tailed).

Table 8.4 Borrowing of features across generic forms

Group name	Total attributes	Campaign		Science		Conservation		HHI
		N	ratio	N	ratio	N	ratio	
Campaign for National Parks	4	4	0.8	0	0.0	0	0.0	1.00
Campaign Whale	4	4	0.8	0	0.0	0	0.0	1.00
CPRE	4	4	0.8	0	0.0	0	0.0	1.00
Environmental Investigation Agency	4	4	0.8	0	0.0	0	0.0	1.00
FoE	4	4	0.8	0	0.0	0	0.0	1.00
Greenpeace UK	4	4	0.8	0	0.0	0	0.0	1.00
World Society for the Protection of Animals	4	4	0.8	0	0.0	0	0.0	1.00
British Mountaineering Council	3	3	0.6	0	0.0	0	0.0	1.00
International Fund for Animal Welfare	3	3	0.6	0	0.0	0	0.0	1.00
Ramblers	3	3	0.6	0	0.0	0	0.0	1.00
WWF UK	5	4	0.8	0	0.0	1	0.2	0.68
Marine Conservation Society	4	3	0.6	0	0.0	1	0.2	0.63
Open Spaces Society	4	3	0.6	0	0.0	1	0.2	0.63
Bat Conservation Trust	6	4	0.8	2	0.4	0	0.0	0.56
Amphibian and Reptile Conservation	5	3	0.6	2	0.4	0	0.0	0.52
Hawk and Owl Trust	6	4	0.8	1	0.2	1	0.2	0.50
Marine Connection	4	2	0.4	0	0.0	2	0.4	0.50
The Shark Trust	4	2	0.4	0	0.0	2	0.4	0.50
Woodland Trust	5	3	0.6	1	0.2	1	0.2	0.44
Council for British Archaeology	7	2	0.4	4	0.8	1	0.2	0.43

The Mammal Society	8	3	0.6	4	0.8	1	0.2	0.41
Buglife	5	3	0.6	2	0.4	1	0.2	0.39
The (Royal Society of) Wildlife Trusts	6	2	0.4	1	0.2	3	0.6	0.39
Universities Federation for Animal Welfare	6	1	0.2	3	0.6	2	0.4	0.39
RSPCA	7	3	0.6	1	0.2	3	0.6	0.39
The National Trust	7	3	0.6	1	0.2	3	0.6	0.39
Badger Trust	4	2	0.4	1	0.2	1	0.2	0.38
RSPB	8	4	0.8	2	0.4	2	0.4	0.38
Association of River Trusts	5	1	0.2	2	0.2	2	0.4	0.36
Froglife	5	2	0.4	2	0.4	1	0.2	0.36
Grassland Trust	5	2	0.4	1	0.2	2	0.4	0.36
Wildfowl and Wetlands Trust	7	2	0.4	3	0.6	2	0.4	0.35
Butterfly Conservation	8	3	0.6	3	0.6	2	0.4	0.34
Zoological Society of London	8	2	0.4	3	0.6	3	0.6	0.34
Plantlife	6	2	0.4	2	0.4	2	0.4	0.33
Pondconservation	6	2	0.4	2	0.4	2	0.4	0.33
Whale and Dolphin Conservation Society	6	2	0.4	2	0.4	2	0.4	0.33

158 *Assembling group identities in nascent fields*

industry sectors. The HHI has, however, been used in political science; and in the study of group mobilization in a public policy context (see Gray and Lowery 2000; Halpin and Binderkrantz 2011; Halpin and Thomas 2012a). As Gray and Lowery (2000, 97) suggest, HHI measures offer *descriptions* of concentration/diversity. It is used here as a convenient way to show the relative mix of the features from each three generic forms utilized by groups in organization-building. A HHI score is calculated for each individual group based on the way they borrow features from across the three broad sources identified above. These scores theoretically range from 0.00 to 1.00 depending on the distribution of each group's borrowing of features. For example, a group might have nine features all up – with three out of five features from each of the three sources. It would have a HHI score (calculated as $(3/9^2)+(3/9^2)+(3/9^2)$) equal to 0.33. By contrast a group that has five features in all, but all from one source – say the campaign source – would have a HHI score (calculated as $(5/5^2)+(0/5^2)+(0/5^2)$) equal to 1.00. Thus, in a situation where a group has a score of 1.00 it shows that all features came from the same category, while a lower index score shows a more mixed and even distribution across all three categories.

In other work, a frequency score is used to assess – at the organizational level – generality *versus* specialization of its identity (see Pontikes 2012, 95, who uses a sum of the number of labels used by firms). Others refer to a similar measure as the 'niche width' within a given identity space (Negro *et al.* 2010a) (see chapter nine). Given that the interest here is in the share of features drawn from across three broad generic forms, the HHI measure serves as a more sophisticated organizational-level measure of this dimension of generality.

So far the analysis has focused on the way groups match up with attributes belonging to generic forms (which themselves have origins many decades ago). But how reliably are these broad generic forms replicated in actual organizations? Table 8.4 provides some hints. Ten groups have a Herfindahl index core of 1.0, which means their attributes are drawn from only one form (in this case the campaign form). This might suggest that the campaign form is more or less reliably replicated in some contemporary groups. Yet the irrefutable result from this analysis is that many groups draw attributes across two, sometimes three, generic forms. There is ample hybridity evident in building group identities.

To examine how distinctive these forms are in this contemporary set of group cases, an alternative approach is to measure label- or categorical-*contrast* (see Hannan *et al.* 2007). This is a shift from the organizational level to the category or generic form level. In essence, it is about assessing the extent to which generic forms are realized in a population. Admittedly this is most salient – and revealing – when attempted in a time-series manner, because one can determine whether generic forms are firming up or softening at the edges. But for now, our static picture provides some clear pointers as to how this work might be attempted in the group field.

In a first step, one measures the Grade of Membership (GoM) of each group in each of the three form categories: this is measured as the proportion of each group's total attributes that are from each form category.[8] The GoM for each group

Assembling group identities in nascent fields 159

in each 'form' is calculated and recorded from 0–1. Then, the degree of fuzzy density of each form is calculated by summing the GoM of each group in each form. This is effectively a proxy for the number of members within a population in a given generic form (Pontikes 2012, 95). The measure for contrast – defined as a measure of boundary strength between categories – is calculated as the fuzzy density divided by the number of non-zero cases (see Pontikes 2012, 94). Contrast is a crucial measure here because it captures the extent to which the generic form itself is actually a clear and firm category. Put another way, while as a researcher I have tried to firm up and justify that each of the three forms is indeed clear and differentiated from one another, this measure assesses the degree to which this turns out to be the case empirically. Given that we are examining a nascent field – the environment movement – we would not expect all categories to be replicated, we expect to see hybridization (borrowing of features across generic forms). These statistics are recorded for the above data in Table 8.5.

The results of these measures at the form level demonstrate that the campaign form is by far and away the most popular form in aggregate. In terms of the extent to which its attributes are broadly spread in 'real' groups in the sample, as measured by fuzzy density, it has the broadest reach. Thought of in something akin to 'whole group equivalents', there are around 22 groups composed of campaign group attributes, with roughly seven each for science and conservation group. What about the degree to which each generic form emerges in our empirical data with the same clarity as it was laid out generically? The data shows that the campaign form also has a relatively high contrast compared to scientific and conservation forms. Put another way, the latter two generic forms are not often reliably replicated in single real organizations. Instead attributes are adopted, for the most part, by groups that are dominated by campaign group attributes.

Conclusion

The organizational studies literature itself struggles with developing persuasive accounts as to how forms emerge over time. Traction over this type of gap requires attention to nascent fields where entrepreneurs *must* try and develop new organizational identities, but amidst uncertainty as to what is appropriate. Here, taking the context of environmental groups in the UK, we could examine and detect the traces of source codes from abutting (and established) fields. This is after the fact, and undoubtedly many groups in this population will have changed or (re)fashioned their identities over time, drawing closer or moving farther away from generic forms.

Table 8.5 Measures of form fuzziness and contrast

Measures	Campaign group	Scientific society	Conservation group
Fuzzy density	22.26	7.14	7.60
Contrast	0.60	0.32	0.30

160 *Assembling group identities in nascent fields*

Those building organizations in nascent fields are confronted with the initial challenge of deciding how to organize in the absence of clear guidance as to the 'proper' way to do so. Interest group entrepreneurs are no different. This chapter illustrates the style of work that can be deployed to trace the material provided by generic forms from which groups fashion their precise identities. Moreover, it suggests tools to assess the empirical coherence of the generic forms that might emerge over time as nascent fields mature.

A more persuasive approach would be to detect the way these traces accumulate (or not) over time. The next chapter takes up this point by tracing the way that forms themselves come to solidify and change over time using explicitly categorical data. Moreover, it starts to develop an audience-perspective on the way groups develop identities from existing categories.

Notes

1 Trying to parse out these approaches is increasingly difficult because they share authors and many key references. For instance, Rao has published with ecologists, institutionalists and those pursuing an explicitly categorical approach. What they have in common, as discussed in Chapter 3, is an identity-based approach to form.
2 Another set of terminologies amount to much the same thing. McKendrick *et al.* (2003) make a distinction between identities of specific organizations and the emergence of forms. The former can exist without them necessarily coalescing into a form recognized by key audiences. They observe that 'disk array' firms existed yet the market did not recognize this as a discrete form – instead preferring to talk of data storage companies, within which disk array technology was one aspect of their business.
3 This may be a set of individuals, but for ease of explanation this is phrased in the singular.
4 This latter point is one reason why institutional approaches are often criticised for not dealing with power – one might validly assume that blueprints represent or embody societal or economic power relations at a given time.
5 There is also a long-standing concern with imprinting processes; specifically the notion that organizations are imprinted with the logic of the time in which they were formed (Stinchcombe 1965). The presumption was always that a 'period effect' would encourage conformance: organizations formed at the same time, facing the same conditions, would resort to similar recipes or blueprints. But more recent work has focused on the breadth of recipes utilized, even among closely knit sets of organizations working in the same field and born concurrently (Baron *et al.* 1999).
6 Powell and Sandholtz (2012, 99) suggest that pearson's r statistics are considered relevant even with small numbers of observations when above the 0.5 level and with $p < 0.05$ level.
7 But see important differences in discussion below between ratio and GoM.
8 Please note that this differs from the ratio reported in Table 8.4. The ratio records how many attributes in each generic form a group manifests. The GoM by contrast simply records how many – out of the total attributes a given group has – are from each generic form. For example, Campaign for National Parks has a 0.8 ratio for campaign form, but this turn out to be a GoM of 1.0 in the campaign form because 100 per cent of its four total attributes come from the campaign form.

9 Evolving group identities

The role of 'categories' and audience

Introduction

A key proposition driving this volume is that when group scholars address the question of organization, they ought to spend more time asking 'what style of organization' is formed, or maintained, or is engaging in policy advocacy. An implication of this approach is that we ought to probe how it is that sets of interests come to adopt the specific organizational designs – or sets of organizational designs – that they do.

As established in Chapter 7, niche-inspired accounts foster expectations of differentiation, but do not provide clear guidance – sufficient to derive testable expectations – with respect to what might shape the dimensions around which difference can be constructed. Further, Chapter 7 established that groups are likely to strategize in a manner that is a balance between difference and similarity. Chapter 8 addressed the population-level picture through the application of institutional and categorical theories from organizational social science. Chapter 8 focused on the establishment of new generic group categories/forms through the emerging identities of environmental groups in the UK. The focus was on how entrepreneurs defined themselves through borrowing and combining practices from abutting fields of endeavour.

In this chapter the aim is to take this perspective further, by problematizing the notion that groups 'fit' fixed group forms. I explore how generic forms – this time conceptualized as categories – themselves evolve through processes of borrowing and (re)combination. In turn, I show how some categories become weak, while others firm up. In addition, I focus on the audience perspective on group categorization. As outlined in Chapter 3, one area where organizational social science scholarship is growing rapidly concerns the role of audiences in establishing and enforcing organizational forms. They use categories – fashioned by intermediaries – to interpret the identity claims of real organizations. In group scholarship to date, identity-based approaches have mostly considered the way groups try and fashion their identity, not how it might interact with audiences. Here the intention is to use data that enables one to take the question of audience seriously when identifying generic forms and how specific organizational entities fashion their specific identities. For ease of discussion and analysis, the same sample of UK environment groups analysed in Chapters 4 and 8 is utilized here.

162   *Evolving group identities*

The British environmental movement: blending and mixing forms

While the general interest group literature is largely silent on the issue of organizational form, sector specialists are more attentive to qualitative differences across sets of related groups, and over time. The literature on the antecedents of the modern UK environment movement observes several broad – but by no means neat or orderly – phases of organizational development. A review of the literature provides a narrative as follows (see also discussion in Chapters 4 and 8).

Very early organizations emerged as 'Societies' in the late 1800s with the aim of preserving specific sites of environmental or conservation value through direct purchase with funds elicited from elites. Legislative aims were pursued by influence owing to personal contacts among wealthy benefactors, ministers and parliamentarians. Many of these groups also had an amateur science or natural history element to them, whereby individuals went on study trips and collected specimens or made observations (Rootes 2009, 205). Post-First World War organizations continued in much the same mode, but targeted new social conditions. The Ramblers targeted the working class and their demand for access to the countryside, while the Campaign to Protect Rural England (CPRE) organized middle-class professionals opposed to pressures for uncontrolled urbanization of rural areas (as soldiers return from war), and achieved influence by virtue of the vocational position of its members (as planners and architects) (Rootes 2009, 206). According to Rawcliffe these groups tended to be based on more decentralized structures – given planning and access emphasis (1998, 16). The post-Second World War period saw development of specialized nature protection groups, such as the Mammal Society.

According to students of the UK environment movement, a key break point was the formation of the WWF UK, in 1961. It was

> A bridge between old and the new, WWF was, like the early nature conservation organizations, an elite initiative to raise funds for wildlife conservation, enjoying royal patronage and relying on wealthy individuals for initial funding. But in a foretaste of what was to come a decade later, it employed mass media to broadcast its message.
>
> (Rootes 2009, 208)

The WWF-UK was launched in the pages of the *Daily Mirror* – a mass-market newspaper – and it was a mass membership group from the beginning. Perhaps the other most well-known organization in this field is the Friends of the Earth (FoE). While it is often considered as at the 'vanguard of the new environmentalism' it is also true that there were 'important continuities' (Rootes 2009, 209). Its dedication to scientific argument and use of old-fashioned 'dossiers of information' to win arguments were consistent with old peers. As Rootes says, perhaps the 'novelty of FoE consisted in the [outsider] *style* of its actions rather

Evolving group identities   163

than the substance of its campaigns' (2009, 209). Greenpeace took over the protest action mantle as FoE cooled off. Both groups were mass member, but never claimed to be internally democratic. They were vehicles to fund activist protest.

What is immediately obvious here is that in the scholarly imaginary, specific (usually well-known) groups serve as symbols of more generic organizational models. This is, of course, one way to get one's head around the idea of variation in form. Key high-profile groups serve as ideal types on one or other set of dimensions. Another is to work with more basic dimensions like aim or key activity. O'Riordan (cited in Rawcliffe 1998, 20) suggests five 'types': those groups that 'manage land for conservation purposes', 'campaign or lobby for policy change', 'service other groups through fundraising, coordination or support services', 'do research or practice environmental education, training' or 'practice civil disobedience'. This type of discussion supports the style of analysis using group form developed in Chapter 4: setting out a limited number of generic forms, and allocating groups to the one they most resemble.

Yet another reading of the above could equally conclude what is more striking than outright difference among groups is the extent to which individual groups *share or blend characteristics*. Indeed, just this point is underlined by Rawcliffe, who reflects that 'the environmental movement in Britain is today a synthesis of both old and new' (1998, 17). If one dwells on it for a moment, this seemingly innocuous statement raises critical questions for group scholars: how does this process of synthesis occur? And what guides this dynamic process? This chapter probes the general processes of (institutional) borrowing, mixing and blending among organizational forms, utilizing the case of UK environmental groups. As will become evident, it does so in a slightly different manner from the preceding chapter: the focus here is on categorical theories which direct attention to forms as cultural objects that emerge and take effect in the context of audience perceptions and assumptions about appropriateness.

Categories, classification and differentiation

Categorical theories have become increasingly influential in organizational social science (see Negro *et al.* 2010b for a comprehensive review). The core focus of such theories is the basic observation that the social world is subject to constant categorization, it makes the world intelligible, and at the same time provides structures and order. Organizations are subject to categorization, which defines 'what organizations are expected to be by their members and other social agents' and in turn 'affects the social, cultural, and material resources available to them' (Negro *et al.* 2010b, 4). Thus scholars in this genre seek to understand the development and impact of categories and classification on social and economic spheres of activity.[1]

The orthodox deployment of categorical theories has been around their value in simplifying the complexity for market participants in locating relevant products. Once established, systems of classification and categorization – often by

164 *Evolving group identities*

third parties (like restaurant reviews, film critics, or bank ratings agencies) – serve as cognitive maps that enable consumers to understand the complexity of the market. Yet, categories are also important for helping organizations relate to others: as Schneiberg and Berk (2010, 256) suggest 'categories help answer the question, "who are my peers?"'. What is highly salient for our present purposes is that 'even without enforcement', they can 'unleash potent pressures for conformity and homogeneity' (Schneiberg and Berk 2010, 256–7). In short categories – as encapsulated in classification systems – are the '*cognitive infrastructures* of markets ... by which firms and others make sense of, locate themselves and others within, and give shape and order to markets' (Schneiberg and Berk 2010, 259).They go further: 'They serve ... as cognitive interfaces by which firms orient their activities towards competitors and trading partners, their own production processes, and even ... their past and future selves' (Schneiberg and Berk 2010, 259). While categorical theories are most often deployed to explain 'mediated markets' (e.g. how markets for restaurants, investment products, actors, and films are structured) they are equally relevant to understanding allied phenomenon in the field of political organization like voluntary associations (Mohr and Guerra-Pearson, 2010) political parties (Karthikeyan and Wezel 2010) and social movements (Minkoff 1999).

Why should realized organizational entities pay attention to generic organizational categories? These categories come to discipline the work of entities in several interesting ways. Most saliently, research has shown how organizations that boundary-cross – span more than one category – face the problem of identity confusion and thus are more prone to mortality and performance hazards. Because categories serve the function of limiting attention and reducing search costs to market participants, firms that are easily recognizable against existing categories risk missing their market. Put simply, 'If categorical divides are accepted by audiences [possessing resources], organizations that do not attend to them meet market disappointments' (Negro *et al.* 2010b, 13). Of course, audiences may not be united in expectations, and from here we might find the origins of diversity – rather than the expectations of isomorphism inherent in early formulations. Moreover, categories can, of course, be fuzzy. Early ecological work treated populations of say universities, as the set of organizations that *fully* shared those core features attributed to that form. More recently, it has been argued that this overplays the crispness of population boundaries and of category belonging: emphasis is now on the *degree* of membership (or GoM) of specific organizations in established categories (Hannan 2010). The same basic sentiment expressed is in the literature on organizational hybridity and hybrid identities (Albert and Whetten 1985, 270).

While category-spanning might be avoided because it leads to audience confusion – and associated loss of legitimacy and resources – there is another mechanism at play that provides incentives for organizations to adopt a form that aligns with single categories. Organizations that focus their attention on a single category will develop knowledge and expertise associated with their line of work (whatever that may be), and thus an (important) by-product is that the quality of

Evolving group identities 165

the organizations with simple identities is likely to be greater than that of those with complex identities (see Hannan 2010). This is easier to detect and test in cases of product categories – say wine production or restaurant quality – than in organizational categories in the group field. Nevertheless, it is an expectation that could be useful as a hypothesis for group scholars to test empirically.

How do categories fit into concepts like organizational form? Categorical theories have required a rethink in terms of operating with the concept of form; specifically a shift to a social constructivist rather than organizational features based approach. This has meant that the mainstream ecological approach has shifted direction: 'The shift of attention to audiences and category boundaries has reoriented work within organizational ecology ... forms are not distinguished by organizational architectures but involve social and cultural typifications' (Negro *et al.* 2010b, 7). In short, whereas early empirical approaches utilized 'industrial or product-market distinctions to specify organizational forms' this categorical approach emphasizes 'the perceptions of audience members when specifying forms and their boundaries' (Negro *et al.* 2010b, 8). This is, however, not to say that we ignore the structures and core features literally embodied in the real organizations we study. Categories in fact *imply* an adherence to an underlying set of features: that is, to retain category membership, an organization must possess (or be *assumed* to possess) the *core* characteristics and properties that are crucial to the category. Thus, the threat of penalties or punishment (such as withdrawal of resources, custom or legitimacy) from deviating away from the form underpinning a category is the force that drives conformance to category/form distinctions (Rao *et al.* 2005, 988).[2]

What about the creation of new categories? The study of the development of film genres shows that film producers take great care in fostering an identity for their new film: an identity which draws on elements of established genres – thus gaining legitimate acceptance from audiences – yet blended with new elements. Over time, such blending can generate new genres altogether (see Jensen 2010). Simply, organizations are often both well aware of the implications of their identity and the difficulties in making tactical switches. Yet they may seek to overcome this constraint through *obscuring* identities. Commercial brewers had trouble authentically presenting themselves as the producers of 'microbrewed' beer, because consumers were purchasing the brewers' identity, and not the features of the beer itself. This forced brewers to obscure their identity through creation of allied brands or spin-off business units that looked like convincing microbreweries (Carrol and Swaminathan 2000). Just this type of phenomenon occurs with interest groups. This explains why a group like the RSPB – an encompassing environmental lobbying organization – would launch and fund smaller groups – like Buglife – rather than take on invertebrate conservation issues 'in-house'.

How does this relate to interest groups? This approach, it is suggested, provides some important cues for how group scholars might proceed in further developing a research agenda based on a concept like organizational form. Groups can be conceived as navigating design decisions with respect to existing

166 *Evolving group identities*

categories – what I have previously called generic forms – that have varying degrees of acceptance among key audiences. Audiences include insiders – in the group context, members or donors – and outsiders – in the group context these are typically policy makers or the general public. These choices to borrow or conform with such generic forms/categories, it is argued, are the 'stuff' that group entrepreneurs build groups from. Thus, in terms of understanding the content – rather than the mechanism – through which group organizational identities are built, categorical theories have much to offer.

To summarize, the specific realized form or identity of a group at a given moment ought to approximate an existing – and legitimate – category (the label) and its realized organizational strategies/features fit the associated schema (key expected features) otherwise it risks lower attention, less resources and poorer performance. However, as discussed in Chapter 7, groups face a twofold strategy. First, to seem like they belong to a category – say an environmental group – but, second, and at the same time, be distinctive enough to be uniquely attractive to key audiences – say an advocacy versus a direct action environmental group. The expectation is of a twofold set of imperatives for group entrepreneurs: to appear to fit existing forms (or even the dominant form) while also seeking to be distinctive among peers (Deephouse 1996; see also Pedersen and Dobbin 2006).

Context and data source

A central challenge in investigating the way organizations utilize categories to shape their identities is finding convincing data. As discussed above, a core mechanism in categorical theories of organizational form and identity is that of audience perceptions of identity. To summarize, audiences interpret claims about identity by first categorizing groups, and thereafter focusing on differences; in response, organizations take efforts to craft identities that respect prevailing categories such that they attract understanding, thus (hopefully) legitimacy and ultimately resources. How might we be able to tap this process in the group universe?

One approach might be to probe contemporary self-presentations offered by groups, say through websites or similar (much like Heaney 2007). Yet, the absence of time-series data based on web pages makes it difficult to explore one of the more interesting aspects of form 'choice', namely the question of how (or if) design changes over time. Moreover, it makes it difficult to see how groups navigate the various 'available' categories in terms of identity: that is, which identity positions do they try to occupy and which do they seek to avoid? An alternative is to utilize some kind of publicly available directory. When categorical approaches are applied to market settings, it is suggested that categories emerge, and are reproduced, by 'middle-men' who reduce the search costs of information gathering and sorting of organizations for 'consumers' in complex organizational landscapes. Thus, scholars tend to use data sources that tap the categories embedded in evaluations and typifications of market intermediaries. For instance, scholars analyse the field of gourmet restaurants by utilizing the *Michelin Guide* (Rao *et*

Evolving group identities 167

al. 2005), the field of Listed Companies by utilizing the categories of investment analysts (Zuckerman 1999), the field of acting and film making by probing the categories utilized by film critics or casting agents (Zuckerman *et al.* 2003).

In this chapter I utilize data on UK environment groups contained in publicly available directories as a way to approximate the category/identity (and mix of categories/identities) that they adhere to at different points in time. This type of source is widely used in population-level studies of organizational dynamics (see Mohr and Guerra-Pearson, 2010; Johnson 2008; Walker *et al.* 2011 to name but a few). Specifically, I utilize the *Directory of British Associations* (hereafter referred to as the DBA), the first volume of which was produced in 1965. In preparation for each edition the compliers ask groups to submit (or revise) their entries, enabling them to adjust their profile. For our purposes this pattern – and adjustments – provide a proxy for a groups projected identity (which categories do they claim to belong to?). A key feature of the directory is that it asks groups themselves to self-report their key activities along a set of more or less constant categories. I use this entry data to approximate the breadth and complexity of the identity of each group against activity categories relevant to all British associations. I assess the mix of such categorical belonging among a discrete set of environmental groups: those that belong to the Countryside and Wildlife Link (as utilized in Chapters 4 and 8).

Why use this data? The DBA has been used elsewhere to approximate the British national group population (see Jordan and Greenan 2012). It is the most reliable single source of data on group populations, and as Jordan and Greenan suggest 'An indicator that the directory *is* reasonably reliable is that it has satisfied its market and has publishing stability; that is, a preliminary pointer to accuracy is its commercial survival' (2012, 80). One might ask, however, to what extent are groups operating in a 'mediated market'? And can the DBA (and its compilers) be considered akin to the role of restaurant review guides or wine guides? The DBA can be taken as a loose approximation of a guide to insiders as to the identity of a given group at a point in time. On the DBA compilers website, one finds comments like, '*It's an excellent guide and one we use on a regular basis* Department for Business, Enterprise and Regulatory Reform (BERR)'. Such comments support the use of the DBA as a mediator of the British market for associative advocacy. Lastly, how useful are the codes I utilize here as a proxy for a given group's projected identity? In discussing the use of these codes, the DBA editors explain that the codes proved necessary because the group name alone did not make a groups' purpose immediately apparent (DBA, various). This illustrates the intrinsic importance of codes to guide the audience as to that substantive form of each group that is listed – names increasingly do not suffice.

In this analysis, data is taken from several volumes of the directory. The first edition in 1965 is selected, then volumes at various increments to give a sense of change over time. While the original data set includes entries from 12 annual editions, our interest here is in broad trends, which can be easily gauged by looking at periodic snapshots.

168 *Evolving group identities*

Results

This section outlines the results of longitudinal analysis of the DBA entries for a selected number of UK environmental groups. Analysis concerns two basic processes. The first concerns the emergence, firmness and relative strength of the generic forms that groups in this population draw upon, as represented by the system categories utilized in the DBA volumes over time. This is an analysis of a system of group forms (operationalized as categories) rather than groups themselves. The second concerns the use of this system of categories/forms by our sample of groups over time. Here we are concerned with (i) the extent to which groups adopt focused or blurred identities (i.e. extent of category-spanning) and (ii) how identity focus changes over time.

How firm are these categories?

While groups might seek to shape their identities through changes in – or mixes of – categories identified in the DBA, this does not tell us whether these categories are themselves firm and robust. As has been pointed out elswhere, there is an important difference bewteen organizations that construct blurry identities – by category-spanning – and those that seek to create a simple identity – by not category-spanning – but are confounded in their efforts by doing so through a blurry category (Pontikes 2012, 94–5). Thus, here we make a distinction between the act of choosing single or simple categories by groups, on the one hand, and the firmness or fuzziness of the categories themselves. The implications here are that fashioning an identity from fuzzy categories will both undermine the value of a focused (simple) identity and further compound the cost of fashioning a diverse and unfocused (complex) identity.

To examine how sharp these categories are, I generate two measures. First, I calculated the Grade of Membership (GoM) of each group in each of the categories *used in that year*. For instance, if in the year 2010 the RSPB nominates k and l as categories it belongs to, then its GoM for that year is 0.5 in each. The GoM for each group in each category is calculated and recorded from 0–1. This measure becomes the raw material for assessing categories themselves. Then, I calculated the degree of fuzzy density of each category by summing the GoM of each group that nominated each category. So, for example, the RSPB would contribute 0.5 to the GoM figure for both the k and l categories. The measure for 'label contrast' – defined as a measure of boundary strength between categories – is calculated as the fuzzy density divided by the number of non-zero cases (see Pontikes 2012, 94). This measure is a proxy for the strength of a given category vis-à-vis other categories in use. If lots of groups claim a very partial membership in category v, but all then have very large membership in category k, the strength of category is going to be low. Thought of more intuitively, using this example, the meaning attributed to category v is low because its essence is hard for audiences to understand. It is hard work out what it stands for.

Table 9.1 Category measures of fuzziness and label contrast, DBA entries selected years

Category	2009		2002		1992		1982		1965	
	Fuzzy density	*Contrast*	*Fuzzy density*	*Contrast*	*Fuzzy density*	*Contrast*	*Fuzzy density*	*Contrast*	*Fuzzy density*	*Contrast*
Breed society (b)	0.33	0.33	0.00	0.00	0.00	0.00	0.00	0.00	0.00	0.00
Education (e)	0	0.00	0.00	0.00	0.00	0.00	0.25	0.25	0.00	0.00
General interest/hobby (g)	3.66	0.61	2.33	0.58	2.50	0.83	0.00	0.00	4.00	1.00
Campaign/pressure group (k)	10.33	0.74	8.50	0.77	6.00	0.75	1.00	1.00	1.00	1.00
Learned/scientific society (l)	1.99	0.40	1.66	0.42	1.83	0.46	1.25	0.42	3.00	1.00
Coordinating body (n)	0.83	0.42	0.83	0.42	1.00	0.50	0.50	0.50	0.00	0.00
Research organization (q)	1.16	0.39	0.83	0.42	0.83	0.42	0.75	0.38	0.00	0.00
Sports (s)	1.33	0.67	2.00	1.00	2.00	1.00	2.00	1.00	1.00	1.00
Vet and animal welfare (v)	2.33	0.58	2.83	0.71	2.83	0.71	2.25	0.75	2.00	1.00
Number of groups	**22**		**19**		**17**		**8**		**11**	

Source: DBA entries, various (authors own data).

170 *Evolving group identities*

Another way to get a sense of trends in 'category strength' over time is to focus on the fuzzy density measure. It can usefully be thought of as a measure something akin to 'whole group equivalents': so, in 2009 we can say that of the 22 groups in the population, 10.33 whole group equivalents identified as campaign groups. This measure enables one to explicitly embrace the fact that real groups will often claim to identify with several organizational forms, and thus it sums up the overall strength to which a population draws on differing forms. However, it is calculated in such a way that makes comparison over time – across years – of the headline figure problematic (especially if the composition and size of the population differs between observations). One solution is to simply divide the fuzzy density measure by the number of cases per observation period, expressed as a percentage. Thus, taking the example above, 10.33 whole group equivalents identified as campaign groups, divided by 22 observations, which gives a percentage of 46. This is referred to here as 'category strength'. One could conclude then that in 2009, the strength of the campaign group form/category was 46 per cent.

Figure 9.1 presents the measures of category strength for the same time series discussed in earlier tables. It may be read as follows. A time-series is presented for each generic category, with the statistic for 2009 on the left and each successive earlier observation to the right. Of course, these measures are somewhat

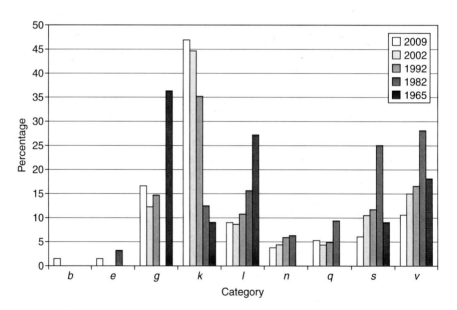

Figure 9.1 Measures of category strength (various years) (source: DBA entries, various (author's own data)).

Notes
Breed society (b), Education (e), General interest/hobby (g), Campaign/pressure group (k), Learned/scientific society (l), Coordinating body (n), Research organization (q), Sports (s), Vet and animal welfare (v).

Evolving group identities   171

volatile owing to the small (and changing) number of observations: thus they need to be read with caution. However, some clear trends are evident. What is clear here is that the number of groups identifying with the campaign category has grown significantly in strength in each successive time period. By contrast, the strength of categories like Learned/scientific society (*l*), Vet and animal welfare (*v*), and General interest/hobby (*g*) have declined within this population. Again, to emphasize, these trends are in *some* way connected to the entry of specific new groups into the sample population analysed here: in that sense new groups with a more campaign-style identity dilute the prevailing strength of scientific society and hobby identities. However, as discussed above, many (well-known) groups have also shifted identities from these categories to a campaign style (in combination, or in total). It is a complex picture.

So, is 'campaign' a core identity? Group scholars may, guided by a definitional starting point, be tempted to assume that interest groups are from the get go orientated primarily to political advocacy or campaigning. Indeed, this is the presumption of much of the US foundational literature, where we see political disturbance as the catalyst for organizational formation (as opposed to organization transformation of extant associations into policy actors). The data on environmental groups self-identification through the DBA provides an interesting window on this question. How many first entries – regardless of formation date, or lag time to entry – include (solely or in combination) identification as a 'campaign or pressure group'? Only four groups in the 37 cases examined started with a singular campaign identity, and retained that identity consistently throughout the time period: Open Spaces Society (1965); Environmental Investigation Agency (1998); Whale and Dolphin Conservation Society (1992); FoE (1974). As is evident, there is no clear period or even size effect here.

Category spanning: simple or complex identities?

A simple reading of categorical theories suggests that the safest strategy for an organization is to align itself with a single category; that is, to avoid category-spanning and to build its identity from a single generic form. This is because audiences will find it hard to 'read' the specific identity of groups if they do not (mostly) resonate with a single category. Moreover, it is likely that spanning will dull attempts by groups to sharpen up relevant capabilities. Thus, made concrete, group leaders need clear signals to be sent in such a way as to differentiate groups providing *services* to rescue abused animals from other groups that focus on *campaigning* to oppose animal cruelty and yet others that might *purchase and conserve* bird habitats. For interest groups in our sample, this would mean projecting a clear identity through selecting a single category in the DBA list. How much category-spanning do we see in this sample?

Figure 9.2 reports the proportion of groups over time that identify with one through to four different categories. The obvious finding here is that, at least on this crude measure, no evident change occurs over time in complexity of

172 *Evolving group identities*

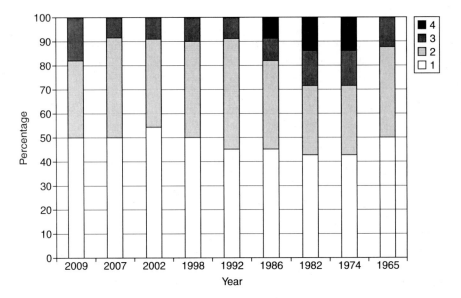

Figure 9.2 Trends in category spanning, selected years.

identity. The modal group sticks to a single category in all time periods. Of course, this does mask a lot of case-level change between time periods. That is to say, individual groups do change the complexity of their identities over time. The Royal Society for the Protection of Birds (RSPB) is a good example. It started with a singular identity of vet and animal welfare. In the 1980s it added campaigning to that, and in the 1990s dropped the animal welfare identity altogether in preference for general interest/hobby group.

In relation to *individual* group identities, we are concerned with the extent to which they are focused or unfocused, complex or simple. In their study of wine production in France, Negro *et al.* (2010a) examine the extent to which individual producers utilize different production styles (they distinguish between three) across successive vintages. To do so, they calculate what they call 'niche width', which is arrived at by calculating the GoM of each firm in each style (on an annual basis) and then summing the square of the three GoMs and subtracting from 1 (Negro *et al.* 2010a, 1412). This conceptualization is consistent with a view of the space being partitioned by organizations as identity-space rather than resource space (see the discussion in Chapter 7). Applied to our data, the niche-width measure captures whether each group has a more or less simple or complex identity. In the UK group data, the maximum number of categories employed at any one time was four, which means the simplest identity (a single category, coded as 1,0,0,0) would elicit a niche width of 0, and the most complex (spanning four categories, coded as 0.25, 0.25, 0.25, 0.25) would elicit a niche width score of 0.75.

Evolving group identities 173

Figure 9.3 reports the average niche width measures over time for our data. The first recorded year, 1965, shows that every group had a simple identity with no category-spanning (hence a score of 0). From this baseline, there is some variation. However, the linear trend line shows a broad upward trajectory in niche width over time. Again, this needs to be read with some caution because the number of cases varies from year to year.[3] What this means is that over time, the population of UK environment groups has on average manifested a more complex identity as it increasingly straddles several categories of group form. Nevertheless, it is salient that in the most recent year (2009), the modal set of groups was those with a simple identity (10 from 21), with the next straddling two categories (7/21) and the smallest grouping straddling three (4/21). Thus, even if the trend is for an average increase in category straddling, the modal groups *still retains a simple identity*.

This aggregate picture is borne out in specific group cases. A large number of groups ($n=12$) of the 26 groups for which records are available for several years since formation instances *retained* a simple identity (a single category identification) over all entries. Only a single group, the Zoological Society of London, developed a simpler identity over time – but that was a move from four categories to three. A more common pattern was that of the RSPB that moved from a simple veterinary/animal welfare identity to a more complex campaign/general interest identity.

What conclusions can we draw from these shifts in expressed identity? The basic point is that category shifting by groups – as measured by their self-selecting choice of DBA categories – serves as a useful proxy for the identities

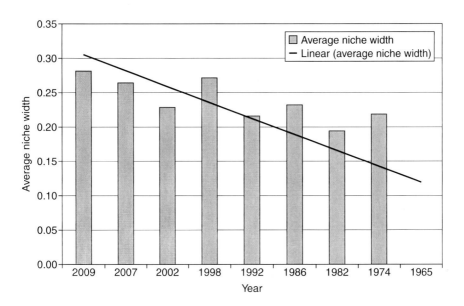

Figure 9.3 Complexity of group identity: average identity niche-width, over time.

174 *Evolving group identities*

that groups try to construct. That is, it indexes the group identity that leaders seek to project to key audiences – both members and policy makers. Of course, what is less clear is whether this identity shapes the reactions of supporters and policy makers. Compared to a restaurant's entry in the *Michelin Guide* or a movies' genre classification by a reviewer, entries in the DBA *alone* are less clearly and directly likely to shape audience reactions. What they do signal is the group's attempt to shift and shape identity: and we can find traces of this in their strategies, if not always in its effect.

Many possible simple and complex identities do not show themselves in realized forms: that is, just because combinations of categories are logically possible does not mean they exist in real organizations. Table 9.2 reports the simple and complex identities actually evident in the data.

In summary, trends are hard to spot, but what is clear is that the 1990s is the turning point after which the number of categories with a campaign component (simple or complex) constituted over half of all group cases. This suggests a shift in the legitimacy of the notion of campaigning as a viable identity for environment and countryside organizations. To be clear, the mechanism here is the entry of new organizations – most new entrants into this population are campaign groups. Only a few existing groups transform their identities.

Table 9.2 Frequency of realized category combination, all years

Category	n
k	30
v	15
g	14
s	13
g, k	10
k, v	7
l, q	7
k, l	6
k, n	4
g, l, n	3
l	3
l, q, v	3
m, s	3
g, k, s	2
l, m	2
b, l	1
b, l, q	1
e, l, p, v	1
e, l, q, v	1
l, g, v	1
l, n	1
Total group cases	**128**

Conclusion

This chapter has pursued an identity-based approach to deploying organizational form, with a specific emphasis on illustrating the ways in which categorical theories of organizational identity-building might be elaborated in group scholarship. The initial focus was on exploring how broad generic group categories perform over time: do they strengthen or weaken? The secondary focus was on how individual groups utilize these generic categories to build their specific identities – and to change identities – over time. In so doing, the intention was to highlight how categorical approaches can help connect up the way individual groups determine identities and the way audiences assess identities: here the DBA served as the mediator, refining generic categories for groups to design and audiences to interpret identities.

It should be self-evident that this is but the start of such a research programme and should be viewed in that spirit: a taster for what might be done with more elaborate data. What might this agenda look like? Most immediately, this work could be upscaled to explore entire group systems over time. The raw data is there, but the challenge of coding categorical alignments remains a substantial one. More broadly, one could imagine utilizing different data sources yet giving them the same theorietical and analytical treatment. For instance, data based on web page self-identifications, records of policy representations, or similar could be used as proxies for generic categories.

While I noted above that one rationale for pursuing a simple identity is functional – they are more likely to avoid the 'jack of all trades' error – this was not able to be explored empirically in this chapter. Yet this seems a worthy pathway for future efforts. This might be usefully extended into assessments of group performance. For instance, one might look at shifts in identity profiles and member recruitment or policy access. On the former, for instance, the Ramblers have not lifted their overall membership numbers in the last decade, even though they have signalled a relaxation of the sports-related identity into a hobby and general interest organization. Such work requires more, and different, data than assembled here. Yet the work involved to do so is likely to provide some fascinating insights on identity complexity and group performance.

Notes

1 It is worth noting here that this literature has blended the theoretical concerns and attention of neo-institutional and ecological scholars to the extent that a recent review found it difficult to identify boundaries (Negro *et al.* 2010a, 24).
2 See a similar, but somewhat more abstract, discussion about distinctions between codes by Hannan *et al.* (2007).
3 The cases in each annual analysis for Figures 9.2 and 9.3 are as follows: 2009 (22), 2007 (12), 2002 (19), 1998 (16), 1992 (17), 1986 (14), 1982 (9), 1974 (8), 1965 (11).

10 Interest group policy capacities

Introduction

For many scholars, the attraction of studying interest groups is that they attempt to exert influence on public policy. Indeed, one core element of definitions of interest groups is that they seek to shape or influence public policy (Jordan *et al.* 2004). But what does the discussion of organizational form (and its adaptation and evolution) have to add or contribute to questions of policy influence? The answer to this question comes in two parts and is elaborated in this chapter.

The first part of the answer is it depends on how one conceives of the 'task' of group influence. I take issue with the dominant (and I argue, narrow) conception of lobbying as 'influence'. I suggest that a focus on outright influence has painted an image of group policy engagement as a straightforward pursuit of control over specific decisions (or non-decisions). The recent resurgence of attempts to measure preference attainment on a specific policy issue has encouraged this view even further. From this perspective, organizational factors seem of only remote interest – perhaps reduced to a proxy like resources. By contrast, I suggest that lobbying by groups is best conceived as diverse policy work, which in turn provides more space to recognize the importance of organizational form as a key variable.

Second, and building on this initial observation, I argue a focus on a concept like group 'policy capacity' is a productive way to play-in the impact of organizational form on the preparedness for groups to engage in policy work (and concerns with influence). The approach here is that resources alone are not enough; they have to be purposefully utilized by groups to generate specific capacities. The concept of policy capacity is a neat way to capture the way the policy work of interest groups is in some way contingent on organizational design issues. Resource levels alone do not tell us about the capabilities groups possess; groups must decide how to put these to use and develop what they see as important abilities. Thus by examining group capacities we probe how fit they are for specific forms of policy work, which has an obvious organizational context. This concept of policy capacity is embedded in much group and public policy literature and I attempt to surface it and package it up for use.

Interest group policy capacities 177

The first sections of this chapter argue that we ought to shift our focus from assessing the 'policy wins' of groups to understanding their policy work. This in turn highlights the importance of group capacity as a focus for analysis. The subsequent section reviews group and public policy literatures to recover the concept of policy capacity and flesh it out in its various guises. Finally, with this concept in hand, the chapter illustrates how it can be employed empirically. Utilizing a range of convenient examples, it explores how group policy capacity is linked to questions of group design, how policy context shapes the value of different group capabilities, and discusses the prospects for groups to shift and develop capabilities over time.

From policy 'wins' to policy 'work'

One reason, I argue, that there has been little direct attention on organizational design issues in group scholarship is that we have become corralled into a rather narrow focus on influence as policy wins.

Understandably, many scholars approach the study of groups with an overriding desire to answer a question like 'Is group x influential?' or 'Is group x more influential than y?' While some counsel that this style of question framing is probably unhelpful if one wants to understand the nature of group engagement in public policy (see Jordan 2009; Leech 2011; Lowery 2013), it is nevertheless an increasingly popular thread in the literature. Viewed in this manner, organizational dimensions are minimal because (attempted) explanations of varied influence derive either from issue context or from general variables like resources (expressed as lobby spend, annual budget or staff numbers). By contrast, if one views the policy engagement activities of groups through a lens of policy work, then organizational dimensions become more central. This is because policy work is multifaceted, which means the not all groups will possess the same abilities to engage in such work.

The focus on influence, and specifically preference attainment, is a fruitful line of inquiry. It is not something I would wish to criticise or whose value ought to be diminished per se. Having said that, I also suggest that scholarly attention, particularly of the emerging generation of scholars, ought not become wholly or disproportionately fixed on this facet of group activity. For, as I discuss below, it encourages a rather stilted and one-dimensional view of the role and contribution of groups in public policy. Simply put, it does not capture the full breadth – or perhaps even the majority – of modes of interest group policy work.

While the contemporary literature is building momentum around assessing policy influence, the group maintenance literature has been built around the observation that group entrepreneurs spend a considerable amount – perhaps even most – of their time on activities other than the pursuit of policy influence (see Chapter 2). It has been long asserted that 'no interest group is just a lobby' but equally that 'membership would never continue their support if lobbying were dropped' (Browne 1977, 48, 52). The evidence, where it has been collected, suggests this is a safe assumption. In a largely overlooked piece, Browne

178   *Interest group policy capacities*

engaged in some very detailed ethnographic research to explore the nature of the entrepreneurial work undertaken by group leaders. He examined the ways in which group leaders went about sustaining their groups, based on their own discussions and reflections. He notes the complex relationship between policy advocacy provision and member-service orientation – suggesting that they are strongly interlinked. One of his respondents explains that 'If the director looks at himself as just a lobbyist, he's dead' (Browne 1977, 50). One instinct is to bring the account in which groups are viewed as single-minded agents for influence closer to the more realistic view that such aims are part of broader agendas such as keeping members happy, remaining relevant to policy makers and surviving as an organization (see Lowery 2007).

Further support for putting questions of influence in their proper context comes from the survey evidence of group representatives, which shows that they spend a remarkable amount of time on organizational matters. In their survey of Washington representatives, Heinz *et al.* (1993, 88–9) conclude that 'On average, and with substantial variation among organizational roles, interest representatives spend a surprisingly large portion of their time on the internal affairs of their organizations.' This finding held regardless of policy domain in which these individuals operated. Perhaps even more salient for our present discussion is their conclusion that 'these data do emphasize the point that external representation and internal management are undertaken by the same people and therefore are closely tied together' (Heinz *et al.* 1993, 89). In sum, there is every reason to see influence in a broader organizational context; not least because group leaders cannot avoid to do anything but assess influence tasks in the context of other group imperatives.

However, in this section I want to push the focus onto an intermediate area: namely, those group activities that *are* policy-relevant, but which are treated as 'noise' in the narrowly drawn discussion of influence in the contemporary literature. It is argued that the quest for identifying interest group influence has encouraged a conceptualization of group policy-related activities which seems rather divorced from the varied type of work engaged in by most groups. The aim here is to illustrate the salience of a slightly broader and richer take on policy work as a prelude to developing the concept of group policy capacity.

The basic claim is based on the reasonable assumption that the modal manner of policy engagement by groups is more akin to what Leech (2011, 550) characterizes as a 'service bureau'. Leech puzzles over why it seems so hard to say something definitive about influence. Her answer: 'we have been measuring the wrong things in the wrong ways' (2011, 535). She contrasts three broadly held perspectives on what policy work aimed at influence is all about: influence is not about buying-off decision makers (not financial muscle), nor about electoral guarantees to elected officials, but about 'groups as service bureaus'. Viewed in such a way, interest groups affect policy by supplying 'information, facts, supporters, media coverage, or strategic expertise' which policy makers require. It is important to note here that Leech is not just talking about supplying 'stuff' – imagined as a packet of information – but also supplying abilities to do things or act in important ways or exhibit important functions. She suggests

Interest group policy capacities   179

Interests groups do many, many things in their efforts to influence public policy and work in many political arenas. So rather than investigating the impact of just words said to a legislator in an office, we should investigate all actions of interest groups aimed at changing public policy

(Leech 2011, 535)

Actions might include 'providing information, mobilizing publics, attracting media attention' (Leech 2011, 550). It might also be extended to things like policy preparation, implementation and even member coordination.

This subtle, but I suggest nevertheless profound, re-orientation is also evident in Grant Jordan's review of the term lobbying for the British audience. He suggests that the term ought to be understood as a repertoire composed of a number of 'means of policy modification' (Jordan 2009, 370). The most usual means of policy engagement is what he calls the 'insider mode', where routine information exchange and 'win:win' consensus-seeking consultations are the means of policy change or stasis (Jordan 2009, 371; see also Grant 2001). These are not the limits. For instance, a group might engage in media-based reframing of a policy issue. Or, a group might mobilize protest or engage in disruptive actions. These 'means' may be relevant for the (relatively) few issues that escape the usual method of processing issues or as tactical addendums or footnotes to insider politics. Like Leech's account, this discussion of lobbying underlines the mixed bag of abilities groups utilize as part of a basic commitment to policy work. Influence is a by-product of policy work when viewed over the long run, but not every act of policy work has detectable policy wins as its guiding tactical imperative.

When we redefine policy influence or lobbying in terms of policy work and approach the policy task of groups from a perspective of something like service bureaus, then the issue of group design starts to become highly salient. That is because not all groups are going to be able to deliver all possible things to policy makers. Thus, we need some term to capture this variation; and in this connection I suggest the notion of group policy capacity.

The concept of group 'policy capacity'

If one accepts that the group contribution to policy work is to provide services to policy makers, then a curious mind might cogitate over (a) how such services are provided, and (b) whether there are variations among groups as to their ability to deliver them. Leech addresses these two points in an indirect way through a discussion of the normative objections to her account of insider politics. She remarks

The trouble arises if some types of interest groups and some types of interests are better able to take advantage of this *ability* to subisidize than others. If, for example, what money buys is the *ability* to mobilize constituencies and the *ability* to provide information to government officials and poorer groups and poorer interests are shut out of this process, then a democratic problem remains.

(2011, 550–1, italics added)

180   *Interest group policy capacities*

Harking back to the phraseology of Schattschneider and Schlozman – the implication of Leech's observation might be to talk of a 'capability bias'.

The salient point here is that noting group resource levels is not in and of itself sufficient to indicate value to policy makers. Groups must make decisions as to how resources are deployed, what they are invested in. These decisions are embedded and evident in the organizational designs of groups, and represent sunk costs that are hard to easily or quickly turn around. As discussed in Chapters 5 and 6, this 'lock-in' process happens at two levels. Not only do investments of resources create real 'capabilities' in certain things, they also foster a reputation for those abilities. Not all groups will likely have the abilities that policy makers see as useful: we ought to anticipate variation in capability. Thus, it may be useful to ponder how abilities coveted by policy makers are generated. The perspective here is that understanding these abilities is at its core about understanding the organizational design issues of groups: group design processes are the engine of policy capacity development.

Echoing the discussion of abilities by Leech (2011), elsewhere I have defined group 'policy capacity' as 'the abilities and skills groups develop in order to contribute to – and affect – the process of policy formulation or/and implementation' (Halpin *et al.* 2011). Some sensible riders are required at this point. This concept does not capture political power that a group may hold due to electoral influence or such like (and of course, a group may hold weak capacities as I define it here, but might be otherwise capable due to structural or electoral power). This might of course help a group be able to act politically, but it is not something that derives from organizational issues. In addition, it is important to keep in mind that groups may well have capabilities, but not in-house. For instance, the rise of economic consultancies that provide well-regarded analysis and modelling have no doubt replaced the in-house economists and analysts that were once standard fare in business associations. Thus capacity is not simply about number of employees or budget, it is about the way that groups expend resources to build specific abilities that assist it to do certain types of policy work. In addition, capacity is not the same as influence. Take a scenario where a group has low capacity, but high influence (measured as access). The National Farmers' Union of Scotland (NFUS) has been stripped of internal independent research capacity, and has a low number of expert staff. It also has a small and shrinking resource base. Yet it is the dominant farm group in Scotland.

While not a requirement, scholarly concepts that proximate the understandings of those in the contexts we study are particularly strong (Gerring 1999). The salience of capacity issues for real public policy making is illustrated by the following example. The then Australian Prime Minister, Julia Gillard, announced in late 2012 that the Australian Government would spend $10 million Australian over a three-year period to 'fund the on-going costs of a non-profit organization with a primary focus on superannuation policy research and advocacy' (Government of Australia 2012). The Superannuation Consumer Centre is somewhat controversial as commentators note there is already a group – the Self-Managed Professionals Association – that arguably covers the similar territory. The

Interest group policy capacities   181

government's move is best interpreted as a move to strengthen the advocacy sector in an area of need. Put another way, governmental actors view the associational landscape through a lens of capacity and sometimes even actively engage in capacity-building where they deem a deficit.

The concept of policy capacity can be fleshed out further by retracing its provenance through various group and public policy literatures: a task to which this chapter now turns.

Retrieving the concept of 'policy capacity' (and its link to organization)

As is by now a common thread in this volume, group scholars need not start with a blank page when it comes to developing a concept like policy capacity. In this section I set out to show how it sits *implicitly* within much of the existing work in several relevant sub-literatures and demonstrate its link to organizational form. The task here is to surface this concept such that it might be more explicitly deployed by group scholars.

The influence literature and 'resources'

Before moving forward, let me take one brief step back. The retrieval of the concept of policy capacity is aided by showing how it is to some extent evident – yet stillborn – within narrowly conceived accounts of group influence. As reviewed in Chapter 2, an emerging emphasis in the literature pursues the fine-grained empirical study of group influence. The fact that policy engagement is a central feature of any definition of an interest group rightly encourages scholarship that scrutinizes, measures or otherwise studies, how it works in practice. The most recent work has emphasized direct measures of influence, where influence is conceptualized as preference attainment on specific policy issues (see Dür 2008; Helbroe-Pedersen 2013). Preference attainment is operationalized in terms of whether a group 'gets what it wants', with all obvious caveats applying that such a measure is still short of the proverbial 'smoking gun'.

However, even in this circumscribed formulation, the issue of capacity intrudes (just). Because of measurement issues, this work on influence is (almost) forced to assume that groups are equally capable, and thus the contest is over preference attainment *among equals*. The organizational aspects of this contest intrude only to the extent that a variable like resources (but operationalized rather narrowly as say advocacy budget or number of policy staff) is included in the analysis. Thus, the influence literature *has* accepted that preference attainment is in some way reliant on resources, but the precise *mechanism* by which resources comes to matter remains somewhat vague. And it is here where a concept such as capacity becomes useful.

While the idea that money buys power is a persuasive one, it is entirely plausible – and indeed my assertion – that the impact of resources is not simply a matter of *actual* spending power, but something about *how it is applied* to the

182 *Interest group policy capacities*

task of policy work. To reiterate the point made by Leech (2011), money matters to the extent that it buys capacity: if money buys economic research or buys media time, and these actions are crucial to policy work, then it matters. To put it another way, in Jordan's terms, different 'means' of policy engagement rely on groups possessing different capabilities. Resources can be understood as the medium by which groups try to develop capacities to engage in one or other – or several – means of policy modification. Yet resources are subject to decisions about capacity generation, resources do not generate capabilities on their own.

Thus, a concept like policy capacity goes much further in reinforcing the idea that organizational form constrains the scope (and effectiveness) of a group's engagement in policy work. I argue that each policy problem or challenge requires a different set of capabilities to make groups relevant to policy makers: and that a groups fit which such desired capacities will render it more or less important (or potentially influential).

The question is how to firm up the types of capacities that might be relevant for groups to expend resources on generating, and to identify factors that shape how they are produced?

Exchange/transaction perspectives

A different picture of policy engagement emerges if one maintains a focus on 'advocacy' but *relaxes* the presumption that this advocacy is about the attainment of objective, well-defined, group preferences. Of note is that this account highlights capacity-related issues more strongly.

The UK (and US) literature has long discussed what Jordan (2009) calls an 'insider form' of policy making: an exchange between policy makers and groups, whereby policy makers confer access (and thus potential influence) to groups in return for resources that groups might provide which aid the policy formulation and implementation process (see also Grant 2001). The exchange or transaction is not conceived as a zero-sum relationship, rather groups and government seek accommodation (give and take). The image 'is not always that groups are clamouring to be heard, and desperately attempting to force concession from a reluctant bureaucracy. The *policy relevant* group can simplify the policy making task' (Maloney *et al.* 1994, 19, italics added). Put simply, policy makers need 'relevant' groups, and often (if not usually) seek them out to aid policy formulation and implementation. And it follows that groups engage in such an exchange without promise (or expectation) of influence (measured as outright preference attainment), but simply that 'theirs was a significant voice in the policy debate' and that this will likely shape outcomes (Maloney *et al.* 1994, 26). Just this type of image is supported by the numerous instances in which groups report – in the confines of interviews and out of earshot of members – an inability to identify instances where their own actions have been decisive or clear cut in winning an issue.

It goes without saying that what makes a group *policy relevant* is open to debate. Unpacking this black box will assist in fleshing out the idea of policy capacities further. Maloney *et al.* (1994, 37) say 'Civil servants look for

Interest group policy capacities 183

characteristics which will assist in policymaking. These may be technical knowledge of the policy area, relevant information, or assistance in determining the "acceptability" of the policy'. In this literature, the emphasis has been on resources that groups posses: indeed Maloney *et al.* (1994, 23) refer to resources as the 'currency for exchange-based behaviour'. The resources in this approach are, admittedly, a little vague. They cite Truman's distinction between political knowledge (who wants what and political consequences of policy alternatives) and technical knowledge (about the content of policy issue), with the latter being most valuable where policy makers have information deficits. It is suggested that groups that lack political or economic power might develop technical knowledge as a strategy to gain 'credibility with policy makers' (Maloney *et al.* 1994, 21). Maloney *et al.* (1994, 36) list the resources that groups might exchange with policy makers for access as 'knowledge, technical advice or expertise, membership compliance or consent, credibility, information, implementation guarantees'. The pay-off for more resources – more capacity – is privileged access.

More recently, Bouwen provided a similar list of resources but refers to them as 'access goods', which he defines as 'specific kinds of information' that groups use 'in order to gain access' to the policy processes (2002, 370). He identifies two broad types of goods: expert knowledge and encompassing interests. The former relates to 'expertise and know-how' required to understand the sector or the issue on which a group is engaged. The latter refers to the provision of information with respect to the 'needs and interests' of its membership (or of the sector or constituency advocated for). Each one broadly fits with Truman's (1971, 333–4) distinction between technical and political knowledge. The latter, Bouwen suggests, is enhanced where the interest is more emcompassing. Encompassingness is aided where the breadth of coverage of a group is broader, and the representativeness of the group is higher (measured as density of potential members in its ranks) (Bouwen 2002, 370). Importantly, Bouwen takes some steps to discuss how (and if, and in what quality or volume) these access goods are generated. In so doing he suggests that 'In order to provide an encompassing access good, different individual interests have to be aggregated within the interest groups', which means that 'more encompassing access goods are provided by interest groups which can aggregate more individual interests' (Bouwen 2002, 371). Thus, the '*capacity* of interest groups to control their members' codetermines the production or generation of access goods (ibid., 371, italics added). But, as he observes, 'Not in all interest groups do the organizational structures and decision-making mechanisms allow a high degree of control over membership' (2002, 371). These basic set of insights are developed into a set of testable propositions for the European institutions.

The degree of access that a group will gain to policy makers is a reflection on the level of access goods a group can provide in an exchange with policy makers. But what about the production or generation of access goods? It is here where the concept of policy capacity explicitly arises.

Bouwen is quite explicit: 'Not all private interests have the same *capacity* to provide access goods' (2002, 375 italics added). He looks to the organizational

184 *Interest group policy capacities*

form of a given organization for hints as to how capable a group will be: focusing particularly on the number of layers within a group, and the complexity of decision making. On the one hand, the higher the number of layers and complexity of decision making the slower access goods can be generated. However, this is not always the case. For instance, he suggests that in the case of 'encompassing access goods', multiple layers in the organization are 'indispensible', he says 'It is only because of the multiple layers that the bundling of the individual interests into an Encompassing Interest is possible' (Bouwen 2002, 376). On this basis, Bouwen is able to provide a 'ranking of capacities to provide access goods' among various types of private actors (2002, Table 2, 378). For instance, in the context of his work on business lobbying in the EU, firms are high on expert knowledge, but low on encompassing interests. Interest groups manifest the reverse settings, low levels of expert knowledge and high levels of encompassing interests.

It is apparent, then, that the transactional and exchange-based literature relies on the generation of access goods, resources, etc., – what might be bundled up and called policy capabilities – which account for various levels of engagement or proximity to policy makers. Yet there is not so much focus on the way such capacities are generated – this is a black box. However, close reading of this literature – especially Bouwen's contribution – surfaces the argument that the organizational form a group conforms to shapes the production of such capacities.

Neo-corporatism and governability

While the literatures have remained largely separate – and kept so by the skirmishes between the different camps of pluralism and corporatism (see Richardson and Jordan 1979) – the concern with group capacity has been more explicit in the neo-corporatist literature. The literature – at least that focusing on policy intermediation – has been concerned with the granting of public status and authority to private groups or associations. In this literature the capacity of groups to translate bargained agreements into action by the rank and file membership is of particular importance when seeking to explain status (see Schmitter and Streeck 1981). Groups are valuable to the state to the extent that they can work on their constituency to achieve 'compliance' and to 'discipline' members: that they have autonomy in their own right. The ongoing viability of such corporatist policy arrangements is closely linked to the ability of business and labour groups to reproduce these core capacities. In the literature several measures are often deployed to get at the capabilities of groups (and group systems). The number of organizations is deployed as a measure of *generalizability*, membership density used as a measure of *associability*, and the number of affiliates to a peak group as a measure of *governability* (see Traxler 1993, 677–8).

In this connection several studies have shown instances where sectoral corporatism has disintegrated or failed due to the lack of capacity by key groups: the case of the Accord on wages and inflation policy in Australia in the 1980s is a classic example where business disunity precluded progress (see Keating and

Interest group policy capacities 185

Dixon 1989; Matthews 1994). It is also worth noting that the work of Mancur Olson (1982), who famously mistrusted the impact of groups on the generation of public goods, did make the concession that encompassing groups – those representing large numbers of members – had less incentive to pursue self-interested and narrow strategies. In this respect, there is a consensus on valuable capacities; and it is linked to a specific set of organizational features.

The neo-corporatist literature is very attentive to the issue of group capacity. After all, it spends considerable time outlining the optimal properties such associations participating in neo-corporatist bargaining ought to possess for successful intermediation. Again, a link is implied between capacity and organizational design. While these properties seem largely unobtainable for many groups, and the account overly prescriptive, the literature serves as a valuable reminder that not all groups are made equal with respect to capacities; and, moreover, that the relevant capacities of groups is in part contingent on the *mode* of engagement by groups in policy.

This literature has paid considerable attention to the organizational tensions implicit in fulfilling intermediation activities (see Schmitter and Streeck 1981). This is also echoed elsewhere. For instance, Coleman (1985, 413) makes the point that groups engaging as 'participants' with government in formulating or implementing policy face different 'organizational and strategic pressures' than those engaging as 'advocates'. This resonates with Jordan's different means of policy modification. Put another way, it might be said that groups who engage in a inside track – regardless of degree of closeness – require different capacities than those who simply push an interest from the outside. Moreover, Coleman argues that these two roles place tensions on groups: one pulling groups to respond to members demands for the exercise of policy pressure, the other suggesting groups show restraint and discipline members.

Whether the crisp distinction in modes of engagement – participant and advocate – exists in most group experiences is open to question. Nevertheless, it does point to that fact that valuable group capacities only really emerge when one conceives of group engagement as more than brute pressure. Advocacy involves developing positions internally, rallying information in support, ensuring member support for the position, and selecting viable strategies for pressure. By contrast, participation mode involves other capacities, such as administrative oversight of implementation of policy, supervising others who implement, dealing with appeals and sanctioning offenders (see Coleman 1985, 418–19). In this latter mode it has to have some distance from members, since it is often engaged in balancing their interests with the need to deliver on implementation targets and punish those who fail to implement or conform to regulations implemented by the group. It is the ambiguity of the group in relation to whether it is an agent for the state or the members' interests that is at the core of this organizational tension. The literature makes clear that one way to gain this independence or distance from members – it is often referred to as autonomy – is to diversify the support base away from members (which typically means gaining financial resources and legitimacy from the state) (see discussion in Coleman 1985, 425, 431).

186 *Interest group policy capacities*

Governance and public policy

While it is true that the neo-corporatist work of the 1970s and 80s has largely faded due to the simple fact that many explicitly corporatist mechanisms were constrained to labour market regulation, and then only to a few select countries (and that arrangements in other sectors are now largely defunct), this basic insight has been picked up in the more fashionable debate around governance and public policy. And it is particularly strong in the comparative study of economic and industrial development in capitalist economies. In such studies the capacities of social actors – by which they refer usually to business associations and unions – are deemed key to the prospects for state-directed or -assisted industrial rejuvenation strategies. The shadow of the exchange-based narrative is evident, but such studies do take a more detailed look at the mechanisms for the generation and deployment of capacities by specific groups in specific instances. While the insider exchange/transaction account might emphasize strategy choice and informational resources as the basic key to unlock access, the governance approach probes deeper into how this access and exchange works specifically on particular policy problems, and especially in implementation.

This broad approach is evident in the general public policy literature that sees 'associative' capacities as critical to generating 'governing', 'policy' or 'transformative' capacity (see Atkinson and Coleman 1989; Peters 2005, 80; Painter and Pierre 2005, 11; Weiss 1998). The central point here is that the relations between groups and the state are not zero-sum interactions: capable groups are a necessary, but insufficient, condition for governing or state policy capacity. This thread in the literature has been particularly interested in explaining the ability of some nation states to modernize their national industries in the face of increasingly competitive globalized trade: the role of capable interest groups in governance arrangements has been implicated as a key explanatory variable.

For instance, Guy Peters (2005, 80) argues that the 'capacities of society' are crucial to a 'capacity to govern'. He says 'If we continue to use the logic of mutual cooption to understand the relationship between private sector actors in governance, then actors who bring little or nothing to the table are of little value as partners'. But what is it that would (ideally) be brought to the table? What capacities are required? Here Peters (2005, 80) identifies 'the capacity to deliver the commitment of its members and/or other actors in the policy sector' – that groups having been involved in decision making will go along with the decision. He also identifies 'information about the wants, needs and demands of their constituents'. Painter and Pierre (2005, 11) suggest that groups help the state 'acquire essential knowledge, while cooperative relations with them also ensure compliance'.

In a similar vein, Bell and Hindmoor (2009, 163) talk of the 'capacities of associations' as crucial factors in the success, or otherwise of 'governance through associations'. Such capacities include, 'high membership density or coverage, effective internal procedures for mediating member interests, and selective incentives to help mobilise members in collective action.' (Bell and

Interest group policy capacities 187

Hindmoor 2009, 163). They draw particular attention to what is referred to as 'private interest government' or private modes of governance (Bell and Hindmoor 2009, 169). Some are classic instances of delegated authority – as in the case of those both representing and regulating professions (e.g. lawyers, doctors, teachers, etc.). Others are cases where governmental or state authority is almost completely absent.

In the former context, groups rely on their capacity to mobilize consent among key members (and their almost saturation coverage of a sector), to discipline defectors (often through public shaming or by state-delegated powers), and to develop schemes of self-regulation. In some cases this does not take off: such as in the Australian organic sector where research shows that the lack of group capacity made progress on an 'industry-owned' national organic labelling slow and ineffective (Halpin and Daugbjerg 2008). A positive example might be how groups are active in educating their members about implementation issues on government policies: for instance, the government funding provided to Australian business associations to run education programmes for members on the new goods and services tax regime (see Bell and Hindmoor 2009). In the latter context, governance relies almost solely on the capacities of groups to develop, implement and manage quite complex systems of private accreditation. To some extent groups can be said to develop organizational capacities similar to not-for-profit businesses. A good example is the organic certification and standards development undertaken by the Soil Association in the UK, which it has recently had to spin off as a separate business for corporate governance reasons. A less well-developed case is where animal welfare bodies, such as the UK RSPCA, develop standards of animal welfare and accredit use of their label where standards are met by farmers. In these two cases, groups develop systems of governance that rely on market-based mechanisms, such as certification or labelling systems, e.g. Rugmark, Forest Stewardship Scheme (Cashore 2002; Wolf 2008). Some schemes are not targeted at changing consumer sentiment through labelling, but internally directed efforts to shift industry practice. An example is the efforts by the Chemical Industry Associations in North America to develop industry standards on handling and transport. In such a role groups solve collective action problems within their constituency that the state would only be able to achieve via formal regulation.

It is important to underline that this governance-orientated research does not ask if an association 'got what it wanted', rather it looks at how groups can become involved in assisting the state in jointly advantageous action or directly in private (not state-based) regimes of governance. In fact, much work emphasizes the way the industry groups need the state to regulate (or threaten to regulate) the industry to sanction free-riding on self-regulatory schemes. In this latter respect, Culpepper's study of training regimes in Germany and France concluded that 'the presence of employers' associations with *capacities* of information circulation, deliberation and mobilization is a necessary condition for reforms premised on securing decentralised cooperation to succeed' (Culpepper 2001, 286 italics added). The success of efforts by German federal states (Lander) in

188 *Interest group policy capacities*

the former East Germany to implement a scheme of industry training was achieved through the capacity of business associations to authoritatively bargain with government (thus no need for firm-based deals over policy) but also the capacity of the groups to enable firms to talk and learn from one another in a non-competitive setting: that is, the group facilitated non-market coordination. Weak uptake in France was explained by very weak – read incapable – business associations even in the face of high levels of state support. Further evidence comes from his study of the successful implementation of the up-skilling of the German banking workforce through youth training contracts. According to Culpepper (2002) it was because the German banking industry association could circulate information to all members and offer a venue to facilitate meaningful dialogue among member firms – and to do so with high levels of legitimacy within the sector. Weak associative capacity can lead to low governing capacity.

This type of analysis is repeated in respect of the modernization of French agriculture (Coleman and Chiasson 2002). In their study of agricultural governance in France, Coleman and Chiasson (2002, 182) conclude that attempts to modernize French agriculture in the face of 'intensifying globalization' is achieved in part by 'reaching out to new interest groups'. They argue that the actual groups that assisted in earlier agricultural transformation and modernization, namely general encompassing farm interest groups, are insufficiently capable to regenerate its transformative capacity. Instead the state seeks to bolster new groups that draw in broader constituencies (such as consumers and environmental groups). The transformative capacity of the state is actually renewed by finding more capable associative partners.

Summary

Table 10.1 summarizes the existing literature, with an explicit focus on its treatment of policy capacity and any links made to organizational form. What is obvious is that the concept of capacity has been explicitly deployed in many sub-literatures, and implicitly in a few others. In all but the basic influence literature, the concept of capacity is linked directly to the question of organizational form. The term organizational form is utilized in the literatures reviewed above in a way that more closely approximates a feature-based understanding (see Chapter 3). It is the group's form, the theory goes, that shapes the generation of specific sets of capacities. An extension of the hypothesis is that groups are formed, or adapted, in specific organizational forms in order to enable them to better produce desirable capacities, and thus gain better access, influence or policy outcomes.

Applying the group 'policy capacity' concept

Having uncovered – even if not in name – the use of a concept like policy capacity from within group and public policy scholarship, it is now time to look at

Table 10.1 The policy capacity concept and its link to organizational form in the existing literature

Outcome	Outcome measures	Group policy capacity	Capacity measures	Organizational form	Organizational form measures
Influence	Preference attainment, position, reputation (Dür 2008)	Produce resources	• Lobby spend • Staff numbers	Not directly discussed	Not directly discussed
Access	Level, quality or frequency of access to policy makers (Maloney *et al.* 1994)	Produce access goods, services	Truman (1971) • Expert knowledge • Political knowledge Maloney *et al.* (2004) • Knowledge, compliance, information, etc. Bouwen (2002, 2004) • Expert knowledge • Encompassing goods	Mission, formal structures, funding method, decision-making process, affiliations	Truman (1971) • Expert staff/internal research • Members/internal deliberation Bouwen (2002/4) • Number of organizational layers? • Democratic decision making? = Encompassing goods
Neo-corporatist interest intermediation	Stable policy intermediation, policy success (e.g. number of corporatist committees, years agreements in place, no of industrial disputes) (Coleman 1985)	Make authoritative binding agreements	• Negotiate peak national/sectoral agreements • Discipline members	Umbrella or peak form Formally democratic decision-making process, filtering hierarchy, survival autonomous from members (Schmitter and Streeck 1981)	Traxler (1993)[+] • Associability • Encompassingness • Governability
Effective governance/ policy outcome	Policy outcome (Halpin *et al.* 2011: growth of organic sector) (Culpepper 2002: implementation of firm-based training model in Europe)	Act (or provide services) in policy-useful ways	Halpin *et al.* (2011) • Aid deliberation, single representative voice, administration-research capability Culpepper (2002) • 'Capacities of information circulation, deliberation and mobilization'	Mission, formal structures, funding method, decision-making process, affiliations	• Representative democratic structures • Broad sector coverage • Limited group competition • Internal venues for member engagement/deliberation • Internal autonomous staff capacity

190 *Interest group policy capacities*

how one might work with it empirically. The review above, of course, points to the many usages of the concept and the link between capacity and form. But here we offer more straightforward questions and detailed examples as pointers for future work.

Assessing variations in capacity?

Groups are surely not all *equally capable*. Thus, an initial question we might pose is what might shape variations in capacity? The answer suggested here is that the organizational form a group manifests at one point of time shapes the range of capacities a group might reasonably generate and thus possess. How does this pan out empirically?

At a basic level, groups with very small budgets will be unlikely to provide the types of capacities listed above *to any useful extent*. But even within groups with similar financial resource levels, approaches will differ based on form. For instance, a group that has no grass-roots membership but a generous benevolent donor is unlikely to choose a policy strategy of local protest and civil disobedience, but perhaps pursue litigation (see McCarthy 2005). The obvious absence of certain organizational features in such a scenario rules out some styles of policy action. In fact, an old discussion in the UK literature contrasting the sectional model with a promotional or campaign group model, highlights assumed differences in capabilities. If one looks hard enough, the literature *does* – albeit tentatively – link this rather rudimentary 'typing' to questions of policy capacity. In the UK, Whiteley and Winyard (1987, 5) explain that a core difference between these two types is in terms of their power to sanction government. They explain that non-producer groups

> supply specialist information to government, and are frequently consulted by government in the development of policy. However, they do lack the sanctions open to producer groups.... They may be able to embarrass governments but they are not really in a position to prevent or obstruct implementation and this makes them very much weaker than some of the producer groups.

These two ideal-type groups imply different types of organizations, and this has impacts on policy capacities. Groups on different ends of this organizational continuum can be expected to hold different policy capacities.

The recent work on net-based organizations also makes clear that group designs have implications for policy capacity. In his work documenting the development of MoveOn and related organizations, Karpf (2012, 16) notes that organizers of internet-mediated groups recognize their capabilities differ compared to long-standing union organizations: the former

> are never going to sit across the table from management and negotiate a new collective bargaining agreement.... Netroots organizers are well aware of

Interest group policy capacities   191

the limitations of their niche.... They know there are capacities that legacy organizations are better able to provide.

He explains that 'There are some critical capacities to which the nimble staff and rapid tactics or internet-mediated organizations are poorly suited.' The capacities he has in mind include in-house scientific and professional expertise, the ability to sit down and negotiate with government officials, or the ability to call on field officers in regional centres across the country. He continues

> Some valuable functions require substantial overhead costs, regardless of the changing information landscape. A few of these tasks have migrated, covered by 'phantom staff' or by netroots infrastructure organizations and vendors. Others, however, represent a troubling net loss for American polit-ical associations and the interests they represent.
>
> (2012, 169)

Here the claim is that certain capacities inhere in different types of organiza-tional forms.

This type of observation is also evident in work on international NGOs. For instance, work on NGOs engagement with the UN establishes that 'the composi-tion of NGOs has an impact on the resources they devoted to representation' (Martens 2005, 159). Specifically, Martens suggests that 'centralist' NGOs ded-icated more resources to representation at the UN than 'federative' ones. Sim-ilarly, she noted the role of group mission mattered: service NGOs hired those with on-the-ground expertise, while advocacy NGOs tended to hire professionals like human rights lawyers. This had an impact on what they can offer to inter-national institutions, and the mode of this engagement. The claim that group form shapes policy salient behaviour is clear.

Policy context and the demand for capacities

It is relatively easy, as evident above, to list off the group capacities that may be considered, in a general sense, to be policy-relevant. But if such formulations are to make sense in identifying the particular contribution of specific groups to gov-erning capacities in a given policy area, we surely need a more nuanced under-standing of group capacity. Not all group capacities (however defined and measured) are equally as valuable across policy contexts or institutions. Context does matter.

A particularly salient example is the cross-national study of capacity develop-ment among organic farming groups. This work makes the point that policy strategies selected by the state provided the context in which the capacity (or otherwise) of key groups was assessed: different governmental policy strategies necessitated or called for different capacities (Halpin and Daugbjerg 2008; Halpin *et al.* 2011). And, in such a context, groups tended to evolve in ways that matched required capabilities. In the UK, where the state had adopted a market

192 *Interest group policy capacities*

strategy, the key group capabilities revolved around generating market-intelligence and networks on demand for organic food that could be 'matched' with work on developing supply from growers. The UK Soil Association (SA) possessed such capabilities by virtue of an investment in relationship-building with retailers and investment in market-research capabilities (its annual report on the UK organic market was authoritative inside and outside government). State engagement flowed to the UK industry from the perception that the British consumer demanded organic alternatives. The SA was set up to keep delivering this impression. By contrast, in Sweden, where the state persisted with a state-directed supply-side strategy, the key organic group resembled the conventional farm association, with a small staff well-suited to lobbying the state direct for subsidies (see Table 10.2).

Other work connects questions of (in)capacity to changing contexts – both policy and constituency based. In his study of the Business Council of Australia (BCA), Bell (2006) shows how its loss of capacity – specifically its in-house research capacity and ability to produce buy-in from key member CEOs – owed to organizational changes brought about by a mix of policy and constituency factors. On the one hand, the macroeconomic reform of the 1980s and 1990s which the BCA had arguably driven through was largely complete, which left it without a clear policy mission. As such, it was a 'victim of its own success'. On the other hand, the impact of further internationalization of capital meant that many 'Australian' companies were now in fact part of multinational corporations, and views of Australian-based management teams were often reflections of decisions made in Europe, North America or Asia. As such, getting buy-in from CEOs was more difficult and meant something different. Put another way, as the organizational model of the BCA is undermined, it in turn reduces the desired policy capacities it can generate.

The renewal of group capacities?

The above discussion also suggests that as specific policy contexts change over time already established groups may need to *renew* capacities to maintain relevance (to both supporters/donors and policy makers). It suggests a focus on the link between *individual* group evolution and questions of capacity development.

It has to be recognized from the outset that the existing public policy literature is rather pessimistic in relation to group capacity development. The line is that groups provide capabilities that matched the moment of their birth, and that once conditions change their relevance recedes. This is the general thrust of Coleman and Chiasson's (2002, 183) evaluation of French agriculture in which they argue that without new more capable groups, 'the likelihood of realizing this new vision for agriculture would be rather low'. The implication here is that innovation requires a new type of group form. Elsewhere pessimism about groups renewing their capacities seems to be confirmed by the observed propensity for established industry groups to 'stick' even under rather adverse conditions and where their 'value' has waned (Coleman 1997; Wanna and Withers 2000).

Table 10.2 Policy strategy and group capacity development

Country	State policy strategy	Group policy capacities
Australia	Non-intervention	No impact as no incentive structure for groups.
UK	Passive market development	Develop communication capabilities to aid market transparency and inform state of market demand.
Denmark	Active market development	In addition to that of UK, develop substantial implementation capacities around retail sale of organic food.
Sweden	Supply-driven	Capacity development directed towards presenting the interests of organic farmers to government and providing information to organic farmers.

Source: summarized from Halpin *et al.* (2011).

194 *Interest group policy capacities*

While admitting that change is not easy, I am less pessimistic that it occurs (see Chapter 6). I argue that the organizational form into which groups crystallize after a formative period shapes the range of capacities a group could be expected to develop. After taking decisions on organizational form and structural set-up groups are not always easy to change – even where circumstances seem to demand it. Yet, I argue that groups can adapt capacities, albeit shaped *by* the group form into which they have crystallized. Capacities are not natural to groups, they must be consciously worked on and developed. Whether capacities are indeed developed is contingent on the extent to which they fit the organizational logic of the group itself.

In the context of discussing union revitalization, Levesque and Murray made the point that 'Resources are not enough; unions *must be capable of using them*'(2010, 333, italics added). In this literature, the extension of union power is through capacity, where 'Capabilities refer ... to sets of aptitudes, competencies, abilities, social skills or know-how that can be developed, transmitted and learned' (ibid., 336). What is the relationship between changing form and capacity? They say 'There are moments in organizational and institutional history when things are just up for grabs' (Levesque and Murray 2010, 346). They continue

> As previous arrangements come unstuck, union capacity weakens, union resources and capabilities increasingly come under the microscope. Some of the old resources need to be reconfigured or invigorated; the capabilities do not seem to be calibrated to the new context.

The point here is that the development or renewal of capacities is not conducted in a vacuum, the requirements of shifting circumstances send signals about the desirability of specific capacities, as well as also undermining or devaluing existing capacities, and it is up to the group to see if it can act on this signal and renew itself.

To summarize, practices commensurate with particular policy capacities are *developed* as part and parcel of overall organizational form. Capacities are hardly likely to be developed unless leaders see them as consistent with establishing stable organizational forms that will endure. The argument here is not some sort of crude functionalism: the claim is not that form determines capacity. Put simply, research strategies focused on policy work and group capacity – as opposed to simplistic notions of influence – will need to be attuned to organizational matters.

Conclusion

This chapter has explored the ways in which an organizational lens provokes different sets of questions about the way we study and conceptualize the influence of groups. It demonstrates that taking the question of group organization seriously pushes us towards – it does not draw us away from – the policy actions of groups. Three are three basic take-homes here.

First, the chapter argued that the focus on influence seeking – and specifically when conceptualized as preference attainment – results in research that overlooks many of the policy activities that groups do engage in. And, as such, ignores the role of organizational design in shaping the policy activities of groups. The suggestion here was to focus on policy work, rather than policy wins. This argument is important because it is, I suggest, a more accurate reflection of what groups do. Second, a focus on policy work raises the question of capacity. Here it was argued that different policy work requires different group capacities. Groups possess (and can develop) policy capacities that make them useful to policy makers in certain circumstances. Thus, we might explain the access or impact of groups on policy work by resort to a concept like group policy capacity. Third, a discussion about capacity – which as I show is a remarkably discussed concept when one looks closely in the public policy literature – raises the question of variations in organizational form. It is here where the organizational design of a group is most obviously relevant. The argument here is that group design privileges the production or generation of a set of capacities, which goes on to shape its policy impact.

While not the focus in this chapter, one could well imagine stretching the concept of group capacity beyond *policy* capacity, where the connection with organizational form is also evident. For instance, there is a debate around the role that groups might play in relation to promoting democratic participation and/or social capital. The capacity of groups to make such a contribution, it is argued, relies on whether groups in fact foster face-to-face interaction of individuals (Skocpol 2003). This is, I believe, a useful extension of the concept.

11 Conclusions

Technological change and the (ongoing) importance of organization

Revisiting the rationale

The broad thrust of this book is rather simple. Group scholars would benefit from explicitly developing sensitivity to issues and processes of organizational design by interest groups. As such, effort has been expended in the preceding pages to highlight how one might make the group organization the unit of analysis in a meaningful and theoretically rich manner.

The timing of this scholarly intervention is important. As I finish this book, there is a detectable resurgence of organizational themes in the corners of the group literature – albeit that it remains diffuse. Yet, at the same moment, others in allied fields, specifically that of political communications, are pondering the demise of organization and the rise of organizing. I come to the latter point in a moment; but for now, the salient point is that having a firm(er) foundation on which to justify and develop an organizational understanding of interest groups is becoming more, not less, of a priority for the field.

This organizational (re)turn is, however, against a backdrop of benign neglect of organizational design issues in the group literature, where the focus has been on explaining individual's behaviour. Researchers became incrementally less interested in the way groups organize themselves: less concerned with questions of design and of change in design. This permeates all aspects of group research. Those concerned with formation ask how do groups overcome collective action problems? Those interested in maintenance puzzle over how these problems remain resolved and what amendments to incentive exchanges are necessitated over time. The population perspective counts the mortality of groups, but does not probe more deeply into how groups within such populations vary in their design. Lastly, the rush to reassess group influence has led scholars away from asking how organizational design facilitates group capabilities which in turn shape their utility to policy makers. Instead they focus on how groups got what they wanted in set-piece policy contests.

The chief message of this book is that groups ought to be appreciated as complex and evolving organizations. It is simply hard to imagine that any group organization that has any kind of lengthy career will be able to sustain itself, to survive, by simply maintaining the shape or form it established during formation.

Moreover, it is not plausible that all groups 'survive the same': populations of apparently like-groups will likely occupy different organizational configurations at any given moment in time. The basic proposition is that grasping the (changeable) form of a group is crucial to comprehending its policy behaviour and capacities.

As straightforward as these propositions may sound, the immediate challenge this sets scholars is to come up with some way of identifying what form or design a group is in at any particular point of time – one that can serve as a basis to track changes in groups over time and communicate variations within populations. How would we know if a group has changed if we could not know how it used to be, and how it is now? How would we know if a population contained diversity if we do not possess a way to identify organizational differences? How do we account for such variation if we don't have frameworks with which to probe processes of group identity-formation and change?

It should be self-evident from the preceding chapters that I am agnostic as to how this might manifest itself in terms of broad approach (feature- or identity-based) theoretical assumptions (ecological, institutional, categorical, etc.), research strategy (comparative case study, population level, single historical case, etc.) and data type (qualitative interviews, documentary analysis, quantitative mapping, etc.). However, the underlying approach is a conviction that group scholars can profit from an engagement with what I call organizational social science. Thus, I go direct to the original scholarly sources in this multidisciplinary field – and admittedly bypass a rich and relevant volume of more applied work, particularly in the social movement field – in order to demonstrate the provenance of concepts such that readers can engage with them and (hopefully) develop them further.

In engaging group scholarship with this more general literature, I have developed three main concepts. Chief among these concepts is that of *organizational form* (and allied concepts like organizational identity). At its broadest, this concept refers to the way groups are put together, their design. But, as is illustrated in Chapter 3, it has many and varied usages, with each underpinned by subtly different conceptualizations of form. The intention here is not to legislate which is better; in fact, the approach I have adopted is to try and point to how each one has its advantages and disadvantages depending on what aspect of organizational design one is most interested in. Indeed, the book utilizes many of these approaches in different chapters, illustrating different modes of working with the concept.

For instance, I anticipate the feature-based approach developed in Chapter 4 will be more useful than others to most scholars simply because it gives a language to discuss, code and evaluate group populations. The theoretically derived parameters, and parsimonious nature, means that it might serve as a useful tool to discuss form; much like party scholars have the lexicon of mass, elite and cartel parties. That being said, the area of innovation in the general organizational literature is definitely around identity-based approaches to form. And this is indeed the approach that filters through most chapters. The single-case study

198   *Conclusions*

work on formation and maintenance in Chapters 5 and 6 will no doubt appeal to many researchers who are concerned with specific group histories, and ought to also hold interest for those struggling to conceptualize why groups end up designed as they are. However, the categorical and institutional approaches to identifying forms at the population level – highlighted in Chapters 8 and 9 – are most indicative of cutting-edge work. Identity-based approaches are far more sociological than the feature-based approach, in part because forms are conceptualized as contextually derived and enforced constructs. This might not be palatable to some group scholars far more comfortable with predefined neat typologies. Yet, it is a growing area of scholarship and links with the diffuse (but I think exciting) wave of group scholars working with the concept of group identity.

The second is the concept of a group career. The line here is that individual groups are likely to face many challenges in their organizational lives, and there is plenty of evidence that they try and adapt to such difficulties. Yet there was no apparent theoretical framework to either conceptualize careers, or to assess types and styles of adaptive change. By linking together debates in historical institutionalism around institutional/organizational change and that on form, these two silences in the group literature have been tentatively addressed. In so doing, the concept of career also links together formation and maintenance questions: rather than treating them as distinct and separate undertakings.

The last concept developed is that of group capacity. Here the emphasis is on drawing out the importance of organizational design in explaining the way groups engage in policy work. If we started having conversations about group capacities then I argue our research would be far closer to the lived experiences of group entrepreneurs who puzzle over and work on design issues constantly. If you ask a group entrepreneur for a copy of their (internal) strategic plan or review, you will find that these design issues around capacity are ubiquitous. That group researchers have consistently overlooked such issues is a weakness. That our public policy colleagues find the term so useful only strengthens the point that capacity ought to become a more explicit part of our scholarly lexicon. Perhaps, surprisingly for some, a renewed focus on issues of group organization leads to a better engagement with policy context – it does not draw us away as the collective action problem is generally conceded to have done (see Baumgartner and Leech 1998; Leech 2011).

This book is also as much about rethinking old topics of scholarship with organizational form in mind. Thus, Chapter 7 approaches niche theories anew. Chapters 5 and 6 rethink formation and maintenance from the perspective of organizational form. And so on. To state the obvious, this is illustrative and indicative, not exhaustive. The intention is to provoke, innovate and inspire group scholars to check their usual approach and to re-work approaches with a mindfulness to organizational issues. It will have been a success to the extent that the examples offered up here are pulled apart, reworked and added to. That being said, this volume has gone to great lengths to explicitly refer to the organizational social science literature. In addition, there has been a conscious effort

Conclusions 199

to illustrate where the group literature implicitly works with important concepts and how these might be developed further. This iterative engagement between group and organizational literatures is to my mind an essential process in developing a convincing organizational literature in our field. It is something I would argue for and defend strongly. If one is not convinced of its potential, look at the rich literature social movement and party scholars have developed and see how they have profited.

Interest groups and communications technology: organizing not organization?

The premise of this book is that group scholars ought to rediscover a legacy – identifiable in Truman – to be sensitive to the forms in which groups organize. So far chapters have, via a range of varied approaches, illustrated how such an explicit concern with group form can reinvigorate the way we examine various important areas of scholarship – formation, maintenance, survival and influence. However, given that the legacy this book seeks to pick up upon is largely a product of the mid-1900s, it is perhaps little surprise that it does not readily speak to the impact of rapid changes in communications technologies. This part of the concluding chapter addresses the way in which this legacy might be projected forward into a world where the Internet and associated technological developments are read by so many as forces for reshaping the way entrepreneurs address organizational design challenges.

Of particular salience is the fact that scholars in the related field of political communications have argued that group scholarship has trivialized (and thus understated) the impact of web-based technologies on the standard way group organization is conceptualized. Indeed, there is a push-back against the style of work pursued in this book that must be recognized, anticipated and responded to. Influential figures in the field suggest that such technology loosens many of the conditions that might justify an exclusive focus on group organization: specifically a clear boundary between members and non-members and the existence of clear constituencies whose interests are organized formally into groups. For instance, in a recent study comparing The American Legion, MoveOn and AARP, Bimber *et al*. (2012) observe that individuals within the same group experience membership very differently. They argue that technology has given individuals enhanced agency to negotiate their own boundaries of belonging and participation with organizations, as opposed to conceptualizing such boundaries as settled or determined by the group organization itself (Bimber *et al*. 2012, 21). Still others engaged in analysing the role of web technologies for protest and collective action argue that group categorization makes little sense because the hallmark of extant groups in such a technological environment is an ability to project multiple identities or forms (Bennett and Segerberg 2012).

This criticism originates from the fact that modern communication technology has the *potential* to reshape the process of collective action itself, and hence the basis for formal group organizing in the first place. Thus, key scholars in the

200 *Conclusions*

field of communications technology and collective political action note 'Not the least of the questions posed by the internet for interest group theory is the problem of specifying the conditions in which a *traditional* interest group is more effective or successful than other organizational forms' (Bimber *et al.* 2009, 78, italics added). The clear implication here is that studying models of organization ought to give way to a study of organizing.

Even if influential, this is not the only view. By contrast, and closer to the approach pursued here, others suggest that the question of organization is still central when considering the impact of new communications technologies. In a recent study of US advocacy groups, David Karpf argues 'The real impact of the new media environment comes not through "organizing without organizations," but through organizing *with different* organizations' (Karpf 2012, 3 italics in original). The line here is that while we have many commentators suggesting that technology places control in the hands of individuals and away from groups who might have brokered collective action, this is not actually evident in any wholesale shift. What *is* evident is that the advent of Internet and related communications technologies has prompted a lot of discussion as to the ways in which it might catalyse new organizational forms or trigger revisions to standing organizational designs (see Vromen and Coleman 2011). The insistence that organizations still matter is underlined below as I assess the impact of technology in a more nuanced way.

The (varied) impact of technology on group organization

The message of this book is that every group – like all organizations – has a history that shapes the ways in which they experience, process and react to evolving environments. Technology might expand the options, but it does not determine them. Following Bimber *et al.* (2009, 74), there are at least three cases to discuss. Existing groups experience these new technologies from a position in which tasks and functions are already settled. One portion will utilize technologies to do existing things in new ways, while the second will utilize technologies to do new things, in new ways. The third set of cases involves new groups that are established amidst an environment flush with new communication technologies.

Old groups, old things, new ways

The preoccupation in the group literature proper has been with the way technologies have enabled groups to do things they always did, in more efficient ways. The UK literature has been particularly explicit in pursuing the idea that large-scale environmental – or public interest – groups have grown *because* they have availed themselves of modern relationship marketing tools, specifically direct mail and web-based equivalents of membership appeals/renewals. This supply-side approach illustrates that technology can be a powerful tool simply because it makes it easier and cheaper to target and proposition those predisposed and

Conclusions 201

able to pay to support such groups. The presumption then is that new communications technologies will *further* shift the transaction costs associated with such organizational activities.

One can see this line of thinking in the 1990s-based literature considering the impact of offline computing technology in the form of direct mail and database management. According to Jordan and Maloney (1997), the deployment of professional business thinking – and in particular marketing disciplines – is central to the emergence of a protest business form. They say 'Modern large-scale campaigning groups which are the product of mail order marketing are ... essentially *protest businesses*' (ibid. 148). A similar approach is taken in the US literature, where it has been argued that this type of technology has enabled the expansion of the environmental group population (Bosso 2005). In sum, the key point here is that mass-mail and computer database technology can *reduce the transaction costs* of recruitment. This general point is (re)made in the Internet age with respect to the role of mass-email propositioning deployed by mass membership groups (see Karpf 2012). On the recruitment side of the ledger, most major groups now have websites that publicize their efforts. And, of those, most would have functionalities for donations, volunteering and at the very least 'joining' the group. These functionalities are straightforward translations of old-school offline magazines and direct-mail joining/donation request letters.

The same process can also be identified in the area of group influence strategies and tactics. The increasingly well developed e-citizenship and e-democracy programmes of governmental actors have made the Internet a useful tool for what some groups themselves call 'e-activists'. Online consultations, for example, provide ample space for groups to encourage members to make the group's policy line known to policy makers. Moreover, the transaction costs of (i) alerting and recruiting members to participate and (ii) the members' actual participation are both substantially reduced. This has led to the phenomenon of the mass-form letter in online consultations. This mode of e-participation/activism has been labeled variously as 'clicktivism' and 'slacktivism'. These labels are meant to convey that the technology has debased conventional and more substantive forms of political participation (see Shulman 2009). However, these seem to be no more than modern equivalents of the letter-writing campaign which was perhaps the basic tool for the rank and file group member or supporter to be directly involved in legitimate forms of lobbying.[1] In fact, precisely this is argued by Karpf (2010, 9 italics in original) when he suggests that

> email action alerts represent an incremental modification of the form letters, postcards, and petitions that have dominated citizen issue campaigning for decades. Though the lowered costs of the new medium modify a few critical organizational processes, they represent a difference-of-degree rather than a difference-in-kind.

As the theory discussed earlier in this volume suggests (see Chapter 6), there is no reason that this technical adaptation might not add-up to substantive change

202   *Conclusions*

in overall form: but for the most part it simply means an easy technical adaptation based on existing strategies and identity.

Old groups, new things, new ways

Technology may also allow *existing* groups to develop hitherto unimaginable *new* functions, activities and tasks. The impact of web-based communications technologies has had an impact on the way groups *decide* to design relationships with supporters. Chadwick has observed 'traditional, even staid, groups are changing their internal organization and building loose networks in previously untapped reservoirs of citizen support' (2007, 291). Many groups utilize their web portals to offer the chance for individuals to 'join' as members for a fee, but *also* offer the chance for individuals to sign-up for no-fee and receive updates on group actions, volunteer, locate like-minded people or even contribute to group positions (Bimber *et al.* 2012, 7). Alongside branch-based members, groups are enrolling online members who will never meet one another. It is the latter development that is novel, and flows directly from technological advancements.

Particular challenges emerge from the way web-based technologies are incorporated into existing models. For instance, the Australian Conservation Foundation (ACF) offers members the chance to join for the fee of $10 Australian. However, on the same site one can sign-up for the 'ACF Community' and in response receive email alerts asking for donations, providing information on ACF actions *and* even a survey seeking to identify the key environmental issues requiring prioritization. This creates several questions. Is the involvement of the non-joining 'community' in the agenda-setting process of the ACF blurring democratic lines of accountability? Moreover, isn't their approach effectively undermining its membership model by providing almost all 'benefits' of membership to the 'community' for free? In Olsonian terms, this is giving away what could be selective incentives for free! What is clear and unambiguous is that many groups (but particularly the mass member variety) now offer a range of varied relationships with supporters, rather than the straightforward member/ non-member model.

Groups have always engaged in some type of networking amongst like-minded peers. Whether coalitions or networks or alliances, groups share resources to pursue common interests. However, web-based technologies have enabled existing groups to *rapidly* project themselves and rebrand themselves on an issue basis. The claim here is that extant and old style bricks-and-mortar groups can use the web to build virtual shop-fronts or façades for transient issues. For instance Animals Australia developed a campaign website to push its agenda of ending factory farming, which sought to inform and educate in addition to seek out issue-based funding (e.g. www.makeitpossible.com). This was separate from its group website that asked for members to join the group as a whole. Groups also increasingly use online social media to try and get their message out in a cluttered public media space, and to manage relationships with individuals beyond their core membership.

Conclusions 203

New groups, new things, new ways

One of the key impacts of Internet technology on US democracy has been facilitating the establishment of a new generation of groups. Key authors describe an 'accelerated pluralism', whereby 'the Internet contributes to the on-going fragmentation of the present system of interest-based group politics and a shift toward a more fluid, issue-based group politics with less institutional coherence' (Bimber 1998, 136, 133). A similar idea is expressed by Klein, who suggests that the Internet enables a different temporal response to issue salience. He suggests

> In response to a crisis or an opportunity, ad hoc associations can be more easily created, and existing associations more easily reactivated. A citizen action can be announced on existing listservs in order to attract participants, and a forum can be created quickly at nearly no cost to participants.
>
> (1999, 219)

There is, of course the phenomenon of the 'virtual group', the single operator and a website trying to project as if a collective organization. And it is undeniable that lobbyists utilize this device to appear as independent citizen groups when they are actually fronts for special interests.

On this score the actions of British tobacco firms is a good example. They have been accused by the anti-tobacco lobby Action on Smoking and Health (ASH) of establishing 'astroturf' websites and associated organizations that look like independent campaigns but are actually fronts for vested interests.[2] The policy director at ASH explained

> The industry dilemma is this: they hope to achieve more credibility by using organizations that look independent, but the more independent the spokesman, the less the tobacco companies are in control. This time they are mimicking online campaign sites like 38 Degrees, recruiting smokers as 'netizens', but retaining maximum control over the content.

This type of activity is enabled by web-based technologies that make virtual shop fronts easy to set up but their authenticity hard to assess or evaluate. Yet it is not just more groups that are hypothesized to emerge from the technological revolution, there is also a discussion of new types or forms of groups. And this is more salient to the themes developed in this book.

While I do not intend to drift into a discussion of organizing without organization (see Bimber *et al*. 2012), it *is* necessary to focus some considerable attention on those cases where technology allows non-traditional group organizational forms to emerge. Skocpol counsels the new generation of group entrepreneurs to 'let their imaginations roam and look for ways to reinvent membership organizations along new lines suited to today's constituencies and technologies' (2003, 275). But what evidence is there that such technologies have recast the dye of group design?

204 *Conclusions*

According to Bimber *et al.* (2009, 79) the typical interest group (what I refer to as the 'traditional' model in Chapter 4) makes sense where there are 'high costs of information and communication, few avenues of horizontal interaction among citizens who are not proximate to one another, and targets for organizing that involve large, slow moving, policy institutions'. Where such conditions do not hold, they suggest that other forms might be more likely to emerge. There is recognition that new technologies are likely to span new organizations.

For instance, Chadwick (2007, 283) argues that some 'organizational types' – he cites MoveOn explicitly – simply 'could not work without the Internet' because they enable 'complex interactions between the online and offline environment', and that existing groups are adopting these new repertoires of organizing to good effect. It has recently been argued that these organizations constitute a new third generation of group organizational form (Karpf 2012). It has been suggested that there is a transformation between three generational models, each having distinctive approaches to defining the limits and expectations of membership and financing. First generation organizational dominated the US in the 1800s–1960s. They were 'membership federations', which drew on key (cross-class) social and economic identities through local branches and elected leaders and decided policy positions based on intensive internally democratic processes. Between the 1970s and up until the early 2000s, these groups were replaced in the US by a newer model Karpf refers to as 'professional advocacy organizations'. These are characterized as having funding based on direct mail or grants from patrons and encourage 'armchair activism'. While the first-generation groups pursued the broad agendas of their constituents, these second-generation groups tended to be highly specialized or focus on a single issue. These first two are familiar from the discussion in Chapter 4, and resonate well with the accounts provided by Skocpol (1999, 2003). In addition, Karpf (2012) suggest that the 2000s witnessed the creation of what he calls 'internet-mediated groups'. Such groups have 'supporters', however they are expected to dip in and out of active engagement with the organization depending on their aspirations, resources and interests. They have what might be described as a 'user-generated' policy agenda, whereby supporters propose and select (by virtue of donations against specific policy action propositions) which actions the group will engage with. Karpf, amongst others, is optimistic and upbeat about the impact this new generation of groups will have in undoing the impact of professionalized groups on participation and engagement by activists.

Still the organizational (re)turn?

It is so easy to be carried along by the impact of web-based technologies on designing advocacy. The rapid decline of print-based media, specifically the daily broadsheet newspaper, and its impending replacement with various online versions is suggestive of the way long-standing logics of organizing are rapidly superseded. It would be easy to think that the context of interest group organization would be subject to the same epic and radical pattern of change as we easily witness in the decline of bricks and mortar retail enterprises or the decline of the printed newspaper. There are some who take just this line. Some have gone so far as to suggest these technologies might foster unmediated communication between governments and citizens, thus rendering redundant traditional linkage organizations such as parties and interest groups altogether (see Bimber 2012, 123).

One acid test for how revolutionary virtual organizations such as GetUp! or MoveOn are is to assess how widespread their modes of organizing have become dispersed. After all, both institutional and ecological theories would use the prevalence of a particular mode of organization as a proxy for legitimation (see Chapter 3). On this score, there is precious little evidence that new or existing organizations are mimicking these groups in terms of overall identity/form. It is evident that there is a more or less emergent organizational form – understood as a generic template for organizational design – around what Karpf calls an Internet-mediated group. And there is evidence that there are several groups across western democratic nations that explicitly claim some family-resemblance: 38 Degrees (UK); GetUp! (Australia), MoveOn (US), and Avaz (Global). Yet these groups are themselves evolving fast. MoveOn has quickly developed an online platform signon.org which effectively places the policy agenda in the hands of users, who generate ideas, and donations are 'crowd-sourced'. When sufficient support is reached an issue is acted on and a campaign initiated. Effectively, it is about creating a platform for broadly progressive individuals to prioritize issues and pursue policy action. The same seems to be developing in Australia, where GetUp! develops the communityrun.org platform.

The above review highlights in a synoptic manner that technological developments, even those as seemingly thoroughgoing and remarkable as the Internet, do not in and of themselves drive organizational design. While it is tempting to see sporadic examples of novel forms – or hybrid forms – that have technological elements as their core modus operandi as the peak of the proverbial iceberg, for the most part technology shapes the work of extant organizations without undermining them. To be certain, they provide tools for existing groups to rethink the techniques they utilize to deploy existing core functions. And, in some cases, they might also inspire previously unconsidered strategies and functions to emerge. But there is no sign of a wholesale shift to new virtual models of group organization. Again, this brings us back to the broader theme of this book; who exploits what forms, why and to what effect?

Notes

1 Of course direct action, such as protests, is also a key method of member involvement. Yet this is part of an outsider strategy, which is perhaps only replicated in technological terms by coordination of protests through social media, and also hacking as a form of protest. The book does not dwell on these approaches.
2 www.guardian.co.uk/society/2013/jun/07/tobacco-firm-stealth-marketing-plain-packaging accessed 10/6/13.

References

Albert, S. and Whetten, D.A. (1985) 'Organizational Identity', *Research in Organizational Behavior*, 7, 263–95.

Aldrich, H. (1999) *Organizations Evolving*. London: Sage.

Aldrich, H. and Reuf, M. (2006) *Organizations Evolving*. London: Sage.

Andrews, K. and Edwards, B. (2004) 'Advocacy organizations in the US Political process', *Annual Review of Sociology*, 30, 479–506.

Atkinson, M.M. and Coleman, W.D. (1989) 'Strong states andweak states: sectoral policy networks in advanced capitalist economies', *British Journal of Political Science*, 19(1), 47–67.

Australian Financial Review (2013) 'Greenpeace raises its sails', 4 May. Available online at: www.afr.com/p/national/arts_saleroom/greenpeace_raises_its_sails_wW5kBbGW0 uMjn9pDgLwq3M (accessed June 2013).

Barakso, M. (2011a) 'Brand identity and the tactical repertoires of advocacy organizations', in A. Prakash and M.K. Gugarty (eds), *Advocacy Organizations and Collective Action*, pp. 155–76. New York: Cambridge University Press.

Barakso, M. (2011b) 'Dissenting doctors: the internal politics of the AMA during the health care reform debate', in A.J. Cigler and B.A. Loomis (eds), *Interest Group Politics*, pp. 97–109. Washington DC: CQ Press.

Baron, J., Hannan, M. and Burton, D. (1999) 'Building the iron cage: determinants of managerial intensity in the early years of organizations', *American Sociological Review*, 64(4), 527–47.

Bassett, P. (1980) *A List of the Historical Records of the Royal Society for the Protection of Birds*. Birmingham: The University of Birmingham.

Baumgartner, F. and Jones, B. (1993) *Agendas and Instability in American Politics*. Chicago, IL: University of Chicago Press.

Baumgartner, F.R. and Leech, B.L. (1998) *Basic Interests: The Importance of Groups in Politics and in Political Science*. Princeton, NJ: Princeton University Press.

Baumgartner, F.R. and Leech, B.L. (2001) 'Issue niches and policy bandwagons: patterns of interest group involvement in national politics', *Journal of Politics*, 63(4), 1191–213.

Baumgartner, F., Larsen-Price, H., Leech, B. and Rutledge, P. (2011) 'Congressional and presidential effects on the demand for lobbying', *Political Research Quarterly*, 64(3), 3–16.

Bell, S. (2006) 'A victim of its own success: internationalization, neoliberalism, and organizational involution at the Business Council of Australia', *Politics Society*, 34(4), 543–70.

Bell, S. and Hindmoor, A. (2009) *Rethinking Governance: Bringing the State Back In*. Cambridge: Cambridge University Press.

References 207

Bennett, W.L. and Segerberg, A. (2012) 'The logic of connective action', *Information, Communication and Society*, 15(5), 739–68.

Bentley, A. (1908) *The Process of Government*. Chicago, IL: University of Chicago Press.

Beyers, J. (2008) 'Policy issues, organisational format and the political strategies of interest organisations', *West European Politics*, 31(6), 1188–211.

Bimber, B. (1998) 'The Internet and political transformation: populism, community, and accelerated pluralism', *Polity*, 31(1), 133–60.

Bimber, B. (2012) 'Digital media and citizenship', in H. Semetko and M. Scammell (eds), *The SAGE Handbook of Political Communication*, pp. 115–26. London: Sage.

Bimber, B., Flanagin, A. and Stohl, C. (2009) 'Technological change and the shifting nature of political organization,' in A. Chadwick and P. Howard (eds), *Handbook of Internet Politics*, pp. 79–85. Abingdon: Routledge

Bimber, B., Flanagin, A.J. and Stohl, C. (2012) *Collective Action in Organizations: Interaction and Engagement in an Era of Technological Change*. New York: Cambridge University Press.

Binderkrantz, A. (2006) 'Interest group strategies: navigating between privileged access and strategies of pressure', *Political Studies*, 53, 694–715.

Black, M. (1992) *A Cause for Our Times: Oxfam, The First 50 Years*. New York: Oxford University Press.

Blyth, M. and Katz, R. (2005) 'From catch-all party to cartelisation: the political economy of the cartel party', *West European Politics*, 28(1), 33–60.

Bosso, C.J. (2005) *Environment, Inc.: From Grassroots To Beltway*. Lawrence, KS: University Press of Kansas.

Bouwen, P. (2002) 'Corporate lobbying in the European Union: the logic of access', *Journal of European Public Policy*, 9(3), 365–90.

Bouwen, P. (2004) 'Exchanging access goods for access. A comparative study of business lobbying in the EU institutions', *European Journal of Political Research*, 43(3), 337–69.

Brittain, J. and Wholey, D.R. (1989) 'Organizational ecology as sociological theory: comment on Young', *American Journal of Sociology*, 95(October), 435–44.

Browne, W.P. (1977) 'Organizational maintenance: the internal operation of interest groups', *Public Administration Review*, 37(1), 48–57.

Browne, W.P. (1990) 'Organized interests and their issue niche: a search for pluralism in a policy domain', *Journal of Politics*, 52(2), 477–509.

Bulmer, S. and Burch, M. (1998) 'Organizing for Europe: Whitehall, the British State and the European Union', *Public Administration*, 76, 601–28.

Carroll, G. and Hannan, M. (2000) *The Demography of Corporations and Industries*. Princeton, NJ: Princeton University Press.

Carroll, G.R. and Swaminathan, A. (2000) Why the microbrewery movement? Organizational dynamics of resource partitioning in the U.S. brewing industry', *American Journal of Sociology*, 106(3), 715–62.

Carroll, G.R. and Wheaton, D. (2010) 'The organizational construction of authenticity: AN examination of contemporary food and dining in the US', *Research in Organizational Behavior*, 29, 255–282.

Cashore, B. (2002) 'Legitimacy and the privatization of environmental governance: how non-state market driven (NSMD) governance system gain rule making authority', *Governance*, 15(4), 503–29.

Chadwick, A. (2007) 'Digital network repertoires and organizational hybridity', *Political Communication*, 24, 283–301.

Cigler, A. (1986) 'From protest group to interest group: the making of American Agriculture

208　*References*

Movement, Inc.', in A. Cigler and B. Loomis (eds), *Interest Group Politics*, 2nd edn, pp. 46–69. Washington, DC: CQ Press.

Clark, P.B. and Wilson, J.Q. (1961) 'Incentive systems: a theory of organisations', *Administrative Science Quarterly*, 6, 129–66.

Clemens, E. (1996) 'Organizational form as frame; collective identity and political strategy in the American labor movement, 1880–1920', in D. McAdam, J.D. McCarthy and M.N. Zald (eds), *Comparative Perspectives on Social Movements*, pp. 205–26. Cambridge: Cambridge University Press.

Clemens, E. (1997) *The People's Lobby: Organizational Innovation and the Rise of Interest Group Politics in the United States, 1890–1925*. Chicago, IL: Chicago University Press.

Clemens, E. and Cook, J.M. (1999) 'Politics and institutionalism: explaining durability and change', *Annual Review of Sociology*, 25, 441–66.

Clemens, E. and Minkoff, D. (2004) 'Beyond the iron law: rethinking the place of organizations in social movement research', in D. Snow, S. Soule and H. Kriesi (eds), *Blackwell Companion to Social Movements*, pp. 155–70. New York: Blackwell.

Coleman, W. (1985) 'Analysing the associative action of business: policy advocacy and policy participation', *Canadian Public Administration*, 28, 413–33.

Coleman, W.D. (1997) 'Associational governance in a globalizing era: weathering the storm', in J.R. Hollingsworth and R. Boyer (eds), *Contemporary Capitalism: The Embeddedness of Institutions*, pp. 127–53. Cambridge: Cambridge University Press.

Coleman, W.D. and Chiasson, C. (2002) 'State power, transformative capacity, and adapting to globalisation: an analysis of French agricultural policy, 1960–2000', *Journal of European Public Policy*, 9(2), 168–85.

Culpepper, P. (2001) 'Employers' associations, public policy, and the politics of decentralized cooperation in Germany and France', in P.A. Hall and D. Soskice (eds), *Varieties of Capitalism: The Institutional Foundations of Comparative Advantage*, pp. 275–306. New York: Oxford University Press.

Culpepper, P. (2002) 'Associations and non-market coordination in banking: France and Eastern Germany compared', *European Journal of Industrial Relations*, 8(2), 217–35.

Culpepper, P. (2003) *Creating Cooperation: How States Develop Human Capital in Europe*. Ithaca, NY: Cornell University Press.

Curtis, R.L. and Zurcher, L.A. (1974) 'Social movements: an analytical exploration of organizational forms', *Social Problems*, 21(3), 356–70.

Danieli, A. and Wheeler, P. (2006) 'Employment policy and disabled people: old wine in new glasses?', *Disability and Society*, 21(5), 485–98.

Deephouse, D.L. (1996) 'Does isomorphism legitimate?', *Academy of Management Journal*, 39(4), 1024–39.

Deephouse, D.L. (1999) 'To be different, or to be the same? It's a question (and theory) of strategic balance', *Strategic Management Journal*, 20, 147–66.

DiMaggio, P. (1991) 'Constructing and organizational field as a professional project: US art museums, 1920–1940', in W. Powell and P. DiMaggio (eds), *The New Institutionalism in Organizational Studies*, pp. 267–92. Chicago, IL: Chicago University Press.

DiMaggio, P. and Powell, W. (1983) 'The iron cage revisited: institutional isomorphism and collective rationality in organizational fields', *American Sociological Review*, 48, 147–60.

DiMaggio, P. and Powell, W. (1991) 'The iron cage revisited: institutional isomorphism and collective rationality in organizational fields', in W.W. Powell and P.J. DiMaggio (eds), *The New Institutionalism in Organizational Analysis*, pp. 41–62. Chicago, IL: University of Chicago Press.

References   209

Dunleavy, P. (1988) 'Group identities and individual influence: reconstructing the theory of interest groups', *British Journal of Political Science*, 18, 21–49.

Dunleavy, P. (1991) *Democracy, Bureaucracy and Public Choice*. London: Harvester Wheatsheaf.

Dür, A. (2008) 'Measuring interest group influence in the EU: a note on methodology', *European Union Politics*, 9(4), 559–76.

Dür, A. and De Bièvre, D. (2007) 'The question of interest group influence', *Journal of Public Policy*, 27(1), 1–12.

Engel, S. (2007) 'Organizational identity as a constraint on strategic action: a comparative analysis of gay and lesbian interest groups', *Studies in American Political Development*, 21(Spring), 66–91.

Erakovic, L. and Powell, M. (2006) 'Pathways of change: organizations in transition', *Public Administration*, 84(1), 31–58.

Fedden, R. (1968) *The Continuing Purpose: A History of the National Trust, its Aims and Work*. London: Longmans.

Fernandez, J.J. (2008) 'Causes of dissolution among Spanish nonprofit associations', *Nonprofit and Voluntary Sector Quarterly*, 37(1), 113–37.

Fiol, C.M. and Romanelli, E. (2012) 'Before identity: the emergence of new organizational forms', *Organization Science*, 23(3), 597–611.

Foreman, P. and Whetten, D.A. (2002) 'Members' identification with multiple-identity organizations', *Organization Science*, 13(6), 618–35.

Galaskiewicz, J. and Bielefeld, W. (1998) *Nonprofit Organizations in an Age of Uncertainty: A Study of Organizational Change*. Hawthorne, NY: Aldine de Gruyter.

Gerring, J. (1999) 'What makes a good concept? A critical framework for understanding concept formation in the social sciences', *Polity*, 33(3), 357–93.

Golden-Biddle, K. and Rao, H. (1997) 'Breaches in the boardroom: organizational identity and conflicts of commitment in a nonprofit organization', *Organization Science*, 8(6), 593–611.

Government of Australia (2012) Ministerial press release. Available at http://ministers. treasury.gov.au/DisplayDocs.aspx?doc=pressreleases/2012/070.htm&pageID=003&min=brs&Year=&DocType= (accessed October 2013).

Grant, W. (1978) *Insider Groups, Outsider Groups and Interest Group Strategies in Britain*. Warwick: University of Warwick Department of Politics Working Paper No. 19.

Grant, W. (2000) *Pressure Groups in British Politics*. Basingstoke: Macmillan.

Grant, W. (2001) 'Pressure politics: from "insider" politics to direct action?', Parliamentary Affairs, 54, 337–48.

Gray, V. and Lowery, D. (2000) *The Population Ecology of Interest Representation: Lobbying Communities in the American States*. Ann Arbor, MI: University of Michigan Press.

Greenwood, R. and Hinings, C.R. (1996) 'Understanding radical organizational change: bringing together the old and the new institutionalism', *Academy of Management Review*, 21(4), 1022–54.

Greenwood, R. and Hinings, C.R. (1988) 'Organizational design types, tracks and the dynamics of strategic change' *Organizational Studies*, 9(3), 293–316.

Greenwood, R. and Hinings, C.R. (1993) 'Understanding strategic change: the contribution of archetypes', *Academy of Management Journal*, 36(5), 1052–81.

Grossman, M. (2012) *The Not So Special Interests*. Stanford, CA: Stanford University Press.

Hall, P. and Taylor, R. (1996) 'Political science and the three new institutionalisms', *Political Studies*, 44, 936–57.

210 *References*

Halpin, D. (2005) 'Introduction', in D. Halpin (ed.), *Surviving Global Change? Agricultural Interest Groups in Comparative Perspective*, pp. 1–30. Aldershot: Ashgate.

Halpin, D. (2006) 'The participatory and democratic potential and practice of interest groups: between solidarity and representation', *Public Administration*, 84(4), 919–40.

Halpin, D. (2010) *Groups, Democracy and Representation: Between Promise and Practice*. Manchester: Manchester University Press.

Halpin, D. and Binderkrantz, A. (2011) 'Explaining breadth of policy engagement: patterns of interest group mobilization in public policy', *Journal of European Public Policy*, 18(2), 201–19.

Halpin, D and Daugbjerg, C. (2008) 'Associative deadlocks and transformative capacity: engaging in Australian organic farm industry development', *Australian Journal of Political Science*, 43(2), 189–206.

Halpin, D. and Daugbjerg, C. (2013) 'Identity as constraint and resource in interest group evolution: a case of radical organizational change', *The British Journal of Politics & International Relations*, doi: 10.1111/1467-856X.12016.

Halpin, D. and Jordan, G. (2009) 'Interpreting environments: interest group response to population ecology pressures', *British Journal of Political Science*, 39(2), 243–65.

Halpin, D. and Jordan, G. (eds) (2012) *The Scale of Interest Organization in Democratic Politics*. Basingstoke: Palgrave.

Halpin, D. and Nownes, A. (2011) 'Reappraising the survival question: why we should focus on interest group "organizational form" and "careers"', in A. Cigler and B. Loomis (eds) *Interest Group Politics*, 8th edn, pp. 52–73. Washington, DC: Congressional Quarterly Press.

Halpin, D. and Thomas, H. (2012a) 'Evaluating the breadth of policy engagement by organized interests', *Public Administration*, 90(3), 582–99.

Halpin, D. and Thomas, H. (2012b) 'Interest group survival: explaining sources of mortality anxiety', *Interest Groups and Advocacy*, 1(2), 215–38.

Halpin, D., Daugbjerg, C. and Schwartzman, J. (2011) 'Interest group capacities and infant industry development: state-sponsored growth in organic farming', *International Political Science Review*, 32(2), 147–66.

Hannan, M. (2005) 'Ecologies of organizations: diversity and identity', *Journal of Economic Perspectives*, 19(1), 51–70.

Hannan, M. and Carroll, G. (1995) 'An introduction to organizational ecology', in G. Carroll and M. Hannan (eds), *Organizations in Industry: Strategy, Structure, and Selection*, pp. 17–31. New York: Oxford University Press.

Hannan, M. and Carroll, G.R. (1992) *Dynamics of Organizational Populations: Density, Legitimation, and Competition*. Oxford: Oxford University Press.

Hannan, M. and Freeman, J. (1984) 'Structural inertia and organizational change', *American Sociological Review*, 49(2), 149–64.

Hannan, M. and Freeman, J. (1987) 'The ecology of organizational mortality: American labor unions 1836–1985', *American Journal of Sociology*, 92, 910–43.

Hannan, M. and Freeman, J. (1988) 'Density dependence in the growth of organizational populations', in G. Carroll, (ed.), *Ecological Models of Organizations*, pp. 7–31. Cambridge, MA: Ballinger Publishing Company.

Hannan, M. and Freeman, J. (1989) *Organizational Ecology*. Cambridge, MA: Harvard University Press.

Hannan, M.T. (2010) 'Partiality of memberships in categories and audiences', *Annual Review of Sociology*, 36, 159–81.

Hannan, M.T. and Freeman, J. (1977) 'The population ecology of organizations', *American Journal of Sociology*, 82(5), 929–64.

Hannan, M.T., Pólos, L. and Carroll, G.R. (2007) *Logics of Organization Theory: Audiences, Codes and Ecologies*. Princeton, NJ: Princeton University Press.

Hay, C. (2006) 'Constructivist institutionalism', in R. Rhodes, S. Binder and B. Rockman (eds), *The Oxford Handbook of Political Institutions*, pp. 56–74. Oxford: Oxford University Press.

Hayes, M. (1986) 'The new group universe', in A. Cigler and B. Loomis (eds), *Interest Group Politics*, 2nd edn, pp. 133–45. Washington, DC: CQ Press.

Heaney, M.T. (2004) 'Outside the issue niche: the multidimensionality of interest group identity', *American Politics Research* 32(6), 611–51.

Heaney, M.T. (2007) 'Identity crisis: how interest groups struggle to define themselves in Washington', in A. Cigler and B. Loomis (eds), *Interest Group Politics*, 7th edn, pp. 279–300. Washington, DC: Congressional Quarterly Press.

Heaney, M.T. and Rojas, F. (2014) 'Hybrid activism: social movement mobilization in a multi-movement environment', *American Journal of Sociology*, conditionally accepted.

Heinz, J.P., Laumann, E.O. Nelson, R.L. and Salisbury, R.H.(1993) *The Hollow Core*. Cambridge MA: Harvard University Press.

Helbroe-Pedersen, H. (2013) 'Is measuring interest group influence a mission impossible? The case of interest group influence in the Danish parliament', *Interest Groups & Advocacy,* 2(1), 27–47.

Hojnacki, Marie, Kimball, D.C., Baumgartner, F.R., Berry, J.M. and Leech, B.L. (2012) 'Studying organizational advocacy and influence: reexamining interest group research', *Annual Review of Political Science*, 15, 379–99.

Holyoake, T.T. (2012) *Competitive Interests: Competition and Compromise in American Interest Group Politics*. Washington, DC: Georgetown University Press.

Hsu, G. (2006) 'Jacks of all trades and masters of none: audiences' reactions to spanning genres in feature film production', *Administrative Science Quarterly*, 51, 420–50.

Hsu, G. and Hannan, M. (2005) 'Identities, genres, and organizational forms', *Organization Science*, 16(5), 474–90.

Hsu, G., Hannan, M.T. and Koçak, Ö. (2009) 'Multiple category memberships in markets: a formal theory and two empirical tests', *American Sociological Review*, 74, 150–69.

Human Rights Watch (2013) www.hrw.org/en/node/75138#11 accessed October 2013.

Hutchinson, G.E. (1957) 'Concluding remarks', *Cold Spring Harbor Symposia on Quantitative Biology*, 22(2), 415–27.

Imig, D. (1992) 'Survival, resource mobilization and survival tactics of poverty advocacy groups', *The Western Political Quarterly*, 45, 501–20.

Imig, D. and Berry, J. (1996) 'Patrons and entrepreneurs: a response to public interest group entrepreneurship and theories of group mobilization', *Political Research Quarterly*, 49, 147–54.

Jacobson, R.D. (2011) 'The politics of belonging: interest group identity and agenda setting on immigration', *American Politics Research*, 39(6), 993–1018.

Janda, K. (1983) 'Cross-national measures of party organizations and organizational theory', *European Journal of Political Research*, 11, 319–32.

Jensen, M. (2010) 'Legitimizing illegitimacy: how creating market identity legitimizes illegitimate products', in G. Hsu, G. Negro and Ö. Koçak (eds), *Categories in Markets: Origins and Evolution* (Research in the Sociology of Organizations, Volume 31), pp. 39–80. Bingley: Emerald Group Publishing Limited.

212 References

Johnson, E. (2008) 'Social movement size, organizational diversity and the making of federal law', *Social Forces*, 86(3), 967–93.

Jordan, A.G. and Richardson, J.J. (1987) *British Politics and the Policy Process – an Arena Approach*. London: Allen & Unwin.

Jordan, G. (2009) 'Lobbying', in M. Flinders, A. Gamble, C. Hay and M. Kenny (eds), *The Oxford Handbook of British Politics*, pp. 365–83. Oxford: Oxford University Press.

Jordan, G. and Greenan, J. (2012) 'The changing contours of British representation: pluralism in practice', in D. Halpin and G. Jordan (eds), *The Scale of Interest Organization in Democratic Politics: Data and Research Methods*, pp. 67–98. Basingstoke: Palgrave.

Jordan, G. and Halpin, D. (2004a) 'Olson triumphant? Explaining the growth of a small business organisation' *Political Studies*, 52(3), 431–49.

Jordan, G. and Halpin, D. (2004b) 'Cultivating small business influence in the UK: the Federation of Small Businesses' journey from outsider to insider', *Journal of Public Affairs*, 3(4), 313–25.

Jordan, G. and Halpin, D. (2006) 'The political costs of policy coherence? Constructing a "rural" policy for Scotland', *Journal of Public Policy*, 26, 21–41.

Jordan, G. and Maloney, W. (1997a) *The Protest Business? Mobilizing Campaign Groups*. Manchester: Manchester University Press.

Jordan, G. and Maloney W. (1997b) 'Accounting for sub-governments: explaining the persistence of policy communities', *Administration and Society*, 29(5), 557–83.

Jordan, G. and Maloney, W. (1998) 'Manipulating membership: supply-side influences on group size', *British Journal of Political Science*, 28, 389–409.

Jordan, G. and Maloney, W. (2007) *Democracy and Interest Groups: Enhancing Participation?* Basingstoke: Palgrave.

Jordan, G., Halpin, D. and Maloney, W. (2004) 'Defining interests: disambiguation and the need for new distinctions?', *British Journal of Politics and International Relations*, 6(2), 195–212.

Karpf, D. (2010) 'Online political mobilization from the advocacy group's perspective: looking beyond clicktivism', *Policy & Internet*, 2(4), 7–41.

Karpf, D. (2012) *The MoveOn Effect: The Unexpected Transformation of American Political Advocacy*. Oxford: Oxford University Press.

Karthikeyan, S.I. and Wezel, F.C. (2010) 'Identity repositioning: the case of Liberal Democrats and audience attention in British politics, 1950–2005', in G. Hsu, G. Negro and Ö. Koçak (eds), *Categories in Markets: Origins and Evolution* (Research in the Sociology of Organizations, Volume 31), pp. 295–320. Bingley: Emerald Group Publishing Limited.

Katz, R.S. and Mair, P. (1995) 'Changing models of party organization and party democracy: the emergence of the cartel party', *Party Politics*, 1(1), 5–28.

Keating, M. and Dixon, G. (1989) *Making Economic Policy in Australia: 1983–1988*. Melbourne: Longman Cheshire.

King, G., Keohane, R. and Verba, S. (1991) *Designing Social Inquiry*. Princeton, NJ: Princeton University Press.

Klein, H. (1999) 'Tocqueville in cyberspace: using the internet for citizen associations', *The Information Society*, 15, 213–20.

Knoke, D. (1990) *Organizing for Collective Action: The Political Economics of Associations*. New York: Aldine de Gruyter.

Koole, R. (1996) 'Cadre, catch-all or cartel? A comment on the notion of the cartel party', *Party Politics*, 2, 507–27.

Kriesi, H. (1996) 'The organizational structure of new social movements in a political

References   213

context', in D. McAdam, J. McCarthy and M. Zald (eds), *Comparative Perspectives on Social Movements*, pp. 152–84. New York: Cambridge University Press.

Lang, J.R., Ronit, K. and Schneider, V. (2008) 'From simple to complex: an evolutionary sketch of theories of business association', in J.R. Grote, A. Lang and V. Schneider (eds), *Organized Business Interests in Changing Environments*, pp. 17–41. Basingstoke: Palgrave.

Leech, B. (2011) 'Lobbying and influence', in J.M. Barry and S. Maisle (eds), *The Oxford Handbook of American Political Parties and Interest Groups*, pp. 534–52. New York: Oxford University Press.

Leech, B.L., Baumgartner, F., LaPira, T. and Semanko, N. (2005) 'Drawing lobbyists to Washington: government activity and the demand for advocacy', *Political Research Quarterly*, 58, 19–30.

Levesque, C. and Murray, G. (2010) 'Understanding union power: resources and capability for renewing union capacity', *Transfer: European Review of Labour and Research*, 16(3), 333–50.

Lewin, A. and Volberda, H. (2003) 'The future of organization studies: beyond the selection-adaptation debate', in H. Tsoukas and C. Knudsen (eds), *The Oxford Handbook of Organization Theory*, pp. 568–96. Oxford: Oxford University Press.

Locke, R. and Thelen, K. (1995) 'Apples and oranges revisited: contextualized comparisons and the study of labor politics', *Politics and Society*, 23(3), 337–67.

Lounsbury, M. (2005) 'Institutional variation in the evolution of social movements: the spread of recycling advocacy groups', in J. Davis, D. McAdam, W.R. Scott and M. Zald (eds), *Social Movements and Organization Theory*, pp. 73–95. Oxford: Oxford University Press.

Lowery, D. (2007) 'Why do organized interests lobby? A multi-goals, multi-context theory of lobbying', *Polity*, 39(1), 29–54.

Lowery, D. (2013) 'Lobbying influence: meaning, measurement and missing', *Interest Groups & Advocacy*, 2, 1–26.

Lowery, D. and Brasher, H. (2004) *Organized Interests and American Government*. Boston, MA: McGraw Hill.

Lowery, D. and Gray, V. (1995) 'The population ecology of Gucci gulch, or the natural regulation of interest group numbers in the American States', *American Journal of Political Science*, 39, 1–29.

Lowery, D. and Gray, V. (2004a) 'A neopluralist perspective on research on organized interests', *Political Research Quarterly*, 57(1), 163–75.

Lowery, D. and Gray, V. (2004b) 'Bias in the heavenly chorus: interest in society and before government', *Journal of Theoretical Politics*, 16, 5–30.

Lowery, D. and Gray, V. (2007) 'Understanding interest system diversity: health interest communities in the American States', *Business and Politics*, 9(2), 1–38.

Lowery, D., Witteloostuijn, A., Peli, G., Brasher, H., Otjes, S. and Gherghina, S. (2013) 'Policy agendas and births and deaths of political parties', *Party Politics*, 19(3), 381–407.

Mahoney, C. (2007) 'Lobbying success in the United States and the European Union', *Journal of Public Policy*, 27(1), 35–56.

Maloney, W.A., Jordan, G. and McLaughlin, A.M. (1994) 'Interest groups and public policy: the insider/outsider model revisited', *Journal of Public Policy*, 14(1), 17–38.

March, J. and Olsen, J.P. (1984) 'The new institutionalism: organizational factors in political life', *American Political Science Review*, 78, 734–49.

214   *References*

Martens, K. (2005) *NGOs and the United Nations: Institutionalization, Professionalization and Adaptation*. Basingstoke: Palgrave.

Matthews, T. (1994) 'Employers' associations, corporatism and the accord: the politics of industrial relations', in S. Bell and B. Head (eds), *State, Economy and Public Policy*, pp. 195–218. Melbourne: Oxford University Press.

McCarthy, J. (2005) 'Persistence and change among nationally federated social movements', in G. Davis, D. McAdam, W. Scott and M. Zald (eds), *Social Movements and Organization Theory*, pp. 193–225. New York: Cambridge University Press.

McCarthy, J.D. and Zald, M.N. (1977) 'Resource mobilization and social movements: a partial theory', *American Journal of Sociology*, 82, 1212–41.

McKelvey, B. (1982) *Organizational Systematics: Taxonomy, Evolution, Classification*. Berkeley, CA: UC Press.

McKendrick, D.G. and Carroll, G.R. (2001) 'On the genesis of organizational forms: evidence from the market for disk arrays', *Organization Science*, 12, 661–82.

McKendrick, D.G., Jaffee, J., Carroll, G.R. and Khessina, O.N. (2003) 'In the bud? Disk array producers as a (possibly) emergent organizational form', *Administrative Science Quarterly*, 48, 60.

McKinney, B. and Halpin, D. (2007) 'Talking about Australian pressure groups: adding value to the insider/outsider distinction in combating homelessness in Western Australia', *Australian Journal of Public Administration*, 66(3), 342–52.

McPherson, M. (1983) 'An ecology of affiliation', *American Sociological Review*, 48(4), 519–32.

Meyer, A., Tsui, A. and Hinings, C. (1993) 'Configurational approaches to organizational analysis', *Academy of Management Journal*, 38(6), 1175–95.

Minkoff, D., Aisenbrey, S. and Agnone, J. (2008) 'Organizational diversity in the U.S. advocacy sector', *Social Problems*, 55(4), 525–48.

Minkoff, D. and Powell, W.W. (2006) 'Nonprofit mission: constancy, responsiveness, or deflection?', in W.W. Powell and R. Steinberg (eds), *The Nonprofit Sector: A Research Handbook*, pp. 591–611. New Haven, CT: Yale University Press.

Minkoff, D.C. (1999) 'Bending with the wind: strategic change and adaptation by women's and racial minority organizations', *American Journal of Sociology*, 104, 1666–703.

Minkoff, D.C. (2002) 'The emergence of hybrid organizational forms: combining identity-based service provision and political action', *Nonprofit and Voluntary Sector Quarterly*, 31(3), 377–401.

Moe, T. (1980) *The Organisation of Interests*. Chicago, IL: University of Chicago Press.

Moe, T. (1991) 'Politics and the theory of organization', *Journal of Law, Economics, and Organization*, 7 (special issue), 106–29.

Mohr, J.W. and Guerra-Pearson, F. (2010) 'The duality of niche and form: the differentiation of institutional space in New York City, 1888–1917', in G. Hsu, G. Negro and Ö. Koçak (eds), *Categories in Markets: Origins and Evolution* (Research in the Sociology of Organizations, Volume 31), pp. 321–68. Bingely: Emerald Group Publishing Limited.

Negro, G., Hannan, M.T. and Rao, H. (2010a) 'Categorical contrast and niche width: critical success in winemaking', *Industrial and Corporate Change*, 19, 1397–425.

Negro, G., Koçak, Ö. and Hsu, G. (2010b) 'Research on categories in the sociology of organizations', *Research in the Sociology of Organizations*, 31(November), 3–35.

NIB (1930–1) *Annual Report 1930–1, National Institute for the Blind*. London: unpublished document. Accessed at RNIB Offices, 2009.

Nownes, A. and Cigler, A.J. (1995) 'Public interest groups and the road to survival', *Polity*, 27(3), 379–404.

References 215

Nownes, A. and Neeley, G. (1996) 'Public interest group entrepreneurship and theories of group mobilization', *Political Research Quarterly*, 49(1), 119–46.

Nownes, A.J. (2004) 'The population ecology of interest group formation: mobilizing gay and lesbian rights interest groups in the United States, 1950–98', *British Journal of Political Science*, 34, 49–67.

Nownes, A.J. (2010) 'Density-dependent dynamics in the population of transgender interest groups in the United States, 1964–2005', *Social Science Quarterly*, 91, 689–703.

Nownes, A.J. and Lipinski, D. (2005) 'The population ecology of interest group death: gay and lesbian rights interest groups in the United States, 1945–98', *British Journal of Political Science*, 35, 303–19.

Öberg, P., Svensson, T., Christiansen, P., Nørgaard, A., Rommetvedt, H. and Thesen, G. (2011) 'Disrupted exchange and declining corporatism: government authority and interest group capability in Scandinavia', *Government and Opposition*, 46(3), 365–91.

Oliver, A. and K. Montgomery (2000) 'Creating a hybrid organizational form from parental blueprints: the emergence and evolution of knowledge firms', *Human Relations*, 53, 33–56.

Olson, M. (1965) *The Logic of Collective Action: Public Goods and the Theory of Groups*. Cambridge, MA: Harvard University Press.

Olson, M. (1982) *The Rise and Decline of Nations*. New Haven, CT: Yale University Press.

Padgett, J.F. and Powell, W. (2012) 'The problem of emergence', in J. Padgett and W. Powell (eds), *The Emergence of Organizations and Markets*, pp. 1–32. Princeton, NJ: Princeton University Press.

Page, E. (1999) 'The insider/outsider distinction: an empirical investigation', *British Journal of Politics and International Relations*, 1(2), 205–14.

Painter, M. and Pierre, J. (2005) 'Unpacking policy capacity: issues and themes', in M. Painter and J. Pierre (eds), *Challenges to State Policy Capacity: Global Trends and Comparative Perspectives*, pp. 1–18. Basingstoke: Palgrave.

Pedersen, J.S. and Dobbin, F. (2006) 'In search of identity and legitimation: bridging organizational culture and neoinstitutionalism', *American Behavioral Scientist*, Special Issue, 49(7), 897–907.

Peters, B.G. (2005) 'Policy instruments and policy capacity', in M. Painter and J. Pierre (eds), *Challenges to State Policy Capacity: Global Trends and Comparative Perspectives*, pp. 73–91. Basingstoke: Palgrave.

Phillips, G.A. (2004) The *Blind in British Society: Charity, State and Community* c.*1780–1930*. Aldershot: Burlington.

Polletta, F. and Jesper, J.M. (2001) 'Collective identity and social movements', *Annual Review of Sociology*, 27, 283–305.

Pontikes, E.G. (2012) 'Two sides of the same coin: how ambiguous classification affects multiple audiences' evaluations', *Administrative Science Quarterly*, 57(1), 81–118.

Powell, W. (1991) 'Expanding the scope of institutional analysis', in W.W. Powell and P.J. DiMaggio (eds), *The New Institutionalism in Organizational Analysis*, pp. 183–203. Chicago, IL: University of Chicago Press.

Powell, W. and Sandholtz, K. (2010) 'Amphibious entrepreneurs and the emergence of organizational forms', available at http://woodypowell.com/wp-content/uploads/2012/03/1_Powell_Sandholtz_12_16_2011.pdf (accessed June 2011).

Powell, W. and Sandholtz, K. (2012) 'Chance chance, necessité, et naïveté: ingredients to create a new organizational form', in J. Padgett and W. Powell (eds), *The Emergence of Organizations and Markets*, pp. 379–433. Princeton, NJ: Princeton University Press.

216 *References*

Prakash, A. and Gugarty, M.K. (2010) *Advocacy Organizations and Collective Action.* New York: Cambridge University Press.

Prestby, J., Wandersman, A., Florin, P., Rich, R. and Chavis, D. (1990) 'Benefits, costs incentive management and participation in voluntary organisations: a means to understanding and promoting empowerment', *American Journal of Community Psychology*, 18(1), 117–49.

Putnam, R. (2000) *Bowling Alone.* New York: Simon and Schuster.

Ragin, C. (1987) *The Comparative Method: Moving Beyond Qualitative and Quantitative Strategies.* Berkeley, CA: University of California Press.

Rao, H. (1998) '*Caveat emptor*: the construction of nonprofit consumer watchdog organizations', *The American Journal of Sociology*, 103(4), 912–61.

Rao, H., Monin, P. and Duran, R. (2005) 'Border crossing: bricolage and the erosion of categorical boundaries in French gastronomy', *The American Sociological Review*, 70(9), 868–991.

Rao, H., Morrill, C. and Zald, M.N. (2000) 'How social movements and collective action create new organizational forms', in B. Staw and R. Sutton (eds), *Research in Organizational Behavior*, pp. 237–81. New York: JAI Press.

Rawcliffe, P. (1998) *Environmental Pressure Groups in Transition.* Manchester: Manchester University Press.

Reed, M. (2004) *Rebels for the Soil: The Lonely Furrow of the Soil Association 1943–2000.* Thesis submitted in fulfilment of the requirements for the degree of Doctor of Philosophy (Bristol: University of the West of England).

Ruef, M. (2000) 'The emergence of organizational forms: a community ecology approach', *American Journal of Sociology*, 106(3), 658–714.

Richardson, J. (1995) 'Interest groups and representation', *Australian Journal of Political Science*, 30(Special Issue), 61–81.

Richardson, J. (1999) 'Pressure groups and parties: a "haze of common knowledge" or empirical advance of the discipline?', in J. Hayward, B. Barry and A. Brown (eds), *The British Study of Politics in the Twentieth Century*, pp. 181–222. Oxford: Oxford University Press.

Richardson, J.J. and Jordan, A.G. (1979) *Governing under Pressure.* Oxford: Martin Robertson.

RNIB (2001) *Annual Report 2001 Royal National Institute of the Blind.* London: unpublished document. Accessed at RNIB Offices 2009.

Romanelli, E. (1991) 'The evolution of new organizational forms', *Annual Review of Sociology*, 17, 79–203.

Rootes, C. (2009) 'Environmental NGOs and the environmental movement in England', in N. Crowson, James McKay and Matthew Hilton (eds), *NGOs Contemporary Britain: Non-state Actors in Society and Politics since 1945*, pp. 201–21. Basingstoke: Palgrave.

Rose, R. and Mackie, T.T. (1988) 'Do parties persist or fail? The big trade-off facing organizations', in K. Lawson and P.H. Merkl (eds), *When Parties Fail: Emerging Alternative Organizations*, pp. 533–58. Princeton, NJ: Princeton University Press.

Rothenberg, L.S. (1988) 'Organizational maintenance and the retention decision in groups', *The American Political Science Review*, 82(4), 1129–52.

RSPB (1903) *Report*, accessed at RSPB, Sandy, Bedfordshire.

Rucht, D. (1999) 'Linking organization and mobilization: Michels's iron law of oligarchy reconsidered', *Mobilization*, 4(2), 151–69.

Ruef, M. (2000) 'The emergence of organizational forms: a community ecology approach', *American Journal of Sociology*, 106(3), 658–714.

References 217

Salisbury, R.H. (1969) 'An exchange theory of interest groups', *Midwest Journal of Political Science*, 13, 1–32.

Salisbury, R.H. (1984) 'Interest representation: the dominance of interest groups', *American Political Science Review*, 78(1), 64–78.

Schmitter, P.C. and Streeck, W. (1981) *The Organisation of Business Interests. A Research Design to Study the Associative Action of Business in the Advanced Industrial Societies of Western Europe.* Berlin: International Institute of Management, Discussion paper IIM/LMP 81–13.

Schneiberg, M. and Clemens, E.S. (2006) 'The typical tools for the job: research strategies in institutional analysis', *Sociological Theory*, 24 (3), 195–227.

Schneiberg, M. and Berk, G. (2010) 'From categorical imperative to learning by categories: cost accounting and new categorical practices in American manufacturing, 1900–1930', in G. Hsu, Ö. Kocak, and G. Negro (eds), *Research in the Sociology of Organizations*, pp. 255–92. Bingley: Emerald Group Publishing.

Schlozman, K., Verba, S. and Brady, H.E. (2012) *The Unheavenly Chorus.* Princeton, NJ: Princeton University Press.

Schmitter, P.C. (1983) 'Democratic theory and neocorporatist practice', *Social Research*, 50(4), 885–928.

Schmitter, P.C. and Streeck, W. (1981) *The Organisation of Business Interests. A Research Design to Study the Associative Action of Business in the Advanced Industrial Societies of Western Europe.* Berlin: International Institute of Management, Discussion paper IIM/LMP 81-13.

Scott, W.R. (1995) *Institutions and Organizations.* Thousand Oaks, CA: Sage.

Shulman, S. (2009) 'The case against mass e-mails: perverse incentives and low quality public participation in U.S. Federal rulemaking', *Policy & Internet*, 1(1), 23–53.

Skocpol, T. (1999) 'Advocates without members: the recent transformation of American civic life', in T. Skocpol and M.P. Fiorina (eds), *Civic Engagement in American Democracy*, pp. 461–509. Washington, DC: Brookings Institution.

Skocpol, T. (2003) *Diminished Democracy.* Norman, OK: Oklohoma University Press.

Soule, S. (2012) 'Social movements and markets, industries, and firms', *Organization Studies*, 33, 1715–33.

Staggenborg, S. (1988) 'The consequences of professionalization and formalization in the pro-choice movement', *American Sociological Review*, 53(4), 585–605.

Stewart, J.D. (1958) *British Pressure Groups: Their Role in Relation to the House of Commons.* New York: Oxford University Press.

Stinchcombe, A. (1965) 'Social structure and organizations', in J.G. March (ed.), *Handbook of Organizations*, pp. 142–93. Chicago, IL: Rand.

Streeck, W. and Thelen, K. (2005) 'Introduction: institutional change in advanced political economies', in W. Streeck and K. Thelen (eds), *Beyond Continuity Institutional Change in Advanced Political Economies*, pp. 3–39. Oxford: Oxford University Press.

Strolovich, D.Z. (2007) *Affirmative Advocacy.* Chicago, IL: Chicago University Press.

Thelen, K. (2003) 'How institutions evolve: Insights from comparative-historical analysis', in J. Mahoney and D. Rueschemeyer (eds), *Comparative Historical Analysis in the Social Sciences*, pp. 208–40. New York: Cambridge University Press.

Thomas, M.G. (1957) *Royal National Institute for the Blind.* Brighton: Brighton Herald.

Tomlinson, I.J. (2007) *Transforming British Organics: The Role of Central Government, 1980–2006.* Thesis submitted in fulfilment of the requirements for the degree of Doctor of Philosophy (Department of Geography, University College London).

Traxler, F. (1993) 'Business associations and labor unions in comparison: theoretical

218   *References*

perspectives and empirical findings on social class, collective action and associational organizability', *British Journal of Sociology*, 44(4), 673–91.

Truman, D.B. (1971) *The Governmental Process*, 2nd edn. New York: Alfred Knopf.

Tsoukas, H. and Chia, R. (2002) 'On organizational becoming: rethinking organizational change', *Organization Science*, 13(5), 567–82.

Voss, K. and Sherman, R. (2000) 'Breaking the iron law of oligarchy: union revitalization in the American labor movement', *American Journal of Sociology*, 106(2), 303–49.

Vromen, A. and Coleman, W. (2011) 'Online movement mobilisation and electoral politics: the case of GetUp!', *Communication, Politics and Culture*, 44(2), 76–94.

Walker, E.T., McCarthy, J.D. and Baumgartner, F. (2011) 'Replacing members with managers? Mutualism among membership and nonmembership advocacy organizations in the United States', *American Journal of Sociology*, 116(4), 1284–337.

Walker, J.L. (1983) 'The origins and maintenance of interest groups in America', *American Political Science Review*, 77(2), 390–406.

Walker, J.L. (1991) *Mobilizing Interest Groups in America*, Ann Arbor, MI: University of Michigan Press.

Wanna, J. and Withers, G. (2000) 'Creating capability: combining economic and political rationalities in industry and regional policy', in G. Davis and M. Keating (eds), *The Future of Governance*, pp. 67–93. St Leonards: Allen and Unwin.

Warhurst, J. 1994. 'The Australian Conservation Foundation: the development of a modern environmental interest group', *Environmental Politics*, 3(1), 68–90.

Weiss, L. (1998) *The Myth of the Powerless State: Governing the Economy in a Global Era*. Cambridge: Polity Press.

Whiteley, P.F. and Winyward, S.J. (1987) *Pressure for the Poor: The Poverty Lobby and Policy Making*. London and New York: Methuen.

Whiteley, P.F. and Winyward, S.J. (1988) 'The poverty lobby in British politics', *Parliamentary Affairs*, XLI, 195–208.

Williamson, O. (1975) *Markets and Hierarchies: Analysis and Antitrust Implications*. New York: Free Press.

Williamson, O.E. (1985) *The Economic Institutions of Capitalism*. New York: Free Press.

Wilson, J.Q. (1995) *Political Organizations*. Princeton, NJ: Princeton University Press.

Wolf, K. (2008) 'Emerging patterns of global governance: the new interplay between the state, business and civil society', in A.G. Scherer and G. Palazzo (eds), *Handbook of Research on Global Corporate Citizenship*, pp. 225–48. London: Edward Elgar.

Wollebæk, D. (2009) 'Age, size and change in local voluntary associations', *Acta Sociologica*, 52(4), 365–84.

Young, M. (2008) 'From conservation to environment: the Sierra Club and the organizational politics of change', *Studies in American Political Development*, 22(Fall), 183–203.

Young, M. (2010) *Developing Interests: Organizational Change and the Politics of Advocacy*. Lawrence, KS: University of Kansas Press.

Young, R.A. and Forsyth, S.M. (1991) ' "Leaders" communications in public-interest and material-interest groups', *Canadian Journal of Political Science*, 24(3), 525–40.

Young, R.C. (1988) 'Is population ecology a useful paradigm for the study of organizations?' *American Journal of Sociology*, 94(1), 1–24.

Zuckerman, E., Kim, T., Ukanwa, K. and von Rittmann, J. (2003) 'Robust identities or nonentities? Typecasting in the feature-film labor market', *American Journal of Sociology*, 108(5), 1018–74.

Zuckerman, E.W. (1999) 'The categorical imperative: securities analysts and the illegitimacy discount', *American Journal of Sociology*, 104, 1398–438.

Index

Page numbers in *italics* denote tables, those in **bold** denote figures.

access goods 6, 183–4
adaptation 27–8, 32, 34–5, 58–9, 65, 98, 102–6, 109, 119, 136, 201–2
agency 10, 25, 34, 76, 102, 104–5, 119, 199
Albert, S. 43, 45–50
Aldrich, H. 27, 32, 39, 42–3, 130
American Agriculture Movement Inc. (AAM) 23, 84
audience 15, 44, 46–9, 51–2, 74–6, 80, 84, 86–7, 97, **105**, 107, *111*, 120, 124, *127*, 132, 134, 137–9, 141, 146–8, 150, 152, 163–8, 171, 174, 178–9

Barakso, M. 9, 10
Baumgartner, F. 1, 13, 16, 28, 29, 37, 109, 130, 198
Berry, J. 20, 31, 84, 85
Bimber, B. 9–11, 199–205
Blyth, M. 59
Bosso, C. 5, 78n17, 112, 141, 201
Bouwen, M. 6, 183–4, *189*
branding 9, 42, 95, 121n5, 131, 141, 165, 202
bricolage 15, 146, 148
Browne, P. 5, *19*, 25, 124–6, *127*, 130, 136, 177–8

Carroll, G.R. 39–40, 42–5, 47–9, 60, 84, 111
categorical theories 15, 54, 161, 163–6, 171, 175
category spanning 49, 164, 168, 171, **172**, 173
Clemens, E. 35, 45, 49, 66, 76, 78n15, 87, 89, 99, 106–7, 146, 148
collective action 10, 18, *19*, 28, 71, 80, 186, 199–200; problem 2, 4, 9, 20, 23, 25, 28, 33, 36–7, 62, 79, 120, 187, 196, 198
Culpepper, P. 6, 74, 78n21, 187–8, *189*

Daugbjerg, C. 9, 90, 103, 116, 187, 191
Deephouse, D. 64, 65, 107, 137–8, *139*, 142, 143n7, 146, 166
differentiation 55n9, 66, 122, 126, 129, 137–9, *139*, 143n1, 161, 163
Dür, A. 181, *189*

ecological theory 6, 48, 124, 133, 205
exchange theory 22, 133, 140, 182–4, 196

Forestry Contractors' Association 91–2
formation 1–4, 14, *19*, 20–2, 27, 32, 36, 62, 74, 79–98, 102, **105**, 113, 125, 131, 148, 162, 171, 196, 198

Gerring, J. 62, 180
GetUp! 9, 205
Grant, W. *19*, 28, 36n5, 51, 179, 182
Gray, V. 2, 3, 5, 6, 8, 11, 13, 16, *19*, 21, 25, 26, 27, 28, 36n3, 37, 38, 65, 66, 76, 76n1, 77n11, 77n14, 79, 109, 123, 124, 125, 126, *127*, 129, 132, 133, 136, 142, 143n3, 158
Greenwood, R. 49, 55n7, 110, 121n6, 146
Grossman, M. 87
group capacity 12, 15, 29, 31, 74, 75, 177, 184–5, 187, 191–2, *193*, 194–5, 198
group career 5, 12, 14, 21, 32–3, 85–6, 102–6, 198
group influence 28–31, 177–9, 181–2, 201
group policy capacity: application 188–94; definition 12; relation to other concepts 181–8; summary 179–81

220 *Index*

Halpin, D. 5, 8,9, 10, 23, 25, 27, 28, 34, 35, 54, 56, 61, *63*, 65, 68, 71, 74, 77n2, 82, 90, 99, 103, 116, 120, 124, 125, 128, 130, 132, 136, 139, 158, 180, 187, *189*, 191
Hannan, M. 39, 42, 43, 44, 45, 47, 48, 49, 54n1, 63, 64, 70, 75, 77n11, 110, 111, 124, 146, 158, 164, 165, 175n2
Hayes, M. 38, 60, 61, 62, 77n5, n6, 78n18
Heaney, M. 87, 107, 120, 121n5, 125–6, *127*, 136, 138, 166
Hojnacki, M. 2, 3, 10, 37
Hsu, G. 42, 45, 47, 48, 133, 134
hybrid forms 147–8, 150, 205
hybrid identity 50, 164
hybridity 11, 15, 49, 50, 67, 158

identity space 15, 123, 133, 134, 136, 142, 158, 172
incentive theory 22–3
incentives 4–5, *19*, 20–5, 32, 37, 119
influence *see* group influence
influence production process 3, 13
institutional change 103, 121n3
institutional theories 66, 147
internet-mediated groups 64, 190, 191, 204, 205
isomorphism 57, 64–7, 76, 137, 150, 164

Jordan, G. 5, 8, 10, 21, 23, 25, 27, 28, 34, 38, 52, 56, 60, 65, 77n8, 99, 109, 112, 113, 120, 125, 132, 136, 139, 167, 176, 177, 179, 182, 184, 185, 201

Karpf, D. 9, 11, 53, 64, 190, 200, 201, 204, 205
Katz, R. 58, 59, 60

Leech, B. 1, 7, 13, 16, 28, 29, 30, 31, 37, 109, 177, 178, 179, 180, 182, 198
Lowery, D. 2, 3, 5, 6, 8, 11, 13, 16, *19*, 21, 22, 25, 26, 27, 28, 36n3, n4, 37, 38, 65, 66, 76, 77n11, n14, 79, 101, 109, 123, 124, 125, 126, *127*, 128, 129, 130, 132, 133, 134, 136, 142, 143n2, 158, 177, 178

maintenance 4–5, *19*, 20, 22–6, 32, 37, 54n5, 67, 84, 98, 99–121, 140, 196
Mair, P. 58, 60
Maloney, W. 5, 21, 25, 28, 29, 34, 38, 54n5, 60, 112, 113, 121n4, 182, 183, *189*, 201
McCarthy, J. 8, 60, 63, 112, 190

McKendrick, D. 40, 42, 44, 45, 48, 145, 147, 160n2
Minkoff, D. 8, 16, 35, 38, 50, 52, 61, 62, 63, 67, 71, 78n24, 88, 99, 112, 136, 143n1, 146, 147, 164
mission 121n5, 137
Moe, T. 3, 4, 11, *19*, 21, 22, 23, 24, 25
mortality 18, 26–8, 32, 36, 75, 120, 164, 196; anxiety 8, 17
MoveOn 9, 190, 199, 204, 205

National Farmers' Union of Scotland (NFUS) 92, 136, 138, 180
National Landlords' Association 94–5
Negro, G. 48, 133, 153, 158, 163, 164, 165, 172, 175n1
niche: fundamental 126; identity 130–2; partitioning 126, 129, 142; realised 126; resource 129; space 132–6; strategy 136–41; theory *19*, 22, 25–6, 54, 62, 75, 123–6, *127*, 126–9, 198 width 158, 172–3
Nownes, A. 5, 6, 9, *19*, 20, 25, 26, 27, 35, 37, 54, 62, 65, 66, 70, 74, 77n11, 78n15, 84, 99, *108*, 120

oligarchy 4, 23
Olson, M. 2, 4, *19*, 20, 22, 24, 28, 37, 54n5, 71, 79, 121n1, 121n4, 185, 202
organizational change 106–10, 142; levels of change 110, *110*, 111, *111*
organizational form 2, 9, 11, 13, 14, 33, 37–9; change *see* organizational change; definitions 39–42, *41* ; emergence 144–9; feature-based *41*, 42–5; generic versus realized 11, 89, 131, 136; generic group 59–64; identity-based 45–50, *41*, 144–9, 163–6, 175; origins 145–9; political parties 57–9
organizational identity 50, 86, 87, 88, 107, *108*, 117, 125, 175; collective 47; complex/simple 168; definition 45–7
Oxfam 112–13
path-dependence 9, 15, 54, 74, 80, 82, 85, 87, 88, 98, 102, 103, 104, 114, 119, 142
People Too 92–3
political party: careers 14, 103; forms and transformation 14, 17n1, 39, 57–9, 63, 64, 103, 197, 199
population ecology (PE) 2, 5, 7, 8, 16, *19*, 25, 27, 32, 34, 38, 54n1, 57, 65, 75, 83, 84, 120, 124, *127*, 129, 130, 141, 142, 144
post-formation 22, **105**, 121n3

Powell, W. 49, 66, 71, 88, 103, 143n1, 145, 146, 147, 148, 152, 160n6
professionalization 4, 5, 24, 53, 55n9

Rao, H. 45, 46, 49, 110, 115, 147, 148, 160n1, 165, 166
representation 10, 11, 21, 22, 27, 52, 68, 82, 105, 117, 118, 125, 175, 178, 191
resource space 15, 25, 122, 123, 126, 131, 133, 134, 142, 147, 148, 172
Romanelli, E. 39, 40, 42, 48, 134, 145
Royal Society for the Protection of Birds (RSPB) 71, *72*, 93, 112–14, *157*, 165, 168, 172, 173
Ruef, M. 42, 48, 54n4

Salisbury, R. 4, 5, *19*, 20, 21, 22, 30, 37, 54n5, 84, 121n1, 121n4
Sandholtz, K. 49, 146, 148, 152, 160n6
Schlozman, K. 8, 180
Sierra Club 81, 88, 130
Skocpol, T. 2, 8, 34, 53, 60, 61, 62, 63, 75, 77n6, 112, 113, 195, 203, 204
social movement: literature 52, 60, 103, 134, 143n1, 197, 199; organizations 14, 38, 49, 63, 164
Soil Association (SA) 90–1, 114–15, 121n7, 187, 192
status 28–9, 52, 55n8, 75, 76n2, 84, 140, 184

Stinchcombe, A. 39, 71, 82, 103, 142, 160n5
strategy: identity-building 166, 171; niche-building 136–40; organizational 93, 104, *108*, 110, 113, 116; policy *19*, 28–30, 52, 76n2, 82, 99; survival 77n3
Streeck, W. 103, 104, 184, 185, *189*
Strolovich, D. 10

Theleen, K. 82, 88, 103, 104
transactional theories 124, *127*, 182–4
Truman D.B. 4, 13, *19*, 20, 38, 60, 71, 74, 79, 82, 103, 183, *189*, 199

Vromen, A. 200

Whetten, D.A. 43, 45, 46, 47, 49, 50, 55n6, 164
Wilson, J.Q. 1, 4, 5, *19*, 21, 22, 23, 24, 25, 38, 126
Wollebæk, D. 34, 35, 96

Young, M. 9, 10, 54, 81, 84, 88, 93, 103, 107

Zuckerman, E. 48, 75, 76, 107, 137, 146, 148, 167

Taylor & Francis
eBooks
FOR LIBRARIES

ORDER YOUR FREE 30 DAY INSTITUTIONAL TRIAL TODAY!

Over 23,000 eBook titles in the Humanities, Social Sciences, STM and Law from some of the world's leading imprints.

Choose from a range of subject packages or create your own!

Benefits for you
- Free MARC records
- COUNTER-compliant usage statistics
- Flexible purchase and pricing options

Benefits for your user
- Off-site, anytime access via Athens or referring URL
- Print or copy pages or chapters
- Full content search
- Bookmark, highlight and annotate text
- Access to thousands of pages of quality research at the click of a button

For more information, pricing enquiries or to order a free trial, contact your local online sales team.

UK and Rest of World: **online.sales@tandf.co.uk**
US, Canada and Latin America:
e-reference@taylorandfrancis.com

www.ebooksubscriptions.com

A flexible and dynamic resource for teaching, learning and research.